DEMOCRACY AND THE PROBLEM OF FREE SPEECH

DEMOCRACY AND THE PROBLEM OF FREE SPEECH

CASS R. SUNSTEIN

THE FREE PRESS
A Division of Macmillan, Inc.
NEW YORK

Maxwell Macmillan Canada
TORONTO

Maxwell Macmillan International
NEW YORK OXFORD SINGAPORE SYDNEY

The Free Press
A Division of Macmillan, Inc.
866 Third Avenue, New York, N.Y. 10022

Maxwell Macmillan Canada, Inc.
1200 Eglinton Avenue East
Suite 200
Don Mills, Ontario, M3C 3N1

Macmillan, Inc. is part of the Maxwell Communication Group of Companies

Printed in the United States of America

printing number

1   2   3   4   5   6   7   8   9   10

Library of Congress Cataloging-in-Publication Data

Sunstein, Cass R.
    Democracy and the problem of free speech / Cass R. Sunstein.
        p.   cm.
    Includes index.
    ISBN 0–02–932271–5
    1. Freedom of speech.   2. Freedom of speech—United States.   I. Title.
JC591.S86   1993   93–5462
323.44'3—dc20   CIP

Contents

Preface and Acknowledgments

HERE ARE SOME RECENT free speech events:

1. A television network plans to show a movie on the topic of abortion. Many advertisers refuse to sponsor the movie. The network decides to run the movie anyway, but it loses a lot of money.

2. A government agency funds artistic projects. In response to a public outcry, it withdraws money from projects that appear to endorse causes associated with feminism and with homosexuals.

3. A male employer makes various suggestive comments to a female employee. He tells her that if she rejects him, she will be fired. She files a complaint with a government agency, contending that her civil rights have been violated. In response, he claims that his right to freedom of speech allows him to say whatever he likes.

4. American companies propose to sell technology to other nations. Some of the technology consists solely of project descriptions, amounting to "words"; but these words could be used to enhance the military capacities of unfriendly countries. The American government tries to stop the exchange. The companies complain that any restriction would violate the First Amendment.

5. The federal government contemplates various methods for improving democracy in America: imposing legal restrictions on private contributions to candidates and to political action committees; allowing free air time for candidates; and prohibiting broadcasters from disclosing polling results during voting. Critics say that any such reforms would abridge free speech.

6. A well-known tobacco company runs a series of advertisements in which black civil rights leaders from the 1960s say that free speech is important to liberty in America. The advertisements are clearly an effort to lay the groundwork for a constitutional attack on legislative efforts to stop advertising for tobacco products.

7. For many years, the Federal Communications Commission required broadcasters to cover public issues and to foster diverse views. The Commission now concludes that these requirements flatly violate the First Amendment, since they tell broadcasters what they may say.

8. In the aftermath of deregulation of the airwaves, there is an explosion of advertising on television for children. Congress proposes the imposition of a ceiling of about twelve minutes of advertising per hour. The President says that the proposal would violate the First Amendment.

9. At the Kitty Kat Lounge in Indiana, much of the entertainment consists of nude dancing. A prosecutor brings suit against the owner of the lounge, contending that nude dancing violates Indiana's ban on nudity in public places. The owner claims that his First Amendment rights would be violated by applying the ban, and he brings this objection to the Supreme Court.

10. There is an increase in incidents of verbal attacks on women, blacks, and homosexuals on the campus of a large university in the Midwest. The university enacts a rule prohibiting hate speech on campus.

11. Various companies create "900" numbers, in which people pay $2 per minute to receive astrological or romantic advice, or to hear prerecorded statements from celebrities. The Federal Communications Commission tries to regulate "900" services to

prevent fraud and abuse of children. The relevant companies complain that any regulation would violate the First Amendment.

We are in the midst of a dramatic period of new thought about the meaning of free speech in America. In this book, I deal with these and many other First Amendment problems. My goal is to set out a general understanding of the purposes of a system of free expression, an understanding that will enable us to address the novel challenges to our most precious constitutional right.

The origins of this book lie in "Free Speech Now," 59 University of Chicago Law Review 255 (1992), an essay that found a somewhat different incarnation as chapters 7 and 8 of *The Partial Constitution* (Harvard University Press, 1993). I am grateful to the University of Chicago Law Review and to Harvard University Press for permission to reprint some of that material here. But this book represents a new departure. Although I have retained a number of the original discussions, the basic argument has been much changed. Most sections have been greatly expanded. I have also added new discussions of many topics, including hate speech, corporate speech, and problems of discrimination in free speech law. There is much more detail here about existing fare on the broadcasting media and about possible reform strategies. In addition, my understanding of several areas has changed a great deal, and the discussion has had to be revised accordingly. I have also tried to make the present volume less technical and more broadly accessible. (Readers interested in how the present volume relates to many other issues in constitutional law and theory might consult *The Partial Constitution*.)

Many friends and colleagues have helped with this book. I cannot thank them all here. But I would like to express a special debt to my editor, Bruce Nichols, for his encouragement and for excellent editorial suggestions; to Gabriel Gore and Richard Madris for research assistance; to Marlene Vellinga for secretarial help; and to the following friends and colleagues for invaluable conversation and comments: Joshua Cohen, Jon Elster, Robert Entman, David Estlund, Stephen Holmes, Elena Kagan, Larry Lessig, Catharine MacKinnon, Martha Nussbaum, Richard Posner, Frederick Schauer, Geoffrey Stone, and David Strauss. For financial support, I am grateful to the Russell Baker Scholars Fund and the James H. Douglas, Jr. Fund for the Study of Law and Government. My final debt is to my students at the University of Chicago, especially the law students in the winter term of 1993, whose comments prompted me to revise the book substantially.

Introduction

"CONGRESS SHALL MAKE NO LAW ABRIDGING the freedom of speech, or of the press." More than anything else in the Constitution, the First Amendment's protection of free speech and free press symbolizes the American commitment to liberty under law. These fourteen words have inspired and provoked not only Americans, but also reformers and constitution-makers all over the world. By prohibiting any law "abridging the freedom of speech," the American Constitution is understood to impose a formidable barrier to official censorship—perhaps the most serious danger to democratic government. The First Amendment, it is often said, forbids government from ordaining any official orthodoxy. It prevents majorities from entrenching their own preferred positions. It even guarantees a large number of outlets for free expression.

All this is conventional wisdom. It contains a good deal of truth. But in light of astonishing economic and technological changes, we must now doubt whether, as interpreted, the constitutional guarantee of free speech is adequately serving democratic goals. It is past time for a large-scale reassessment of the appropriate role of the First Amendment in the democratic process. In this book I propose such a reassessment—one that adapts an old amendment to new controversies and technologies for which the past is an uncertain and perhaps even treacherous guide.

On Text and History

The Constitution does appear to offer broad protection to speech; but standing by itself, it is much more ambiguous than it first appears. The current state of free speech law in America cannot really be attributed to the Constitution's words, or even to the aspirations of the people who wrote them and made them a part of America's founding document. To some readers, the words seem quite rigid, absolute, demanding, clear. On reflection, however, they are anything but that. What does it mean for Congress to "abridge" the freedom of speech? Does regulation of libelous, obscene, or defamatory speech necessarily count as an "abridgement"? How about a ban on attempted bribery, or threats, or perjury, or nude dancing, or false commercial advertising? Or what about speech that most people think entirely unconnected with the First Amendment—price-fixing, contract-making, firing someone for racial reasons, placing bets on horses? Free speech absolutists claim the authority of the supposedly plain meaning of the First Amendment, but they cannot fairly rely on the text alone. By themselves, the words "abridge" and "freedom of speech" do not tell us how to handle disputed free speech cases.

If the text is ambiguous, perhaps the history can help. But if we are especially concerned about the specific views of those who wrote the First Amendment, we will find many puzzles, and we will **probably end up with what everyone would consider an** unacceptably narrow understanding of the free speech principle. We will find, for example, that some framers thought that many government restrictions on free speech were not really "abridgments." As a matter of history, the notion of an "abridgment" was a limited one; it was not coextensive with the notion of a restriction.[1] The word "abridgment," read in light of history, therefore introduces a large degree of ambiguity at the outset.

And—a separate question for interpretation—what does the history say about "the freedom of speech"? If we turn to history, we will find some evidence that in the founding period, the phrase "the freedom of speech" was a term of art, one with a highly specialized meaning. The term may well have referred primarily or even exclusively to protection against what are described as "prior restraints." Prior restraints consist mainly of two things: (1) licensing systems before speech can reach the public (for example, a requirement that you submit your sexually explicit book to a licensor before you can publish); and (2) court-ordered injunctions against expression, banning speech in advance (for example, a court order stopping you from printing a dissident political tract).

A criminal penalty, even a large one, is not a prior restraint. If "the freedom of speech" is limited to protection against prior restraints, subsequent punishment for speech raises no constitutional issue at all. To say the least, this is a jarring conclusion. If the framers intended the free speech principle to apply only to prior restraints, the First Amendment, as originally understood, offered precious little protection against what amounts to official censorship. There is a major obstacle to free speech if someone who utters a criticism of the President is subject to a sentence of life imprisonment; but there is no prior restraint. Most censorship occurs through subsequent punishment, and perhaps the framers did not intend to ban subsequent punishment at all. If this is so, the history reveals an extraordinarily narrow free speech principle.

Thus William Blackstone, a large influence on the framers, wrote:

> [W]here blasphemous, immoral, treasonable, schismatical, seditious, or scandalous libels are punished by the English law . . . the **liberty of the press, properly understood, is by no means infringed** or violated. The liberty of the press is indeed essential to the nature of a free state; but this consists in laying no *previous* restraint upon publications, and not in freedom from censure for criminal matter when published. Every freeman has an undoubted right to lay what sentiments he pleases before the public . . . ; but if he publishes what is improper, mischievous, **or illegal, he must** take the consequences of his own temerity.[2]

Thus Joseph Story, probably the leading early commentator on the Constitution, could write:

> It is plain, then, that the language of this amendment imports no more, than that every man shall have a right to speak, write, and

print his opinions upon any subject whatsoever, without any prior
restraint, so always, that he does not injure any other person in his
rights, person, property, or reputation; and so always, that he does
not thereby disturb the public peace, or attempt to subvert the
government. It is neither more nor less, than, an expansion of the
great doctrine . . . that every man shall be at liberty to publish
what is true, with good motives and for justifiable ends.[3]

The view that the First Amendment is limited to prior
restraints has considerable historical support; nonetheless, it is
probably too extreme as a simple matter of history. Many members of the founding generation believed that the First
Amendment banned at least some forms of subsequent punishment. But even if this is so, it seems clear that during the founding period, much of what we now consider "free speech" was
thought to be unprotected, and that government could regulate
much speech if it was harmful or dangerous. Consider the infamous Sedition Act of 1798, which broadly prohibited "false, scan-
dalous, and malicious writings against the government of the
United States, or either house of the Congress of the United
States, or the President of the United States." The Sedition Act
operated as a formidable barrier to public criticism of government, including dissenting opinions published in popular newspapers. In contemporary textbooks, as well as in modern Supreme
Court opinions, the Sedition Act is commonly described as an act
of evil and unquestionably unconstitutional censorship. But it is
highly revealing that soon after the founding period, many and
perhaps most people thought that the Act was constitutionally
acceptable.[4] If many of the founders did not think that the
Sedition Act offended the First Amendment, we cannot now
claim that the constitutional protection of free speech, understood in its original context, is a self-applying, rigid protection of
expression.

All this means that there is much ambiguity in the seemingly
clear text. The text of the First Amendment is not rigid and it is
not absolute. The history confirms the ambiguity of the text. It
shows that the founders' conception of free speech was a good
deal narrower than ours, though it does not reveal a clear-cut
understanding of what speech was protected and what speech was
not. A simple lesson emerges from all this. However tempting it is

to pretend otherwise, the hard First Amendment cases cannot plausibly be resolved simply by invoking the text or history of the First Amendment. As a guide to our current dilemmas, insistence on the text is basically unhelpful, even fraudulent. I will be insisting on this point throughout. When we consider the issues that now cause great controversy—like campaign finance laws, rights of access to the media, conditions on funding of the arts, scientific speech, pornography, hate speech, commercial speech—we cannot rely on the text alone.

How should we deal with the history? I suggest that the First Amendment should be taken to set out a general principle of free expression, and that the contours of that principle should not be limited to the particular understandings of those who wrote and ratified it.[5] For one thing, those understandings are ambiguous. For another, it is unclear that the people who wrote the First Amendment wanted their particular views to control the future. For yet another, it is unclear that the framers' interpretive views should be binding on us even if the framers wanted them to be. Without circularity, we cannot say that the framers' views are binding simply because they intended them to be. Some sort of argument must be offered to support the view that the framers' particular views control us; and at least in the context of freedom of speech, it is not easy to see how that argument could be made persuasive.[6]

The proposition that the Constitution sets out general principles rather than particular historical understandings is of course controversial, and I will not defend it in detail here. It is notable that in the First Amendment area, even those who usually emphasize history tend to see free speech as a broad and evolving concept.[7] In any case, most Americans—including judges of otherwise different persuasions, legislators, presidents, indeed ordinary citizens—understand the free speech principle in this way. I will be relying on that understanding here. This does not mean that history is irrelevant; on the contrary, I will make historical arguments throughout. It means only that the concept of free speech should take the original constitutional vision at a certain level of generality and abstraction. The concept should not be tied to historically specific understandings if those understandings turn out to be indefensibly narrow as a matter of principle.

In this light, the arguments I will offer should be understood as an effort to give appropriate content to the ambiguous term "the freedom of speech," not to ignore the First Amendment or to call for a new constitutional amendment. If the free speech principle is to extend beyond the framers' narrow understanding—and everyone seems to think that it must—it is we who must decide on its content and structure.

The Madisonian First Amendment

The Supreme Court now understands the First Amendment to offer broad and wide-ranging protection to freedom of speech. In light of the ambiguity of text and history, we might be led to think that the current understanding of free speech in America has little to do with historical understandings. Perhaps the modern Supreme Court has taken a narrow amendment very far beyond its original purpose. Perhaps history, even if understood at a high level of abstraction, really has little to offer. But this conclusion would be far too strong. In one sense, there is a large degree of continuity between current practice and the original understanding of the First Amendment. Because this is so, we can identify a conception of free expression that draws strong support from history and that is also attractive in principle.

The continuity lies above all in the distinctive American contribution to the theory of sovereignty. In England, sovereignty lay with the King. "In the United States," as James Madison explained, "the case is altogether different. The People, not the Government, possess the absolute sovereignty."[8]

The placement of sovereignty in "We the People," rather than the government, may well have been the most important American contribution to the theory of politics. That contribution required large revisions in much of English political theory and practice; it also carried important lessons for freedom of speech. It created an ambitious system of "government by discussion," in which outcomes would be reached through broad public deliberation. It put a premium not on authority or privilege, but on the arguments set out in and resolved through general discussion. It set out a defining principle of political equality, in which no citizen counted for more or less than one.

As Madison understood it, this new conception of sovereignty ultimately required a judgment that any "Sedition Act" would be unconstitutional. "[T]he right of electing the members of the Government constitutes . . . the essence of a free and responsible government," and "[t]he value and efficacy of this right depends on the knowledge of the comparative merits and demerits of the candidates for the public trust." Indeed, the power represented by a Sedition Act ought, "more than any other, to produce universal alarm; because it is levelled against that right of freely examining public characters and measures, and of free communication among the people thereon, which has ever been justly deemed the only effectual guardian of every other right."[9]

What I will call the Madisonian conception of free speech appears principally in the passages from which these sentences are taken, in which Madison explicitly linked the First Amendment to the American revision of sovereignty and to a particular conception of democracy.[10] I do not mean to say that all of the arguments in this book are directly connected with the views and aspirations of James Madison. Many of them of course deal with issues that he could not have foreseen, and in bringing Madison's thought to bear on current dilemmas, we inevitably exercise discretion. But Madison did place a high premium on political (not economic) equality and on the deliberative functions of politics. He understood the free speech principle of the American Constitution, for which he above all was responsible, in the light of these commitments.[11] It therefore seems reasonable to describe the Madisonian conception as one that associates free speech with his distinctive understanding of politics.

Keeping Madison's pronouncements in mind, we might even think of the American tradition of free expression as a series of struggles to understand the relationships among this new conception of sovereignty, the commitment to political equality, the belief in democratic deliberation, and the system of free expression. Indeed, we might understand the extraordinary protection now given to political speech to be an elaboration of the American understanding of sovereignty.

My goal in this book is to evaluate the current system in light of the relationship between political sovereignty and the free speech principle. My largest conclusion is that an effort to root freedom of speech in a conception of popular sovereignty suggests that many of our current understandings are off the mark. I will therefore argue for substantial changes in the theory and practice of free speech. Above all, I suggest that there is a large difference between a "marketplace of ideas"—a deregulated economic market—and a system of democratic deliberation. Our current understandings have tended toward the former and thus disserved the latter. The extraordinary transformation of the First Amendment from a Madisonian principle into a species of neoclassical economics—into a celebration of laissez-faire and the "invisible hand" for speech—is an important and largely untold story.[12] New understandings, self-consciously focussed on democratic principles, would make for a better system of free expression. They would carry forward the Madisonian conception of speech into the dramatically new conditions offered by modern technology.

I will make a number of more particular suggestions. Some of these suggestions will be quite controversial, and in identifying them now, I must hope that the skeptical reader will be willing to suspend judgment. Currently American law protects much speech that ought not to be protected. It safeguards speech that has little or no connection with democratic aspirations and that produces serious social harm. Invoking the rhetoric of absolutism, it refuses to engage in sensible and salutary balancing.

I think that this is a mistake. I will thus be arguing that government has reasonably broad power to regulate (among other things) commercial speech, libelous speech, scientific speech with potential military applications, speech that invades privacy, disclosure of the name of rape victims, and certain forms of pornography and hate speech. I will also argue that in other areas, government is now given excessive power over speech, and that large steps are needed to strengthen constitutional protection. This is so, for example, with speech that is affected by the selective use of government funds and with allegedly libelous speech that really bears on democratic processes but is directed against private persons.

I also believe that current constitutional law threatens to invalidate, as it should not, legitimate and even crucial democratic efforts to promote the principle of popular sovereignty. We are now in the midst of a process of rethinking democratic structures in many areas—including campaign finance regulation, broadcasting law, and the electoral process in general. The First Amendment should not be an obstacle to this process of rethinking. Much of my argument will consist of an attempt to explain how democratic reforms that are now thought to compromise First Amendment principles, or even to amount to "censorship," would actually promote those very principles. We should not reflexively invoke "the freedom of speech" in order to invalidate reforms that would serve Madisonian goals.

I will devote particular attention to the possibility that government controls on the broadcast media, designed to ensure diversity of view and attention to public affairs, would help the system of free expression. Such controls could promote both political deliberation and political equality. In such reforms, I contend, lies the best hope for keeping faith with time-honored principles of democratic self-government under modern conditions.

In these ways I will be calling for something like a "New Deal" with respect to speech. Here I will apply some of the reasoning of President Franklin Delano Roosevelt's New Deal to current questions of First Amendment law and theory—though I will not be endorsing the New Deal's enthusiasm for dictation of social outcomes by large, centralized bureaucracies. My approach would produce significant changes in our understanding of the free speech guarantee. It would call for a large-scale revision in the view about when a law "abridges" the freedom of speech. At a minimum, it would mean that many imaginable democratic interferences with the autonomy of broadcasters or newspapers are not "abridgments" at all. On the contrary, such autonomy, guaranteed as it is by law, may itself be an abridgment of the free speech right. For the moment this argument must remain a bit abstract and obscure; I will offer many details in chapters 2 and 3.

I will also discuss the threats to the system of free expression that come from government control over government funds and over the speech of corporations. Government has often used its power over the purse to affect political, academic, and artistic choices. In recent controversies, it has tried to allocate funds so as to promote its own favored causes. I will deal in some detail with this issue, which promises to be among the most important in the next generation of free speech law. My conclusion is that there are sharp limits on government's power to be selective in the allocation of taxpayer funds for purposes of speech. I will also suggest that the government should have little power to regulate the political speech of corporations. Restrictions that are limited to corporations are unacceptably selective, even though government might well be permitted to limit the distorting effects of wealth in political campaigns.

My general conclusions can be summarized in this way. Deregulated economic markets are neither a sufficient nor a necessary condition for a system of free expression. In the first half of the book, I emphasize that free markets are not sufficient and that the relationship between deregulated markets and Madisonian goals is only partial and contingent. Reform of the market should therefore be upheld against constitutional attack. In the second half of the book, I emphasize that free markets are not constitutionally necessary, in the sense that legal controls on nonpolitical speech should often be upheld.

We should of course recognize the plurality and diversity of values served by a system of free expression. The First Amendment is not concerned only with politics; it has to do with autonomy and self-development as well. Any simple or unitary theory of free speech value would be obtuse. But we can acknowledge all this within the confines of a First Amendment that accords distinctive protection to political speech, and that is readier to allow regulation of nonpolitical speech.

Ultimately, I argue that many of our free speech disputes should be resolved with reference to the Madisonian claim that the First Amendment is associated above all with democratic self-government. The resulting system would resolve most of the current problems in free speech law without seriously compromising the First Amendment or any other important social values. But in order to reach this conclusion, it will be necessary to abandon or at least to qualify the basic principles that have dominated judicial, academic, and popular thinking about speech in the last generation.

Chapter 1

The Contemporary First Amendment

AMERICAN CHILDREN WATCH A GOOD DEAL of television—about twenty-seven hours per week—and American television contains a good deal of advertising. The average hour of television contains nearly 8 minutes of commercials. During most of its history, the Federal Communications Commission (FCC) imposed limits on the amount of advertising that could be screened on shows aimed at children. In 1984, however, the FCC eliminated the limits.

In the wake of deregulation, some stations show between 11 to 12 minutes per hour of commercials during children's programming on weekends, and up to 14 minutes on weekdays.[1] Some shows are actually full-length commercials, because the lead characters are products.[2]

In 1990 Congress tried to return to the pre-1984 period by enacting a law imposing, for children's programming, a limit of 10½ minutes of television commercials per hour on weekends, and 12 minutes on weekdays. But President Bush withheld his approval, invoking the First Amendment to the Constitution. According to the President, the Constitution "does not contemplate that government will dictate the quality or quantity of what Americans should hear—rather, it leaves this to be decided by free

1

media responding to the free choices of individual consumers."[3] The President did "not believe that quantitative restrictions on advertising should be considered permissible."

The Children's Television Act of 1990 nonetheless became law. Eventually it may be challenged on constitutional grounds. Perhaps the constitutional attack will be successful. Certainly the plausibility of the argument has played a central role in the debate over controls on children's advertising. It has deterred stronger efforts to encourage high-quality broadcasting for children. It has also contributed to the singularly weak enforcement of the 1990 Act, which produced no real changes well into its third year on the books.

This little-noticed episode is itself of considerable interest. But it reveals a broader point. Something important and perhaps even strange is happening to the First Amendment. In the 1940s, 1950s, and 1960s, the principal First Amendment suits were brought by political protestors and dissidents. The key cases of that period involved political extremists on the left or the right, or victims of McCarthyism, or civil rights protestors, or people challenging war efforts. Thus, for example, the great *Dennis* case, emblematic of the period, involved a federal prosecution of someone charged with criminal conspiracy because of his academic enthusiasm for the ideas of Marx and Lenin.[4] Most of the celebrated cases between 1930 and 1970 involved dissidents offering controversial contributions to democratic deliberation on public issues. Most of the victims of censorship were people who were rejecting current political orthodoxy.

Many of the modern debates have a strikingly different character. They involve free speech claims by owners of restaurants featuring nude dancing; by advertisers who have shown false, deceptive, or misleading commercials; by companies objecting to securities laws; by pornographers and sexual harassers; by businesses selling prerecorded statements of celebrities via "900" numbers; by people seeking to spend huge amounts on elections; by industries attempting to export potential military technology to unfriendly nations; by speakers engaging in racial harassment and hate speech; by tobacco companies objecting to restrictions on cigarette advertising; by newspapers disclosing names of rape victims; and by large broadcasters resisting government efforts to promote quality, public affairs programming, and diversity in the media. In these and other areas, people invoke the First Amendment not to ensure the preconditions for democratic deliberation, but to bring about a system in which speech is responsive to (in President Bush's words) "the free choices of individual consumers."

Many people think that a well-functioning economic market in speech is both necessary and sufficient for a well-functioning system of free expression. At most, we need a reliable antitrust law to break up monopolies; if we can do this, it is sometimes said, our basic problems will have been solved. The shift from the mid-century effort to protect political dissenters to a system of free speech "laissez-faire"—one that may or may not promote broad democratic debate—is surely a major one. How has all this happened?

In this chapter I try to answer this question. I do so by recovering an old debate in free speech cases and by showing how the resolution of that debate has led to the two key distinctions in current law. These are (1) the distinction between "low-value" and "high-value" speech and (2) the distinction among content-based, content-neutral, and viewpoint-based regulations of speech. With these distinctions in mind, we can identify the basic principles of current First Amendment doctrine, and we can see how the modern debates have come to take such surprising form.

A Dormant Debate

I have noted that President Bush's disapproval of the Children's Television Act reflects the mounting identification of free speech principles with free economic markets. Indeed, the identification has become so strong that it is sometimes hard even to see that the identification is both new and controversial, or that the free speech guarantee might be understood quite differently. For example, it may seem natural or even obvious to include commercial speech within the free speech guarantee; but for most of the nation's history, no serious person thought that commercial speech deserved constitutional protection. It may seem natural or even obvious that free markets in broadcasting are part and parcel of a system of freedom of expression; but until the 1980s, the dominant view was otherwise.

In 1949, the Federal Communications Commission famously

stated that the basic purpose of broadcasting is "the development of an informed public opinion through the dissemination of news and ideas concerning the vital public issues of the day."[5] The most striking development in free speech law is that marketplace thinking has become so dominant, and the competing views so dormant, that it is difficult even to identify those competing views. To begin to understand what has happened, we must step back a bit.

The American system of free expression is surprisingly young. The First Amendment has been in the Constitution since 1791, and our general tradition may well seem to be fiercely protective of free speech. But the free speech tradition really began well into America's second century, and in its speech-protective form, it has lasted for much less than half of our history. Before 1919, there were very few free speech cases in the federal courts. Government censorship did occur, and courts rarely concluded that such censorship violated the free speech principle. For example, and somewhat astonishingly, it was reasonably clear that the government was permitted to stop people from criticizing America's participation in a war. There were two governing ideas in the courts: the First Amendment was limited to "prior restraints"; and government could restrict speech so long as the speech had a tendency to cause harm.[6] This "harmful tendency" approach allowed government to restrict a wide range of material, including criticism of the nation during wartime and advocacy of left-wing causes.

It was not until a series of remarkable cases involving suppression of political speech during the World War I period that the Court moved slowly in the direction of a more protective standard, one that would allow government to suppress speech only if it could show a "clear and present danger." In the 1920s, the clear and present danger test became a serious alternative to the "harmful tendency" approach, and it received prominent support among the justices, particularly Justices Brandeis and Holmes.[7] In this period, the Court started to consider the possibility of offering a large degree of constitutional protection at least to political protests. Free speech had begun an era of dramatic expansion that has continued to this day.

It was in a period of about forty-five years—the central but relatively short era in American free speech law—that current understandings took on their present shape. From about 1925 to 1970, these understandings emerged during a long debate. That debate divided lawyers and judges—and the American public—along clear lines. On the one side were people approaching or even endorsing a form of First Amendment "absolutism." Their central claim was that the First Amendment is "an absolute," allowing no or very few exceptions. On the other side were the advocates of "reasonable regulation," calling for a form of balancing between the speech interests in the individual case and the harms feared by the state. The two sides could be identified by their attitudes toward five central ideas. I develop the competing views at some length, for they are of great relevance to current attitudes about the free speech principle both inside and outside the courts. Our contemporary debates are very much a product of these old disputes. Here, then, are the defining claims of the absolutists.

The first and simplest idea is that the government is the enemy of freedom of speech. Any effort to regulate speech, by the nation or the states, threatens the principle of free expression.

Second, the First Amendment should be understood as embodying a commitment to a strong conception of neutrality. Government may not draw any lines between speech it likes and speech that it hates. All speech stands on the same footing. The protection given to speech extends equally to Communists and Nazis, the Ku Klux Klan and the Black Panthers, Martin Luther King, Malcolm X, Huey Long, and George Wallace. Government should ensure that broadcasters, newspapers, and others can say what they wish, constrained only by the imperatives of the marketplace. Neutrality among different points of view is the government's first and most fundamental commitment. This conception of neutrality has emerged as a central feature of current law.

Third, the principle of free expression is not limited to "political" speech, or to expression with a self-conscious political component. There are two reasons for this conclusion. First, it is extremely difficult to distinguish between political and nonpolitical speech. Indeed, any such distinction is likely itself to reflect politics—in the form of the point of view of the judge—and this may well be illegitimate. Who is to say that literature or art is "nonpolitical"? How would we be able to know that this is true? Second, and quite apart from issues of judicial bias and administrability, nonpolitical speech, like political speech, fully warrants constitutional protection, for it too promotes important social values. In the period from 1925 to 1970, few people claimed that all speech was entitled to the same high degree of protection as political speech. But many people believed that any exceptions should be few, narrow, and sharply defined.

On this view, the free speech principle extends not simply to speech that contributes to democratic deliberation, but also and equally to such forms of expression as sexually explicit speech, music, art, scientific speech, and commercial speech. It follows that the First Amendment should be understood to set out a principle not limited to its particular historical well-springs, which were largely political. "Speech" within the meaning of the First Amendment extends at a minimum to most forms of expression that are literally words; it covers other forms of expression as well, like art and "conduct," such as draftcard-burning, that are intended to set out some kind of message.

Fourth, any restrictions on speech, once permitted, have a sinister and nearly inevitable tendency to expand. Principled limits on government are hard to come by. To allow one kind of restriction is in practice to allow many other acts of censorship as well. Lawyers generally like "slippery slope" arguments—arguments to the effect that once you allow one, seemingly narrow outcome, you are on a "slippery slope" toward a range of outcomes that you will deplore. In the period from 1925 to 1970, as in the current era, many people thought that "slippery slope" arguments deserve an especially prominent place in the theory of free expression. This is because the risk of censorship is so serious and omnipresent, and because seemingly small and innocuous acts of repression can turn quickly into a regime of repression that is anything but innocuous.

Fifth, and finally, "balancing" of competing interests ought so far as possible to play no role in free speech law. Judges should not uphold restrictions on speech simply because government seems to have good reasons for the restriction in the particular case. Judges should not examine "the value" of the speech at issue, compare it against the "harm" of that speech, and announce a judgment based on weighing value against harm. In any such judgments, there is far too large a risk of bias and discrimination. If judges were to balance harm against value, they would be likely to uphold a wide range of laws censoring political dissent, literature, and other forms of speech.

In the past quarter-century, ideas of this general sort commanded enormous respect. They were set out most prominently by Justices William O. Douglas and Hugo Black in judicial writings in the 1950s and 1960s.[8] They were advocated with special enthusiasm by the press itself. But variations on these ideas came from many teachers in the law schools and the political science departments, and of course from numerous litigators, most notably those representing newspapers and the American Civil Liberties Union.

In the same period, the components of the opposing position are also easy to identify.[9] The opponents were led most vigorously by Justice Felix Frankfurter, who waged a crusade for balancing and against absolutism under the First Amendment and indeed in every area of constitutional law. Justice Frankfurter and others argued that balancing is a healthy and even an inevitable part of a sensible system of free expression. Judges should take into account the various conflicting interests that are inevitably at stake. Speech that threatens real harm may be stopped. This category includes speech calling for violent overthrow of the government, libel of racial groups, and speech threatening a judge with reprisal if he rules against one of the parties. "Reasonable regulation" should be upheld. The First Amendment should be understood by reference to history, including the relatively limited aims of the framers and the complexities of the Supreme Court's own precedents, which hardly point toward free speech absolutism.

On this view, certain kinds of speech fall outside of the First Amendment altogether. The amendment does not protect advocacy of crime, commercial speech, hate speech, obscenity, and libel of individuals and groups. The government should also be allowed to maintain a civilized society. This principle means that government may guard against the degradation produced by (for example) obscenity, the risks to social order posed by speech advocating overthrow of the government, and the threats to equality and civility produced by racial hate speech.

It is increasingly difficult to remember the vigor and tenacity with which the two opposing camps struggled over their respective positions. Many of the basic commitments of the absolutist position are now cliches, even dogma—and this is so even though absolutism, taken as a whole, has failed to win over a majority of the members of the Supreme Court. Even if absolutism has had incomplete success, it is fair to say that the absolutist position is at least relatively ascendent, and that its basic commitments have left have a huge mark on the law. This is a remarkable development, for free speech absolutism was genuinely novel. As we have seen, the insistence on the supposedly unambiguous text—made most vivid in Justice Black's free speech writings[10]—was remarkably unpersuasive. Despite valiant efforts, the absolutists could never muster a lot of historical support on their behalf. Nonetheless, they have now won a dramatic number of victories in the Supreme Court. This is so especially with government efforts to restrict speech on the basis of its content. Here special judicial scrutiny and invalidation are routine, except for quite narrow categories of unprotected or partly protected speech (obscenity, "fighting words," private libel, and a few others).

The concrete results are nothing short of extraordinary. Constitutional protection has been given to commercial speech; to most sexually explicit speech; to many kinds of libel; to publication of the names of rape victims; to the advocacy of crime, even of violent overthrow of the government; to large expenditures on electoral campaigns; to corporate speech; to flag-burning; and to much else besides.[11]

Where We Are Now: The Two-Tier First Amendment

It is not an overstatement to say that, taken all together, these developments have revolutionized the law of free expression. We now appear to have a relatively simple system of law, one that makes it necessary to ask two separate questions. First: Does the speech at issue qualify as "low-value"? A distinction between low-value and high-value speech clearly operates in the cases, even though the Court has not made clear by what standard it distinguishes between the two. Second: Has government regulated the relevant speech in a sufficiently neutral way? The two questions are cross-cutting. As we will see, government may not regulate "low value" speech if it does so on a discriminatory basis, and it may regulate even "high value" speech if it does so with the requisite neutrality.

Because current law makes it necessary to ask whether speech qualifies as "low value," it is clear that in spite of the important successes of the free speech absolutists, all speech is not the same. Here the law reflects a kind of compromise between the absolutists and the balancers. Some speech lies at the free speech "core." Such speech may be regulated, if at all, only on the strongest showing of harm. Other speech lies at the periphery or outside of the Constitution altogether. This "low value" speech may be regulated if the government can show a legitimate, plausible justification.

Ordinary political speech, dealing with governmental matters, unquestionably belongs at the core. Such speech may not be regulated unless there is a clear and present danger, or, in the Court's words, unless it is "directed to inciting or producing imminent lawless action and is likely to incite or produce such action."[12] Under this standard, a speech containing racial hatred, offered by a member of the Ku Klux Klan, is usually protected; so too with a speech by a member of the Black Panthers, or by Nazis during a march in Skokie, Illinois, the home of many survivors of concentration camps. The ordinary remedy for harmful speech is more discussion and debate, not suppression. But much speech falls into the periphery of constitutional concern. Commercial speech, for example, receives some constitutional protection, in the sense that it qualifies as "speech" within the meaning of the First Amendment. Truthful, nondeceptive advertising is generally protected from regulation. But government may regulate commercial advertising it if it is false or misleading.[13]

Or consider the law of libel. Here we have an explicit system of free speech tiers. To simplify a complex body of law: In the highest, most speech-protective tier is libelous speech directed against a "public figure." Government can allow libel plaintiffs to recover damages as a result of such speech if and only if the speaker had "actual malice"—that is, the speaker must have known that the speech was false, or he must have been recklessly indifferent to its truth or falsity. This standard means that the speaker is protected against libel suits unless he knew that he was lying or he was truly foolish to think that he was telling the truth. A person counts as a public figure (1) if he is a "public official" in the sense that he works for the government, (2) if, while not employed by government, he otherwise has pervasive fame or notoriety in the community, or (3) if he has thrust himself into some particular controversy in order to influence its resolution. Thus, for example, Jerry Falwell is a public figure and, as a famous case holds, he is barred from recovering against a magazine that portrays him as having had sex with his mother.[14] Movie stars and famous athletes also qualify as public figures. False speech directed against public figures is thus protected from libel actions except in quite extreme circumstances.

But there is also a second tier of libelous speech, developed for libel suits brought by people who are not public figures. In these cases, actual malice need not be shown. The plaintiff may recover if he can show that the speaker was merely negligent. It is not necessary to demonstrate that the speaker knew that the statement was false or that he spoke with reckless indifference to the matter of truth or falsity.[15] There are some constitutional limits on libel actions by people who are not public figures, but the states have much more flexibility to punish libelous speech. Thus, for example, some speech that is constitutionally protected if directed against celebrities—say, a claim that a famous rock star is a drug addict—is not protected when the object of the libel is not famous. The important point here is that the Court has made a distinction between different kinds of libelous speech and thus created an explicit system of free speech "tiers."

Or consider the area of obscenity, one of the most controversial current areas of free speech law. I will devote a good deal of space to the subject of sexually explicit speech (see chapters 5 and 7). For the moment, the key point is that speech that qualifies as "obscene" is entirely without First Amendment protection; it is effectively defined outside of the First Amendment. Obscenity is understood to include a narrow category of speech that appeals to the prurient interest, is patently offensive, and lacks serious social value.[16] By contrast, ordinary art and literature are almost always protected. They may be regulated only on the basis of the strongest showing of harm; this is so even if the material is sexually explicit, indeed filled with graphic sexual acts. For constitutional purposes, most art is high-value. Obscenity is low-value.

There are many other kinds of "low-value" speech. Consider threats, attempted bribes, perjury, criminal conspiracy, price-fixing, criminal solicitation, unlicensed medical and legal advice, sexual and racial harassment. All these can be regulated without meeting the ordinary, highly speech-protective standards for demonstrating harm.

The Court has not set out anything like a clear theory to explain why and when speech qualifies for the top tier. At times the Court has indicated that speech belong in the top tier if it is part of the exchange of ideas, or if it bears on the political process.[17] But apart from these ambiguous hints, it has failed to tell us much about its basis for deciding that some forms of expression are different from others.

Where We Are Now: Different Methods of Abridgement

The second major building block of current law involves not the value of the speech, but the particular method by which government regulates speech. Here we are not concerned with whether the speech is high-value or part of the exchange of ideas; instead the issue is exactly what sort of line the government has drawn between what is permitted and what is proscribed. We need to distinguish among three possible kinds of restrictions on speech: content-neutral restrictions; viewpoint-based restrictions; and content-based restrictions.[18] The basic points are quite straightforward.

Often restrictions on speech are content-neutral, by which I mean that the content of the expression is utterly irrelevant to whether the speech is restricted. Imagine, for example, that the government bans all speech on billboards. Here the content of the speech does not matter to whether the restriction applies; it is in this sense that the restriction is content-neutral. Republicans and Democrats, Communists and Fascists, liberals and conservatives— everyone is treated exactly alike. We do not even need to know what the speech is in order to know whether it is banned. The restriction applies no matter what the speaker wants to say.

By contrast, some restrictions on speech are based on viewpoint, in the sense that government makes the point of view of the speaker central to its decision to impose, or not to impose, some penalty. The government might, for example, ban anyone from criticizing a war, or from favoring homosexuality, or from speaking against the incumbent President, or from arguing on behalf of affirmative action programs. Here the government is trying to protect a preferred side in a debate and to ban the side that it dislikes. A viewpoint-based restriction is distinctive in the sense that it comes into effect only when a particular viewpoint is expressed. We know that we are dealing with a viewpoint-based restriction if and only if the government has silenced one side in a debate.

Third, some restrictions on speech are viewpoint-neutral but content-based. For example, the government might ban all political speech in a certain place, or say that people may not discuss racial issues. Here the content of speech is indeed critical; we do have to know what the speech is in order to know whether it is regulated. But the viewpoint of the speaker is not crucial, or even relevant, to the restriction. A viewpoint-neutral, content-based regulation does not depend on what side the speaker takes. A prohibition on political speech, or on speech dealing with race, applies regardless of whether the speakers are liberal or conservative, Marxist or Fascist, Democrats or Republican, or anything else. In this sense, such a restriction has a degree of neutrality.

Viewpoint-based restrictions are a subset of the category of content-based restrictions. All viewpoint-based restrictions are, by definition, content-based; government cannot silence one side in a debate without making content crucial. But not all content-based restrictions are viewpoint-based. The key difference between a content-based and a viewpoint-based restriction is that the former need not make the restriction depend on the speaker's point of view.

The method of restriction is extremely important to current constitutional law. Whether a restriction will be upheld depends in large part on whether it is viewpoint-based, content-based, or content-neutral. Moreover, and significantly, this issue is entirely independent of the question of whether the speech at issue does or should belong in the upper tier. We could easily imagine *content-neutral restrictions on political speech*. Suppose, for example, that government bars anyone from distributing leaflets in airports, and that this ban is applied to the political statements made in such leaflets about a presidential election. Here we have a content-neutral restriction on "high-value" speech. Or suppose that government prohibits any speeches in subway stations. Someone who seeks to use a free space in the subway to protest civil rights policy might contend that his free speech rights have been violated. It is clear that his speech is political. It is not clear, however, that his constitutional rights have been abridged. The Court might uphold this content-neutral restriction on high-value speech, because the speaker has other means by which to communicate his message.

We could also imagine *viewpoint-based restrictions on low value speech*. Assume, for example, that government makes it a crime for anyone to engage in libelous speech[19] that is directed against conservatives. Or suppose that government imposes special penalties on threats directed against Democrats. Here we have viewpoint-based restrictions on unprotected speech.

Under current law, there is the strongest of presumptions against viewpoint-based restrictions. These restrictions are almost automatically unconstitutional. By contrast, a balancing test is applied to content-neutral restrictions, regardless of whether the speech at issue falls in the upper tier. The Court looks at the extent of the effect on speech and at the nature and strength of the government's interest. Frequently the Court is quite willing to accept the government's claim that its interest is sufficient to justify content-neutral restrictions. Thus the Court often accepts content-neutral restrictions on speech.

Finally, content-based restrictions face a strong, though not irrebuttable, presumption of unconstitutionality. In a few well-defined areas, content-based restrictions are perfectly acceptable. For example, government may regulate obscenity, false or misleading commercial speech, and private libel, even though all of these restrictions are content-based. (Notably, none of these restrictions is viewpoint-based; the bans apply regardless of the viewpoint of the speaker.) Moreover, some viewpoint-neutral, content-based restrictions have been upheld quite outside the context of the few well-defined areas of unprotected speech. Thus the Court has allowed government to ban political advertising on buses, and it has said that partisan political campaigning can be prohibited at army bases.[20]

So much for the structure of current law. How should we evaluate it? Some people think that the new law is an occasion for a sense of triumph and, perhaps, a belief that the principal difficulties with First Amendment doctrine have been solved. The remaining problems might be thought ones of applying this hard-won legal wisdom to the ever-present threats of censorship. Thus some observers think that the current efforts to censor pornography, often coming from feminist groups, are just the same as the old, discredited efforts to censor Joyce's *Ulysses* and Lawrence's *Sons and Lovers*. Others think that the new efforts to control racial hate speech are merely a new version of the old efforts to forbid speech by Communists and other political dissidents. This is indeed the view that emerges from most recent writing on freedom of speech.[21] Perhaps modern law has settled on an admirable set of principles. Perhaps our only task is to apply those principles to current dilemmas.

I think that we should hesitate before accepting this view. In the last decade, the commitments that emerged from the previous generation of free speech law have come under severe strain. At the very least, we should be willing to examine whether the commitments applied to the issues of the 1960s continue to make sense for the new issues of the 1990s and beyond. Consider the problems raised by campaign finance regulation. Should a candidate be allowed to spend unlimited sums to broadcast his message? If Congress cannot restrict expenditures on campaigns, might not the democratic process be skewed by wealth? Other hard questions arise in cases involving pornographic services over the telephone, speech in connection with the sale of securities, sexual and racial harassment in the workplace, scientific speech, nude dancing, commercial advertising, pornography, and regulation designed to produce quality and diversity in broadcasting. With these developments, previous alliances have come badly apart. Sometimes the old belief in "reasonable regulation" has been resurrected for the new disputes.

There are abundant ironies in all this. For one thing, the new coalitions have spurred plausible arguments of hypocrisy and brinksmanship. Free speech advocates say that the liberal's commitment to free speech has been abandoned as soon as it turns out that the commitment is inconvenient, or requires protection for causes that are unpopular with liberals. Hence it is said that some people have abandoned their own principles in order to endorse the "politically correct" orthodoxy of campus hate speech codes, or the new fashions said to have been brought about by the feminist attack on pornography. Indeed, it has been charged that for many, the apparently strong commitment to free speech stands revealed as merely contingent and convenient, and far from principled at all.

On the other hand, the broad enthusiasm for application of free speech principles to the new settings seems ironic as well, especially when it comes from conservatives usually respectful of tradition and of the need for restrained use of the Constitution. The constitutional protection given to commercial speech, for example, is extremely new, and it was rejected by (among many others) Justices Douglas and Black,[22] probably the most vigorous advocates of free expression in the history of the Supreme Court. The notion that the First Amendment protects libel of ethnic groups, or hate speech, is itself a quite modern development (to the extent that it is a development at all, an issue I take up in chapter 6). Indeed, libel on ethnic and racial grounds is prohibited in many flourishing democracies, with apparently little harmful effect on the system of free expression. The First Amendment has not until recently been thought to cast any doubt on the laws regulating speech connected with the sale of stocks and bonds. Before the last few decades, the states had very broad authority to regulate sexually explicit material. How the free speech principle interacts with campaign spending and broadcasting surely raises complex and novel issues.

In these circumstances, it may seem a bit puzzling or even cavalier to insist, as many do, that any regulatory efforts in these areas will really endanger the kind of freedom that is a prerequisite for democratic government, or reflect convenience rather than principle, or inevitably pave the way toward many dangerous incursions on speech. Insistence on the protection of all words and pictures seems especially odd when it is urged by people who otherwise proclaim the need for judicial restraint, for the liberation of democratic processes from constitutional compulsion, and for a firm attention to history. Such ideas would, in these contexts, argue most powerfully against use of the First Amendment. Often, at least, they would suggest that courts should respect the outcomes of democratic processes, even when those processes produce some controls on speech.

Through a series of remarkable judicial interpretations, we have acquired a new First Amendment. The past forty years have witnessed nothing short of a revolution. But the law now faces new constitutional problems raised by campaign finance laws, hate speech, pornography, rights of access to the media and to public places, and government funds accompanied by conditions on speech. These problems have shattered old alliances, and they promise to generate new understandings of the theory and practice of freedom of expression. Might anything be done about an electoral process that places a high premium on wealth, "soundbites," and short-term sensationalism? What can be said to victims of hate speech and violent pornography? Might legal controls improve television programming for children? What forms of public deliberation can government encourage?

In coming to terms with these questions, I propose that at a minimum, we should strive to produce an interpretation of the First Amendment that is well-suited to democratic ideals. As we will see, a reconnection of the First Amendment with democratic aspirations would require an ambitious reinterpretation of the principle of free expression. But the reinterpretation would have many advantages. It might help bring about an alliance among those who appear on both sides of old and new debates. It might even help promote a New Deal for speech, one that is simultaneously alert to time-honored free speech goals and to the novel settings in which those goals might be compromised. It is to this possibility that I now turn.

Chapter 2

A New Deal for Speech

FOR THE MOST PART, the system of free expression in America is now approaching a system of unregulated private markets.[1] Its operation is broadly similar to that of other markets, like those for cars, brushes, cereal, and soap. Through this market, you will indeed be widely heard if you can persuade a newspaper or a broadcasting station to allow you to speak. Of course if you have enough money to buy access to a newspaper or a broadcasting station, many people will hear what you have to say. Both political electioneering and commercial advertising offer countless examples; the recent efforts of Ross Perot, whatever else they may reveal, show the extraordinary power of money in bringing speech to the attention of the public. And you will have an especially wonderful opportunity to communicate your message to a large audience if you have enough money to own a newspaper or a radio station.

Newspapers and broadcasting stations in turn operate largely, though far from exclusively, on the profit principle. They will allocate the right to speak largely in accordance with the goal of increasing financial returns. Of course many owners are willing to sacrifice money in return for better performance. The norms and principles of the newspaper and television businesses affect the

17

content and delivery of news and media "product." But in general, these businesses will be far more receptive to speakers who can help them acquire a large audience than to speakers who cannot. They will be particularly attentive to the wishes of advertisers, who usually want a large audience, but who sometimes want a general pro-business atmosphere that does not perfectly correspond with the goal of increasing the number of people who view or listen (see chapter 3 for details).

Is this a healthy system of free expression? Certainly we could do much worse. The U.S. government is rarely if ever involved in specific decisions about which speakers can have access to which stations or newspapers. In the United States there are many broadcasting stations on both radio and television; there are many newspapers as well. All in all, we have extraordinary diversity in speech outlets. Some current critics speak of "monopoly" of the broadcasting or print media; but there are no real monopolies here. Many people, and many points of view, are able to have access to some part of the media. On every important count, a market system of this kind is much better than a system of centralized government control of speech. For this reason, it sometimes seems as if we are, and should be, moving toward a conception of free expression in which the dominant understanding is one of antitrust law. Once we have broken up all interferences with the operation of the free market, and ensured against any vestige of monopoly, our free speech problems will be solved. This is how economists and many others normally think of commodities in a free enterprise system. Why should speech be any different?

It is important, however, to ask whether unregulated markets actually promote a well-functioning system of free expression. We should not simply assume that the answer is affirmative. To approach this question, we need to have a sense of the features of a well-functioning system. Following the Madisonian conception, I suggest that such a system is closely connected to the central constitutional goal of creating a deliberative democracy.[2] In such a system, politics is not supposed merely to protect preexisting private rights or to reflect the outcomes of interest-group pressures. It is not intended to aggregate existing private preferences, or to produce compromises among various affected groups with self-interested stakes in the outcome. Instead it is designed to have an important deliberative feature, in which new information and perspectives influence social judgments about possible courses of action. Through exposure to such information and perspectives, both collective and individual decisions can be shaped and improved.

Thus, for example, the public might see that some familiar statement about the facts with respect to (say) nuclear power is simply wrong; that a proposed policy for welfare reform will have surprising and unfortunate consequences; that it is necessary to make choices of a certain kind between competing goals, including reduction of the deficit and environmental protection. Or the process of public deliberation might show the real nature and consequences of some social practice, like sexual harassment or abortion.

The system of free expression is the foundation of this process. One of its basic goals is to ensure broad communication about matters of public concern among the citizenry at large and between citizens and representatives. Indeed, we might even define political truth as the outcome of this deliberative process, assuming that the process can approach or meet the appropriate conditions.[3] Those conditions include adequate information; a norm of political equality, in which arguments matter but power and authority do not; an absence of strategic manipulation of information, perspective, processes, or outcomes in general; and a broad public orientation toward reaching right answers rather than serving self-interest, narrowly defined. It is not necessary to claim that the result of any such deliberative process will be unanimity or even consensus. Sometimes people genuinely disagree, and discussion will not bring them together. It may even tear them apart. We should also acknowledge that real-world processes do not conform to these conditions. But under the right circumstances, the system of public discussion should improve outcomes and help move judgments in appropriate directions.[4]

In this system of "government by discussion,"[5] private preferences and beliefs are not taken as fixed and static. What people now prefer and believe may be a product of insufficient information, limited opportunities, legal constraints, or unjust background conditions.[6] People may think as they do simply because they have not been provided with sufficient information and opportunities. It is not paternalistic, or an illegitimate interference with competing conceptions of the good, for a democracy to promote scrutiny and testing of preferences and beliefs through deliberative processes. (Of course there must be rights-based constraints on what might occur in, or as a result of, those processes.) Existing preferences should be subjected to general public discussion, rather than taken as the inevitable building-blocks for government outcomes.

Moreover, the system of deliberative democracy is premised on and even defined by reference to the commitment to political equality. At least in the public sphere, every person counts as no more or no less than one. In markets, "votes" are measured by dollars, which of course vary from rich to poor. In public life, a different norm of equality plays a key role. The constitutional principle of one person-one vote is simply the most recent effort to concretize the traditional constitutional commitment to political equality. It follows that in the deliberative process, arguments are to count if good reasons are offered on their behalf. The identity, the resources, and the power of the speaker do not matter. To institutionalize the idea that the force of an argument is independent of the person who makes it, the system of deliberative democracy must incorporate this principle of political equality.

So much for the aspirations of the Madisonian system. There are many ways for that system to fail in practice. The ideal conditions are extremely demanding and unlikely ever to be met in the real world.[7] To succeed at all, the system must have two minimal features. First, *it must reflect broad and deep attention to public issues.* An absence of information and attention is a decisive problem for the system. If many or most people are without information, or if they do not attend to public issues, the Madisonian system cannot get off the ground. It follows that government should not suppress ideas and information. It also follows that serious issues must be covered, and they must be covered in a serious way. Indeed, the mere availability of such coverage may not be enough if few citizens take advantage of it, and if most viewers and readers are content with programming and news accounts that do not deal well or in depth with public issues. If sensationalistic scandals and odd anecdotes not realistically bearing on substantive policy issues are the basic source of political judgments, the system cannot work.

It may seem controversial or strange to say that there is a problem for the Madisonian system if people do not seek serious coverage of serious issues. Perhaps this suggestion is unacceptably paternalistic; perhaps we should take people however we find them. But as I have noted, the system of deliberative democracy is not supposed simply to implement existing desires. Its far more ambitious goal is to create the preconditions for a well-functioning democratic process. If current preferences disfavor the acquisition of information about political affairs, there is a serious problem with the system. To be sure, no political regime can or should insist that citizens be thinking about politics all, most, or even much of the time; people have many other things to do. But lack of interest in information about government should not be taken as inevitable or as a product of "human nature." We know enough to know that lack of interest is often a result of inadequate education, perceived powerlessness, unsatisfactory alternatives, or a belief that things cannot really be changed. Indifference to politics is frequently produced by insufficient information, the costs of gaining more knowledge, poor educational background, or, more generally, an unjust status quo.

The appropriate remedy for this state of affairs is far from clear. But a polity that does not show the requisite attention cannot create or benefit from genuine citizenship. It follows that if deregulated markets do not deal with public issues, or do so only superficially, the Madisonian aspiration has not been fulfilled. We might therefore understand the Madisonian system to build on the basic democratic commitment to education for all. A system of free expression is designed to benefit from and to complement and extend that commitment. From this point it emerges that if most people do not select options that produce information about public issues, there is a severe problem, though again the remedy remains obscure.

But education and attention to public issues are not enough. The second requirement is that *there must be public exposure to an appropriate diversity of view*. What counts as appropriate diversity is of course controversial. I suggest only that a broad spectrum of opinion must be represented, that people must be allowed to hear sharply divergent views, and that it is important to find not merely the conventional wisdom and the reasons that can be offered on its behalf, but also challenges to the conventional wisdom from a variety of different perspectives. People should see, for example, that there are strong arguments for and against affirmative action policies, for and against a constitutional right to abortion, for and against government funding of the arts, for and against aggressive government action to combat certain environmental risks.

It is important to ensure that government does not suppress dissident views. It is also important to ensure not merely that diversity is available, but also that a significant part of the citizenry is actually exposed to diverse views about public issues. As part of this requirement, no group of citizens should be deprived of exposure to diverse views because of its race or its economic status. Without broad exposure, or with selective limits on available information, public deliberation will be far less successful, and the Madisonian conception will be badly compromised. That conception envisages a high degree of heterogeneity as a precondition for political deliberation. In the absence of different perspectives and a wide range of information, the system cannot function. It will fail to expose errors of fact. It will fail to shed the kind of light that comes only from diverse perspectives about public issues. It will simultaneously violate the commitments to political equality and political deliberation. If everyone thinks the same thing, or nearly the same thing, there will be too few alternatives to allow for genuine discussion.

Of course, our expectations for a system of free expression should be realistic, not utopian. Busy people cannot be expected or required to devote all or most of their time to public issues. One of the advantages of a representative system—not to mention one with a large bureaucracy—is that it allows the citizenry to devote its attention to subjects other than politics. But it is hardly unrealistic to assess a system of free expression by examining whether it generates broad and deep attention to public issues, and whether it brings about public exposure to an appropriate diversity of view. These are not utopian goals.

On both of the key counts, the record of the current American system is at best quite mixed. I will offer many details below. But it would not be an overstatement to say that much of the free speech "market" now consists of scandals, sensationalized anecdotes, and gossip, often about famous movie stars and athletes; deals rarely with serious issues and then almost never in depth; usually offers conclusions without reasons; turns much political discussion into the equivalent of advertisements; treats most candidates and even political commitments as commodities to be "sold"; perpetuates a bland, watered-down version of conventional morality on most issues; often tends to avoid real criticisms of existing practice from any point of view; and reflects an accelerating "race to the bottom" in terms of the quality and quantity of attention that it requires. The current system also makes it difficult for many views, especially dissenting views from the right or the left, to get a serious hearing at all.

If anything like this is true, the current system of free expression is nothing to celebrate. And if anything like this is true, it is, I believe, the law—not nature, not "freedom," and not "private decisions"—that is responsible. It is the law that creates the system operated by the broadcasting media; it is even the law that creates the system operated by the print media. Both systems are an artifact, or a product, of a very distinctive set of legal requirements. For the moment these suggestions may seem obscure. We can give them more content by exploring the possibility of a "New Deal" for speech. This New Deal, I suggest, should parallel President Franklin Delano Roosevelt's New Deal during the 1930s. Without indulging the New Deal enthusiasm for large administrative agencies, it should be rooted in substantially similar concerns.[8]

Brandeis vs. Holmes

We must begin, however, in the generation before Roosevelt, with Justices Oliver Wendell Holmes and Louis Brandeis, two of the greatest figures in the entire history of American law. Much of their greatness stems from their remarkable work on the First Amendment. In historic cases in the early part of the century, Holmes and Brandeis wrote extraordinary dissenting opinions, rejecting the conventional view that the government could ban political speech merely because the speech was dangerous.[9] In the key cases, Holmes and Brandeis argued that the government could not constitutionally punish the dissident writings of people protesting against war efforts or proclaiming their allegiance to radical causes, including socialism. Much of the current protection of speech stems from the analysis in these opinions. The highly protective "clear and present danger" test, to take only the most prominent example, owes its origin to the dissents of Holmes and Brandeis. A good deal of modern free speech theory is taken from these dissents.

The two justices often seemed to speak as one. Holmes joined in Brandeis' dissents, and Brandeis joined in Holmes' separate First Amendment opinions. For several generations Holmes and Brandeis have been grouped together as the outstanding libertarians of the First Amendment—indeed, as jurisprudential twins. If we look at their opinions, however, we will find striking differences, and the differences bear intriguingly on current dilemmas. Let us look first at a passage from Holmes' greatest free speech opinion, written in *Abrams v. United States*.[10] Abrams had circulated leaflets calling for a general strike, attacking capitalism, and complaining of the American decision to send marines to Vladivostok and Murmansk. The Court upheld a criminal conviction under the Espionage Act of 1917. Holmes responded:

Persecution for the expression of opinions seems to me perfectly logical. If you have no doubt of your premises or your power and want a certain result with all your heart you naturally express your wishes in law and sweep away all opposition. . . . But when men have realized that time has upset many fighting faiths, they may come to believe even more than they believe the very foundations of their own conduct that the ultimate good desired is better reached by free trade in ideas—that the best test of truth is the power of the thought to get itself accepted in the competition of the market, and that truth is the only ground upon which their wishes safely can be carried out. That at any rate is the theory of our Constitution. It is an experiment, as all life is an experiment. Every year if not every day we have to wager our salvation upon some prophecy based upon imperfect knowledge. While that experiment is part of our system I think that we should be eternally vigilant against attempts to check the expression of opinions that we loathe and believe to be fraught with death, unless they so imminently threaten immediate interference with the lawful and pressing purposes of the law that an immediate check is required to save the country.

Holmes' opinion builds strong protection for speech on two foundations: skepticism about prevailing understandings of truth and the metaphor of "competition in the market." Truth itself is defined by reference to what emerges through "free trade in ideas." For Holmes, it seems to have no deeper status. The competition of the market is the governing conception of free speech. On his view, politics itself is a market, like any other. Holmes does not appear to place any special premium on political discussion. *Abrams* involved a political dissenter, but Holmes does not emphasize this point. His reasoning seems to apply to all speech, whether political or not. Finally, the value of speech is instrumental in the sense that it is connected with the emergence of truth. Holmes does not suggest that freedom of speech is a good in itself.

This is clearly and self-consciously a marketplace conception of free speech, one that is closely connected with Holmes' marketplace theories of politics.[11] The two foundations of the basic view—skepticism and "competition in the market"—are not entirely compatible. To think of speech as instrumental to truth, it seems necessary to have a way of defining truth that is hardly skeptical and that is independent of the procedure of market competition. The point creates some confusion in the Holmes opinion and indeed in the marketplace metaphor as a whole. Does market competition really *define* truth, or does it instead lead to truth, which is independently defined? If market competition defines truth, we need to have a description of the appropriate preconditions for such competition, for it seems odd to say that any particular market will inevitably yield understandings that should be taken as "truth." Unrestricted marketplace competition in commercial advertising, for example, may well produce falsehoods. If the market does not define truth but merely leads to it, we need to understand exactly how and when this process occurs. It is not easy to explain these points.[12]

In its most attractive form, the market metaphor builds on the pragmatic view of truth associated with Charles Sanders Peirce, a strong influence on Holmes.[13] On this view, political truth is what emerges in a well-functioning democracy, one that allows open discussion under ideal or at least acceptable conditions. Truth is defined as the beliefs that emerge through discussion under these circumstances. But Holmes' skepticism, and his insistence on "free trade," give his conception a distinctive flavor of its own. In all his writings on free speech, Holmes pays little attention to the appropriate conditions under which free trade in ideas will ensure truth, a gap that is probably attributable to his skepticism about whether truth, as an independent value, is at issue at all. Thus Holmes concludes one of his other great free speech opinions with the remarkable suggestion that if, "in the long run, the beliefs expressed in proletarian dictatorship are destined to be accepted by the dominant forces of the community, the only meaning of free speech is that they should be given their chance and have their way."[14]

Now let us turn to the key passages in Brandeis' greatest opinion, set out in *Whitney v. California*.[15] Whitney was convicted for her attendance at the national convention of the Communist Labor Party, which had urged the overthrow of the American government. The Supreme Court upheld the conviction. Justice Brandeis wrote separately:

> Those who won our independence believed that the final end of the state was to make men free to develop their faculties; and that in its government the deliberative forces should prevail over the arbitrary. They valued liberty both as an end and as a means. They believed liberty to be the secret of happiness and courage to be the secret of liberty. They believed that freedom to think as you will and to speak as you think are means indispensable to the discovery and spread of political truth; that without free speech and assembly discussion would be futile; that with them, discussion affords ordinarily adequate protection against the dissemination of noxious doctrine; that the greatest menace to freedom is an inert people; that public discussion is a political duty; and that this should be a fundamental principle of the American government. . . . Those who won our independence by revolution were not cowards. They did not exalt order at the cost of liberty. They did not

fear political change. To courageous, self-reliant men, with confidence in the power of free and fearless reasoning applied through the process of popular government, no danger flowing from speech can be deemed clear and present, unless the incidence of the evil apprehended is so imminent that it may befall before there is opportunity for full discussion. If there be time to expose through discussion the falsehood and fallacies, to avert the evil by the processes of education, the remedy to be applied is more speech, not enforced silence. Only an emergency can justify repression.

There is an obvious overlap between the Holmes and Brandeis opinions. The overlap includes their strongly speech-protective stance and their shared desire to prohibit government from interfering with deliberative processes. But in Brandeis we have a quite distinctive understanding of the free speech principle. In place of Holmes' hard-headed skepticism, Brandeis offers an exceedingly optimistic, even romantic account of the contribution of political deliberation to both democratic government and the development of human faculties.[16] The origins of Holmes' thought lie in modern interest-group pluralism—in the belief that politics consists of the outcomes of struggles for power among self-interested groups. Brandeis' opinion, recalling Pericles' funeral oration, has altogether different roots. Those roots can be found in classical republican thought, with its emphasis on political virtue, on public-spiritedness, on public deliberation, and on the relationship between character and citizenship. There is no market metaphor here. Brandeis does not speak of "free trade." Brandeis's opinion emphasizes not all speech, but the distinctive properties of political discussion and political debate.

Moreover, and crucially, Brandeis thinks that a democracy requires a certain sort of person, one who takes citizenship seriously. Hence the contrast between "fear" and "courage," a contrast that permeates the opinion. Hence—in words foreign to Holmes—Brandeis writes that "the greatest menace to freedom is an inert people"; hence "public discussion is a political duty"; hence the free speech principle is connected with faith in "the deliberative forces" in government. In Brandeis' conception, free speech is emphatically "a means" insofar as it is connected to the achievement of a certain conception of democratic government, one that contains and promotes political discussion. But freedom is also "an end" insofar as a certain understanding of liberty is an intrinsic rather than merely instrumental good. It is an intrinsic good—a form of liberty—to be able to develop one's capacities in a way that promotes courage, self-mastery, virtue. We might suggest that in all these ways, Brandeis sets out a civic conception of free speech—civic because of its deep connection with citizenship and democracy. We might also connect Brandeis' view with Madison's association of the free speech principle and the American revision of the concept of sovereignty. For Brandeis, as for Madison, the First Amendment is part of the commitment to the experiment in self-government.

For many years, the sharp differences between Holmes and Brandeis were basically irrelevant for purposes of constitutional law, and the differences could be safely ignored. When government tries to suppress political dissent, the two conceptions could march hand-in-hand. Holmes and Brandeis could be grouped together as free speech heroes. But this is only a contingent alliance. What if a marketplace of ideas allows for little in the way of political deliberation and discussion? What if the marketplace yields little attention to public issues and diversity of view? What if expenditures on speech reflect large disparities in wealth? What if the marketplace sometimes helps produce an "inert people"? What if government tries to regulate the marketplace in the interest of promoting attention to public issues and diversity of view? Here Holmes and Brandeis would be split apart. Here the marketplace conception of speech would compete with the civic competition. The two would be antagonists, not allies. I suggest that this is exactly what is happening to freedom of speech in the modern era.

What the New Deal Meant

I am going to propose a sort of New Deal for speech; it is therefore important to have a sense of what happened during the New Deal in the 1930s. In that period, many related disputes were prominent in political and legal debate, largely outside of the context of free speech. It is in this period that the conflict between unregulated markets and constitutional goals received its most explicit attention in the United States. The conflict produced a significant reformation of the American constitutional framework.[17] The New Deal created the modern regulatory state. It self-consciously rejected the system of laissez-faire. It gave rise to an extensive national government, with a wide array of regulatory agencies displacing market arrangements. Some of the debate in the period is unhappily abstract; but it is worth close attention, since an understanding of the New Deal reformation will shed a great deal of light on current free speech dilemmas.

Before the New Deal, the Constitution was often understood as a constraint on government "regulation," just as it is now with respect to speech. In practice, this understanding meant that the Constitution frequently prohibited government from interfering with existing distributions of rights and entitlements.[18] Hence minimum wage and maximum hour laws, now pervasive in the law of all industrialized democracies, were invalidated on constitutional grounds. Courts treated these laws as unjustifiable exactions—as "takings"—from employers for the benefit of employees and the public at large.[19]

The Constitution thus insulated private arrangements and economic markets from public control, especially if the government's goals were paternalistic or redistributive. According to the Supreme Court of the early twentieth century, the government must be "neutral" in general, and between employers and employees in particular. Neutrality was defined by reference to existing distributions, or to what people currently had. Government departures from existing distribution signaled partisanship; government respect for those distributions signaled neutrality. A violation of the neutrality requirement, thus understood, would count as a violation of the Constitution.

On the pre–New Deal view, existing distributions marked out the boundary between neutrality and partisanship; but this was not their only function. They also created the very division between inaction and action. Government inaction was defined as respect for existing distributions. Government action was understood as interference with them. The rallying cry "laissez-faire" captured such ideas. (The parallel with current free speech law should be obvious by now.) Market ordering, and respect for existing distributions, was said to "leave everything alone." The fear and the very conception of "government intervention" followed from this view.

The New Deal reformers argued that this entire framework was built on fictions. Their basic response is captured in President Franklin Delano Roosevelt's reference to "this man-made world of ours"[20] in arguing for social security legislation, and in his insistence that "we must lay hold of the fact that economic laws are not made by nature. They are made by human beings."[21] Roosevelt claimed in this way that the social and economic world was a product of human beings, rather than of nature and nature's laws. People, rather than nature, had created economic markets and existing distributions. Laws underlay markets and made them possible. If they had good reasons for doing so, people might change those markets and existing distributions.

On this view, a major problem with the pre–New Deal framework was that it treated the existing distribution of resources and opportunities as prepolitical and presocial—as given rather than chosen—when in fact it was not. It saw minimum wage and maximum hour laws as introducing government into a private or voluntary private sphere, when that sphere was actually itself a creation of law, and hardly purely voluntary. When the law of trespass enabled an employer to exclude an employee from "his" property unless the employee met certain conditions, the law was crucially involved. Without the law of trespass, and accompanying legal rules of contract and tort, the relationship between employers and employees would not be what it now is; indeed, it would be extremely difficult to figure out what that relationship might be, if it would exist in recognizable form at all.

Most generally, the legal rules of property, contract, and tort had produced the set of entitlements that yielded market hours and wages. Those rules specified who owned what and who could do what to whom. All this was a creation of law. The market system, so often described as the realm of purely voluntary interactions, was actually pervaded by law. All this did not mean that individual behavior and initiative were irrelevant to social outcomes. On the contrary, private efforts of course played a role in producing wealth. But the reward of a certain definition of "effort," and the protection of that reward by the state, were emphatically legal. Nor did the New Dealers suggest that voluntary interactions were not possible, or that such interactions were not facilitated by common law rules. They placed a high premium on free choice and they believed that free markets often promoted free choice. They insisted only that those rules embodied certain forms of coercion as well, and that we should closely investigate the role of freedom and coercion in particular cases.

As used in the pre–New Deal period, the traditional understandings of "regulation" and "government intervention" therefore seemed misleading. The government did not "act" only when it disturbed existing distributions. What people had, in markets, was a function of the entitlements that the law conferred on them. The notion of "laissez-faire" thus stood revealed as a conspicuous fiction. In a system of free markets, government did not leave everything alone. It allocated rights of property; it decided on the law of contract and tort. To the extent that property rights played a role in market arrangements—as they inevitably did—those arrangements were a creature of positive law, including, most notably, the law that gave some people a right to exclude other people from "their" land and resources.[22]

On this view, market wages and market hours did not come from the sky. Rather than superimposing regulation on a realm of purely voluntary interactions, minimum wage laws simply substituted one form of regulation for another. If I start a company, and make a good deal of money, it is in large part because the law of property, tort, and contract has enabled me to do so. The law allows me to own property, and it protects my rights against private and public incursion. The law says that the contracts that benefit me must be enforced. The law identifies the kinds of harms that cannot be imposed on me without compensation. Corporate law may even give me special benefits, such as limited liability, favorable tax treatment, and perpetual life, that help me to accomplish my goals. To repeat: These points do not disparage the role of individual effort and initiative in market arrangements. But without legal rules of certain kinds, entirely different winners and losers would emerge. Who knows who would benefit and lose in a system in which property, contract, corporation, tax, and tort law did not exist, or took on quite different forms?

The New Dealers were well-aware that the fact that an existing distribution is not natural or prepolitical provides no argument against it. Nothing in their account means that markets are unjust. Eyeglasses are not natural, but this does not make them a bad idea. Laws prohibiting murder are social creations, but we should not repeal them. "Naturalness" is generally irrelevant from the point of view of law, politics, and morality.[23] When one regulatory system is superimposed on another, it is not true that we cannot evaluate the two for their role in diminishing or increasing human welfare or liberty. A system of private property is a construct of the state, but it is also an important individual and collective good. The fact that it is socially created is not a reason to eliminate it. At least most of the time, a market system—in general or for speech—indeed promotes both liberty and prosperity, and its inevitable origins in law hardly undermine that fact.

To their basic point, however, the New Dealers added a claim that existing distributions were sometimes inefficient or unjust. Different forms of governmental ordering had to be evaluated pragmatically, not dogmatically or through axioms, and directly in terms of their consequences for social efficiency and social justice. As the legal realist Robert Hale wrote, "the next step is to . . . realize that the question of maintenance or the alteration of our institutions must be discussed on its pragmatic merits, not dismissed on the ground that they are the inevitable outcome of free society."[24] Morris Cohen, writing just before the New Deal, put the point similarly: "[T]he recognition of private property as a form of sovereignty is not itself an argument against it. . . . [I]t is necessary to apply to the law of property all those considerations of social ethics and enlightened public policy which ought to be brought to the discussion of any just form of government."[25]

The fact that markets are a creature of law meant not that they were impermissible, but that they would be assessed in terms of what they did on behalf of the human beings subject to them. The New Dealers were not socialists; they generally appreciated the contributions of free markets and private property to prosperity and freedom. They thought that we would have to look at the particular justification for intruding on market ordering in different areas. Perhaps consumers lacked relevant information, and therefore needed protection against unfair dealing; perhaps workers were competing against each other to their collective detriment; perhaps a company was imposing external harms on people who were not parties to any transaction. Possibilities of this kind would have to be investigated in individual cases. At the very least, a democratic judgment that markets constrained liberty—embodied in, say, a law calling for maximum hours or minimum wages—could be plausible and was entitled to judicial respect. That judgment should not be foreclosed by constitutional law.

An oddly overlooked fact is especially important for present purposes: Many of the New Deal institutions actually regulate speech. The Securities and Exchange Commission (SEC) restricts what people may say when they sell stocks and bonds; it pervasively controls expression. Indeed, the SEC imposes old-fashioned prior restraints, requiring government preclearance before speech may reach the public. The Federal Communications Commission (FCC) oversees the broadcasting system under a vague "public interest" standard. It is clear that the New Dealers anticipated that the FCC would regulate the content of speech. Indeed, they sought content-based regulation as a corrective to market forces. The Food and Drug Administration (FDA) pervasively controls the labeling and communicative practices of people who sell foods and drugs. Speech is one of its central targets. The National Labor Relations Board (NLRB) imposes severe restrictions on what may be said by employees, union officials, and especially employers. The Federal Trade Commission (FTC) controls unfair and deceptive trade practices. Many of those practices—indeed most of them—consist of speech.

Some important unifying themes run through all of these areas of New Deal regulatory law. The New Dealers conspicuously rejected the view that speech was absolutely immune from government control. Many of their agencies were a response to the perception that in light of the existing distribution of rights and entitlements, legal controls on speech may actually turn out to promote a well-functioning system of free expression. Is an unregulated securities market necessarily the best system of free speech? The New Dealers thought that it was not, and that government controls on what sellers could say would make for a better process of discussion and free choice. Without legal controls on what employers may say during a union election, do we really have a healthy "marketplace of ideas"? In view of the employer's power over the employee, the New Dealers thought that government may legitimately control speech, including an employer's threat to eliminate the business in the event of unionization. The New Dealers believed that the deliberative process could actually be improved by legal controls on employer speech.

In all of these cases, we might conclude that the New Dealers were trying to regulate speech in order to protect the *deliberative autonomy* of everyone involved. They sought to do this by limiting certain forms of coercion and deception that had otherwise been made possible by law. Restrictions on the sharp or coercive practices of people who sell securities, food, and drugs, or who manage broadcasting stations, might well promote the system of free expression.

Theory

Despite the existence of New Deal institutions regulating expression, New Deal ideas have played remarkably little role in the constitutional law of free speech. For purposes of constitutional understandings of the free speech principle, contemporary understandings of neutrality and partisanship, or action and inaction, are identical to those that predate the New Deal. The whole category of government "intervention" is defined accordingly. It is through precisely this route that Holmes' marketplace metaphor has come to dominate the field, and that we have lost a sense of its potentially sharp contrast with Brandeis' civic conception.

I believe that the recent First Amendment debates confirm the wisdom of the New Deal reformation on this score. We should not be so reflexively opposed to "government regulation." Speaker autonomy, made possible as it is by law, may not promote constitutional purposes. For example, if government requires free air time for candidates, it need not be thought impermissibly to intrude on a law-free private realm. So too, campaign finance laws need not be seen as impermissible government intervention into the private sphere. If designed well, they could even promote the democratic goals of the First Amendment.

With respect to freedom of expression, I think that American constitutionalism has failed precisely to the extent that it has not taken the New Deal reformation seriously enough. The failure stems from the fact that the real purposes of the protection of free speech—its roots in the Madisonian conception of sovereignty, its concern to bring about broad deliberation, including attention to public issues and to diverse views—have often played little role in thinking about the meaning of the First Amendment. Unlike our New Deal predecessors, we do not attempt a pragmatic assessment of the relationship between any particular regulatory regime and full and varied discussion of public affairs. Instead we simply assume that government "intervention," reflexively understood in a distinctive, pre–New Deal way, is the intrinsic evil to be eradicated through constitutional law. We do this without exploring whether this approach to the First Amendment serves or disserves Madisonian goals.

In calling for a free speech New Deal, I do not suggest that speech rights should be freely open to politics or that restrictions should be immunized from constitutional constraint, as are (say) current laws about occupational safety and health. I certainly do not mean to argue that large national bureaucracies should be overseeing our system of free expression for "political correctness" or for good content. There are severe risks in any system of government oversight of speech content. Viewpoint discrimination, whether explicit or implicit, should be ruled out of bounds. Any free speech New Deal must take the various risks into account, and attempt to counter them. Nor do I mean to suggest that free markets in speech are generally abridgments of speech, or that they usually disserve the First Amendment.

I do mean to say that at a minimum, what seems to be government regulation of speech might, in some circumstances, promote free speech as understood through the democratic conception associated with both Madison and Brandeis. If so, such regulation should not be treated as a constitutionally impermissible abridgment at all. I will offer many examples in chapters 3 and 4; for the moment, consider campaign finance laws, which may well improve democratic processes by reducing the distorting effects of wealth. Broadly similar arguments might be made for requirements of public interest programming on television, rights of reply for dissenting views, controls on the power of advertisers to influence programming content, and limitations on advertising time during children's programming. I mean also to argue that in some cases, what seems to be free speech in free markets might, on reflection, amount to an abridgment of free speech. Consider, for example, a shopping center owner's use of the trespass law to exclude political protestors from the only place in town where people convene and are available to read and listen.

It will be tempting to think that my arguments amount to a broad and perhaps bizarre plea for "more regulation" of speech. Many of the practices and conditions that I will challenge are commonly taken to involve private action, and not to implicate the Constitution at all. The outcome of the "market" for expenditures on electoral campaigns, and the practices of broadcasters and managers of newspapers, are generally treated as raising no constitutional question. People think that it is only "government regulation" of "the market" that is problematic. According to this view, we cannot stop a candidate from spending money, or require a broadcasting company to offer free air time to candidates, even if the expenditures and the absence of free air time have corrosive effects on democratic processes.

I do not argue that private acts are governed by the Constitution. In fact we should enthusiastically agree that the First Amendment is aimed only at governmental action, and that private conduct raises no constitutional question. The constitutional text aims at "Congress," not at the owners of newspapers and radio stations. A central principle of American constitutionalism is that the most serious risks to liberty come from government, which has a monopoly on the legal use of force. This principle is far from uncontroversial; private power can be an obstacle to liberty, including liberty of expression. But freedom is often promoted if we allow the private sector to operate without constitutional constraint. In any case, there can be no violation of the First Amendment unless some government action has "abridged the freedom of speech." That action must usually take the form of a law or regulation.

But if the lesson of the New Deal is taken seriously, it follows not that the requirement of government involvement is unintelligible or incoherent, but that governmental rules lie behind and create rights of property, contract, and tort. This is so especially insofar as legal rules grant people rights of exclusive ownership and use of property. If CBS is allowed to exclude people from the airwaves, it is largely because of the law, which backs up the efforts at exclusion. If a shopping center decides not to allow political activity on its premises, it can make that decision effective only through the law. Simply as a matter of fact, property rights are creations of law.

From this it does not follow that private acts are subject to constitutional constraint, or even that the legally conferred rights of exclusive ownership usually violate the First Amendment or any other constitutional provision. Private acts are not controlled by the First Amendment. To find a constitutional question, we always need to find some genuine exercise of public power. And to find a constitutional violation, we always need to show that public power has genuinely compromised some constitutional principle. But a claim on behalf of—for example—government efforts to promote greater quality and diversity in broadcasting is a claim for a new regulatory regime, not for "government intervention" where none existed before. The same conclusion would apply even if we moved, as some people suggest, in the direction of completely free economic markets in communications. In such a system, ownership of broadcasting rights would be like ownership of anything else; the relevant rights could be freely bought and sold on markets. But (as people in Eastern Europe have learned) free markets require a large role for law, in the form of legally defined and enforced property, contract, and tort principles. Property rights of some kind are generally indispensable to freedom and prosperity; but unrestricted property rights in speech can compromise Madisonian goals.

What I want to suggest here is, first and foremost, that legal rules designed to promote freedom of speech should not be invalidated if their purposes and effects are constitutionally valid, even if they conspicuously intrude on the rights of some property owners and even some speakers. The issue of constitutional validity should be assessed in Madisonian terms: Do the rules promote greater attention to public issues? Do they ensure greater diversity of view? If these are the relevant questions, a governmental requirement of free air time for candidates would be constitutional. We may also conclude that some legal rules of property ownership do violate the First Amendment, and in some surprising places, if and when such rules are invoked by property owners to "abridge the freedom of speech" by preventing people from speaking at certain times and in certain places.

Forbears for the Free Speech New Deal

These general proposals, which I particularize below, might seem unconventional. In fact, however, they have a clear foundation in no lesser place than *New York Times v. Sullivan*,[26] one of the greatest cases of modern free speech law. There the Court concluded that a public official could not bring an action for libel unless he could show that the speaker had "actual malice," that is, knowledge of or reckless indifference to the falsity of the statements at issue. The Court therefore reversed an Alabama court requiring the *New York Times* to pay $500,000 to L. B. Sullivan, an Alabama police commissioner, simply because it published certain fairly minor factual errors in an advertisement on behalf of a civil rights organization.

Many people see the *Sullivan* case as the largest legal symbol of broad press immunity for criticism of public officials. Even more, *Sullivan* is often understood to reflect the conception of freedom of expression associated with James Madison and explicitly advocated by the philosopher Alexander Meiklejohn.[27] This is a conception of democratic self-government, connected to the Madisonian conception of sovereignty and built on the need to ensure that political expression is not inhibited by government (see chapter 5). The Court invoked this conception in holding that the law of libel could not be used to punish the press for publishing stories or advertisements that were critical of government's racially discriminatory practices.

In these circumstances, it is striking that in *Sullivan*, the lower court held that the common law of tort, and more particularly libel, was not government action at all, and was therefore entirely immune from constitutional constraint.[28] A civil lawsuit, on this view, is a purely private dispute. The Supreme Court quickly disposed of this objection, and it seems obviously right to have done so. If a court—composed after all of government officials—imposes a damages penalty for speech, the state is surely involved. The use of government tribunals to punish speech in this way is conspicuously government action. What is interesting is not the

Supreme Court's rejection of the argument, but the fact that the argument could be made by a state supreme court as late as the 1960s. How could reasonable judges think that the judge-made rules of tort law, ordering a newspaper to transfer money, are purely private, and do not regulate speech at all?

The answer lies in the surprising persistence of pre–New Deal understandings—to the effect that common law rules simply implement existing rights, or private desires, and do not amount to "intervention" or "action" at all. The view that the common law of property should be taken as prepolitical, nonregulatory, indeed as a refusal to use government power—the view that the New Deal rightly repudiated—was precisely the same as the view of the state supreme court in *Sullivan*. It is especially notable that at common law, reputation is protected because it counts as a property interest. Just as in the pre–New Deal era, the protection of property interests did not appear to the Alabama court to involve government action at all.

The Supreme Court's rejection of that claim seemed inevitable in *Sullivan* itself, and indeed this aspect of the case is largely forgotten. But much of current law is based on very much the same understandings as underlie the forgotten view of that obscure court. Current law, too, tends to take common law rules as prepolitical, nonregulatory, and a refusal to use government power. It refuses to evaluate those rules for their effects on Madisonian aspirations. In coming to terms with current understandings, we might generalize from *Sullivan* the broad idea that protection of property rights, through the common law, must always be assessed pragmatically in terms of its effects on speech. In a system of property rights, there is (I repeat) no such thing as "no regulation" of speech; property rights inevitably allow property owners to exclude prospective speakers. The question is what forms of regulation best serve the purposes of the free speech guarantee.[29]

Consider, for example, the issues raised when citizens try to improve the democratic character of media coverage—thus raising issues that are likely to become increasingly important in the next decades. Suppose that people request the government to regulate broadcasting to increase attention to public issues and diversity of view. Take the example of political campaigns. Suppose that most broadcasters deal little or not at all with issues of public importance, generally restricting themselves to dramatic sound bites, to issues of "who has momentum," to stories about movie stars, or to sex scandals. Suppose too that there is little diversity of view on the airwaves, but instead a bland, watered-down version of conventional morality. If anything like this is so, a large part of the problem for the system of free expression is the governmental grant of legal protection—rights of exclusive use—to large institutions that dominate speech processes. The government licenses television channels, and it confers rights of exclusion. Under plausible factual assumptions, both political deliberation and political equality are thereby compromised. There is not enough in the way of political deliberation, for there is too little attention to public issues and too little diversity of view. There cannot be political equality, because access to popular channels of communication is made a function of the amount of resources that people have and the amount of resources that advertisers are willing to pay for time featuring the speech in question.

The relevant government grants of exclusionary power—sometimes through the common law, sometimes through licensing decisions, sometimes through statute—are usually taken not to be a grant of government power at all, but instead to be purely "private." Current law sees no constitutional problems in the exclusion of certain people and views from the airwaves. The Supreme Court's theory appears to be that the act of exclusion is private; it comes from broadcasters, not from government.[30] Often campaign finance restrictions and rights of access to the media are thought to involve perverse appeals for governmental intervention into the private sphere; so too with attempted government requirements of quality and diversity.

In *New York Times v. Sullivan*, the Supreme Court said that common law rules should be inspected for their conformity with the overriding principle that government may not restrict freedoms of speech and press. "The test is not the form in which state power has been applied but, whatever the form, whether such power has in fact been exercised." We should apply this view to our current problems. If the First Amendment is regarded as an effort to ensure that people are not prevented from speaking, especially on issues of public importance, then current free speech law seems wrong or at least inadequate. A pro-life protestor seeks a right of access to CBS and is denied; he might be understood to be complaining about the governmentally conferred right of exclusion that is operating to his detriment. If the protestor is not allowed on the air, it is largely because government will back up the exclusion. Otherwise we would have a show of force, and who knows what the outcome would be?

In this light, a government effort to require quality and diversity would be simply another regulatory system, with different requirements and exclusions. The current conception of government "regulation" turns out to misstate certain issues and sometimes disserves the goal of free expression itself. The present system is pervasively regulated. The notion of "laissez-faire" is no less a myth—a conceptual error—for speech than it is for property.

It might be responded that *New York Times v. Sullivan* is really unhelpful for the point at hand, because it is fundamentally different from most cases in which property law is invoked to suppress speech. If the *New York Times* refuses to accept my piece, I can always try other newspapers and even set up my own. If CBS refuses to allow me air time, perhaps I can have success elsewhere. These freedoms are indeed important. They show that because many outlets are available, the content-neutral restrictions embodied in property law can be far less severe than other restrictions. We should therefore distinguish between content-neutral restrictions that leave open other adequate options and content-neutral restrictions that do not. This distinction is highly relevant when we are deciding whether the First Amendment permits any particular content-neutral restriction. My point here is not that the law of property is generally offensive to the Constitution. Of course it is not. I am claiming only that property law, like all other law, should be assessed in individual cases for conformity with the free speech guarantee, and here *New York Times v. Sullivan* is a key precedent. The existence of alternative outlets is a big part of that assessment.

We might at this point offer a further distinction. Some content-neutral restrictions on speech are not *specifically directed at speech*, but instead affect speech as part of a large class that includes conduct as well as speech. The law that confers exclusive property rights, for example, is not aimed at speech alone, but at the activity of all trespassers, including but hardly limited to trespassers who speak. The restriction on speech is in this sense "incidental." By contrast, some content-neutral restrictions—like a ban on door-to-door solicitation or on speech on billboards—are specifically directed at speech. This is a distinction between two kinds of content-neutral restrictions, not between restrictions and something else entirely. But perhaps the distinction does make some difference. If it does, it is because explicitly speech-directed content-neutral restrictions should give rise to mild concerns about an underlying censorial motive on government's part. If the government bans all speech at airports, perhaps it is actually seeking to foreclose a certain form of dissent; perhaps it is seeking to ban dissent altogether; perhaps it is undervaluing the need to ensure expressive outlets and overvaluing the need for security. The same is harder to say if government bans all people, whether or not they are speakers, from a certain area. In a case of this kind, we might be less suspicious of the government's reasons for regulation, and think that it is really trying to serve legitimate goals.

In general, however, the distinction between incidental and nonincidental content-neutral restrictions should probably not make a lot of difference. Whether a content-neutral restriction is permissible should depend on a range of contextual factors. For example, a ban on speech on a particular billboard in Chicago is directed at speech, and is not an "incidental" restriction; but it is still not much of an intrusion on speech. By contrast, a ban on any private use of major city squares is aimed at conduct as well as speech, and only incidentally and indirectly affects speech. But it is potentially a huge intrusion on the system of free expression. These examples are by no means exotic. They have close analogues in real cases. The Supreme Court invalidated a ban on speech on billboards on highways, a highly controversial ruling in light of the fact that there are legitimate aesthetic reasons for the ban.[31] By contrast, the Court upheld the use of the trespass laws to exclude speakers from shopping centers.[32] This is a controversial conclusion in light of the fact that the result may be to eliminate speakers from the only meeting place in town, and for perhaps inadequate reasons, since the shopping center is made open to the public in any case and so no real privacy interests are at stake.

I conclude that some content-neutral restrictions that "incidentally" affect speech are much worse than some restrictions that are particularly aimed at speech. It is true that the speech-restrictive rules of property law are usually far less troublesome than content-based restrictions on speech (see chapter 6). It is even true that the speech-restrictive rules of property law can be less troublesome than other content-based restrictions. But these issues should not be decided in the abstract. We need to know about the particular rule at issue. We need to investigate the details.

What cannot be sustained is the idea that legal rights of exclusive ownership are always compatible with a system of free expression. None of this means—I reiterate—that a system of private property, or market ordering with respect to speech, is unjust or bad from the standpoint of liberty. It does mean that this is the question to be addressed, and we cannot do this a priori, or with slogans.

Let me be more specific. Some regulatory efforts, superimposed on regulation through current legal rules, may promote free speech. A governmental requirement of free time for presidential candidates is a possible example; so too for a governmentally conferred "right of reply." Some regulatory efforts might not be "abridgments" of freedom of speech; they might increase free speech. To know whether this is so, it is necessary to understand their purposes and consequences.

Less frequently, the use of the current statutory or common law rules that foreclose efforts to speak might represent impermissible restrictions on speech. To know whether this is so, it is again necessary to assess the effects of such rules in terms of their consequences for the system of free expression. In any case, both reform efforts and the status quo must be judged by their effects, not by question-begging characterizations of "threats from government."

Private Power, Public Power

It is tempting to understand this argument as a suggestion that the New Dealers were concerned about private power over working conditions, and that modern constitutional courts should be more interested in the problems raised by private power over expression or over democratic processes.[33] But this formulation misses the real point, and it does so in a way that suggests its own dependence on pre–New Deal understandings. The central problem is not that private power is an obstacle to speech; even if it is, private power is not a subject of the First Amendment. The real issues are that public authority creates legal structures that restrict speech, that new exercises of public authority can counter the existing restrictions, and that any restrictions, even those of the common law, should be assessed under constitutional principles precisely because they are restrictions.

Return, for example, to a case in which the owners of a large shopping center exclude from their property abortion protestors who believe that the center is the best place to draw attention to their cause. The Supreme Court thinks that the First Amendment is not implicated, since no government regulation of speech is involved. All that has happened is that private property owners have barred people from their land.[34]

In fact, this is a poor way to understand the situation. It is actually the state court's view in *Sullivan*. The owners of the shopping center are able to exclude the protestors only because government has granted to them a legal right to do so. To be sure, without government, property owners might be able to rely on "self-help," that is, their capacity to use force on their behalf and to hire others to do the same. Without government, property rights would consist only of what people could hold onto through such means. But this would be so dramatically different a world that its relationship to existing "property rights" is most obscure. The public grant of such rights—what we really mean by property rights—is an exercise of state power. It is this action that restricts the speech of the protestors. It is a real question whether the grant of exclusionary power violates the First Amendment, at least in circumstances in which it eliminates the only real way of making a protest visible to members of the local community.

Or consider a case in which a network refuses to sell advertising time to a group that wants to discuss some public issue or to express some dissident view. The group might want to argue that abortion is a form of murder, or that homosexual marriages should be legal. Under current law, the refusal raises no First Amendment question, in part because a number of the justices—perhaps now a majority—believe that there is no "state action."[35] But broadcasters are given property rights in their licenses by government, and their exercise of those rights is a function of law in no subtle sense. Clearly state action underlies the grant and deployment of property rights to exclude people from the television networks.

It is commonly responded that for purposes of constitutional theory and politics, we need to distinguish sharply between "freedom" and "power," or between government coercion on the one hand and compulsion by private persons or "by mere circumstances" on the other. If I am unable to buy a plane ticket to Rome, or advertising time on CBS, I am said to lack power, not freedom; no government official is stopping me from doing what I want. The real problem, it might be said, lies with my circumstances, rather than with government coercion or with opposition through the will of some public official. Often this distinction is made crucial for thinking about constitutional law. Why should we not understand free speech in this way?

This is a conventional way to think about things, but it is an inadequate description of the relevant situation, indeed a species of pre–New Deal conceptions of "laissez-faire." To be sure, my inability to buy a plane ticket or airtime on CBS does not by itself implicate government power. But when an airline uses the trespass laws to evict me from the airport, and when CBS calls the police to remove me from the station, there is indeed government coercion, not compulsion by simple circumstance. When public officials use public force to exclude private people from areas in which government has conferred exclusive ownership rights, government is indeed intruding on freedom. Its intrusion may also serve freedom, properly understood, and may be well-justified on balance. But this is a different point.

In the context of speech, the real distinction is between the relatively impersonal, content-neutral restrictions imposed by property law, as opposed to the more personal, content-based restrictions of the sort that tend to produce the most intense judicial scrutiny. As I will emphasize in many places, this is an extremely important distinction. But it is not a distinction between freedom and power.

Nothing I have said is inconsistent with the view that it is generally good for people to live in a system in which government creates ownership rights in property or free markets in speech, just as it is usually a good idea for government to create rights of ownership, and free markets, in property. It is indeed important that anyone can start a newspaper if she can obtain the means to do so. We should not overlook the fact that the absence of the necessary means is a by-product of the system rather than government's specific intention in individual cases. But for present purposes, the key point is that a right of exclusive ownership in a television network or anything else is governmentally conferred. The exclusion of would-be speakers is backed up, or made possible, by the law of (among other things) civil and criminal trespass. It is thus a product of a governmental decision.

Negative Rights, Positive Rights

It might be tempting to say in response that the Constitution creates "negative" rights rather than "positive" ones, or at least that the First Amendment is "negative" in character—a right to protection "against" the government, not to subsidies "from" the government. So stated, the claim certainly captures the conventional wisdom. Any argument for a New Deal for speech must therefore come to terms with the view that the Constitution does not create positive rights, and should not be understood to do so.

I have two responses to this view. The first and most fundamental is that no one is asserting a positive right in these cases. Instead the claim is that government sometimes cannot adopt a legal rule that imposes a (negative) constraint on which people can speak, and where they can do so. When someone with one view is unable to state that view in a shopping center or on the networks, it is because the civil and criminal law prohibits him from doing so.[36] No positive right need be claimed.

This is the same kind of negative right that is at stake in a wide range of more familiar arguments in the Court's cases. Consider the attack on government bans on door-to-door soliciting. An attack on such a ban is not an argument for "positive" government protection at all. It is merely a claim that legal rules that stop certain people from speaking in certain places—here too through the law of property—must be reviewed under First Amendment principles. Everyone recognizes that this is a legitimate claim; the ban on door-to-door soliciting is unconstitutional. In fact the response that a New Deal for speech would create a "positive right" trades on untenable, pre–New Deal distinctions between positive and negative rights.[37]

My second point is that the distinction between negative and positive rights fails even to explain current First Amendment law.[38] There are two possible counterexamples. The Supreme Court has come very close to saying that when an audience becomes hostile and threatening, the government is obligated to protect the speaker. Under current law, reasonable crowd control measures are probably constitutionally compelled before the speaker can be silenced. This is so even if the result is to require a number of police officers to come to the scene.[39] In this way, the right to speak includes a positive right to governmental protection against a hostile private audience, at least in the sense that the government must protect the speaker rather than silence him.

Or return to the area of libel. By imposing constitutional limits on the common law of libel, the Court has held, in effect, that people who are libeled must subsidize speakers, by allowing their reputation to be sacrificed to the end of broad diversity of speech. Even more than this, the Court has held that that government is under what might be considered an affirmative duty to "take" the reputation of people who are defamed, in order to promote the interest in free speech. The First Amendment requires a compulsory, governmentally produced subsidy from personal reputation for the benefit of the system of free speech.[40]

Cases of this sort reveal that the First Amendment, even as currently conceived, is not entirely a negative right. It has positive dimensions as well. Those positive dimensions consist of a command to government to take steps to ensure that the system of free expression is not violated by legal rules giving too much authority over speech to private people. In the hostile audience cases, government is obliged to protect the speaker against private silencing. In the libel cases, government is obliged to do the same thing, that is, to provide an extra breathing space for speech even though one of the consequences is to intrude on—even to violate—the common law property interest in reputation.

We would do well to build on these ideas. A constitutional

question might well be raised by a broadcasting system in which government confers on the major networks the right to exclude certain points of view. In principle, the creation of that right is parallel to the grant of a right to a hostile audience to silence controversial speakers, subject only to the speakers' power of self-help through the marketplace (including the hiring of private police forces). In the hostile audience setting, it is not enough to say that any intrusion on the speaker is private rather than governmental. It is necessary instead to evaluate the consequences of the system by reference to the purposes of the First Amendment—just as it is necessary to evaluate the consequences of any system in which property rights operate to hurt some and benefit others.

None of this shows, as a factual matter, that property rights and free markets fail to produce broad diversity of views and an opportunity to speak for opposing sides. If we do obtain these good things, the market system created by law is constitutionally unobjectionable on the merits. But it is surely imaginable that a market system will have less fortunate consequences.

Madisonianism and Modern Technology

We should glance at this point at the Court's remarkable opinion in the *Red Lion* case.[41] There the Court upheld the so-called "fairness doctrine," which required broadcasters to attend to public issues and to allow a chance to speak for opposing views. (At least it required these in theory; the doctrine was rarely enforced in practice.)[42] In the *Red Lion* opinion, the Court actually seemed to suggest, though it did not expressly conclude, that the doctrine was constitutionally compelled. According to the Court, the fairness doctrine would "enhance rather than abridge the freedoms of speech and press," for free expression would be disserved "by unlimited private censorship operating in a medium not open to all."

The Court wrote:

[A]s far as the First Amendment is concerned those who are licensed stand no better than those to whom licenses are refused. A license permits broadcasting, but the licensee has no constitutional right to be the one who holds the license or to monopolize a radio frequency to the exclusion of his fellow citizens. There is nothing in the First Amendment which prevents the Government from requiring a licensee to share his frequency with others and to conduct himself as a proxy or fiduciary with obligations to present those views and voices which are representative of his community and which would otherwise, by necessity, be barred from the airwaves.[43]

Thus the Court emphasized that

the people as a whole retain their interest in free speech by radio and their collective right to have the medium function consistently with the ends and purposes of the First Amendment. It is the right of the viewers and listeners, not the right of the broadcasters, which is paramount. It is the purpose of the First Amendment to preserve an uninhibited marketplace of ideas in which truth will ultimately prevail, rather than to countenance monopolization of that market, whether it be by the Government itself or a private licensee. It is the right of the public to receive suitable access to social, political, esthetic, moral, and other ideas and experiences which is crucial here. That right may not constitutionally be abridged either by Congress or by the FCC.[44]

Compare this very different suggestion from the head of the FCC during the deregulatory enthusiasm of the 1980s: "It was time to move away from thinking about broadcasters as trustees. It was time to treat them the way almost everyone else in society does—that is, as businesses. [T]elevision is just another appliance. It's a toaster with pictures."[45]

Red Lion sets out a striking vision of the First Amendment, one with clear connections to Justice Brandeis' civic conception and to Madison's original understanding. This vision does not emphasize unrestricted economic markets in ideas. It does not stress the autonomy of broadcasters (made possible only by current ownership rights operating through law) from regulation. It is based instead on the need to promote democratic self-government by ensuring that people are presented with a broad diversity of views about public issues. In a market system, this goal may be severely compromised. It is hardly clear that "the freedom of speech" is promoted by a regime in which people are permitted to speak if and only if other people are willing to pay enough to allow them to be heard.

This argument applies most conspicuously to broadcasters, since the government has such an obvious role in allocating their licenses. But the argument has force for newspapers too. The property rights of newspapers also come from a legally conferred power to exclude others. The *New York Times* is given the legal power to exclude people who want to write for it. Simply as a matter of fact, that power is a creation of the state. It is a function of the law of property. If I want to write for the *New York Times*, and if I am stopped from doing so, it is in significant part because the *Times* is able to invoke the law of trespass to back up its exclusionary decision. Without the law of trespass, we would be in the state of nature, and we can hardly purport to know what would be published in that strange and obscure place. The system in a regime of property rights may well be fine or even wonderful; but it should be assessed in terms of its consequences for speech.

If all this is right, some of the core commitments of current First Amendment law come under severe strain. The idea that threats to speech stem from government is undoubtedly correct, but as usually understood, it is far too simple. Sometimes threats come from what seems to be the private sphere, and, much more fundamentally, these threats could not be made without legal entitlements that enable some private actors but not others to speak and to be heard. And when this is so, a large risk to a system of free expression, not even visible to current law, is the existence of legal rules that diminish opportunities to exercise rights of free expression.

Moreover, the idea that government should be neutral among all forms of speech seems right in the abstract, but such neutrality is often thought, wrongly, to be exemplified in the use of "free" economic markets to determine access to the media and thus an opportunity to be heard. This form of neutrality actually ensures that some will be unable to speak or to be heard at all, and at the same time that others will be permitted to dominate expressive outlets. Markets generally promote both liberty and prosperity.

But when the legal creation of a market has harmful consequences for free expression—and it sometimes does—then it must
be reevaluated in light of free speech principles. If our
Madisonian goal is to produce attention to public issues, and
exposure to diverse views, a market system may well be inadequate. A New Deal may therefore be necessary.

Chapter 3

Broadcasting, Politics, Liberty

A CORE INSIGHT OF THE *Red Lion* case is that when the law promotes the interest in private autonomy from government (made possible in the first place only by government's rules), it is not always acting consistently with our effort to promote democratic self-governance. Here we see a sharp initial split between Justice Holmes' marketplace understanding and Justice Brandeis' civic conception. If we give broadcasters unrestricted property rights and then immunize them from government control, we may compromise both quality and diversity in broadcasting. We may undermine the constitutional commitments to political deliberation and political equality. If so, our actions may not be consistent with the First Amendment's own aspirations. If so, current First Amendment rhetoric might actually disserve free and open debate about public choices; and such rhetoric may be playing a harmful role with Congress and the executive branch as well as with the courts. Of course we must always be concerned about the risks of government ignorance or bias, or interest-group power, in any use of regulatory institutions to oversee efforts to improve the operation of market forces. This consideration will play a large role in my specific recommendations.

If we wanted a First Amendment "New Deal," one that would

be alert to all of the relevant risks, we would consider a large set of proposals for constitutional reform. I deal in this chapter with broadcasting regulation, which poses some of the most important issues in contemporary democracies. I offer a number of suggestions for change. The suggestions are united by the goal of using Madisonian aspirations in a new era of technology for communications.

Broadcasting, Citizenship, Diversity

For much of its history, the Federal Communications Commission (FCC) imposed the so-called "fairness doctrine" on broadcast licensees. As I have noted, the fairness doctrine required licensees to spend some time on issues of public importance, and it created an obligation to allow speech by people of diverse views. The fairness doctrine was hardly a terrific success on its own terms, and as we will soon see, it is poorly adapted for contemporary problems. But an examination of the issues raised by the doctrine will pave the way for an exploration of both constitutional issues and new strategies for reform.

The last decade has witnessed a mounting constitutional assault on the fairness doctrine and on *Red Lion* itself. Licenses are no longer technologically scarce, thanks in part to cable television; the spectrum can be made available to remarkably many people, and the numbers are increasing. Indeed, most cities have far more radio and television stations than major newspapers. In 1987, the FCC concluded that the fairness doctrine now violates the First Amendment, because it involves an effort, by government, to tell broadcasters what they may say.[1] Because licenses are not scarce, the doctrine can no longer be justified as an effort to promote diversity in programming. According to the FCC, the market already provides the requisite diversity.

The FCC therefore concluded that the fairness doctrine is a form of impermissible government intervention into the private sphere of choice by producers and audience. It is constitutionally impermissible. The doctrine violates the government's obligation of neutrality, reflected in respect for market outcomes. Influential judges and scholars have reached the same conclusion.[2] The mode of analysis—in particular the notions of neutrality and inaction—

is highly reminiscent of that of the pre–New Deal Supreme Court. In both cases, certain government policies are said to be impermissible because they reflect partisan intervention into an otherwise voluntary and law-free private sphere. Laissez-faire is the rallying cry, the very definition of constitutional liberty.

The Constitution does forbid any "law abridging the freedom of speech." But is the fairness doctrine such a law? This is by no means clear. Certainly the proposition cannot be established merely by the constitutional text. To its defenders, the fairness doctrine actually promotes "the freedom of speech," by ensuring diversity of views on the airwaves—diversity that the market may fail to bring about. It is true that the market responds to private consumption choices—the place where people fix the dial. But this does not solve the problem, at least if we look at things from the Madisonian point of view and place a special premium on attention to public issues and exposure to diverse political views. The FCC's attack on the fairness doctrine is especially unpersuasive insofar as it asserts, without a serious look at the real-world consequences of different regulatory strategies, that the doctrine involves governmental invasion of a law-free private marketplace. As we have seen, the marketplace is made possible only by legal rules, and a system of markets in expression makes it possible to exclude, through law, many people who would very much like to speak and be heard.

People trying to interpret the Constitution should deal with the fairness doctrine and other regulatory approaches by exploring the relationships among a market in broadcasting, alternative systems, and the goals, properly characterized, of a system of free expression.[3] Let us start with some general points, and then turn to some facts.

On the one hand, it seems clear that a free market will provide a large degree of diversity in available offerings, especially in a period with numerous outlets. So long as the particular view is supported by market demand, it should find a supplier. Free markets in speech do offer an extraordinary range of opinions and options. For this reason, the broadcasting status quo is far preferable to a system of centralized command-and-control regulation of the sort that could be found, for example, in many communist nations before (and even after) their liberation from Soviet domination. Any command-and-control system, if it restricted diversity of view and attention to public affairs, would indeed abridge the freedom of speech and should be held unconstitutional.

In thinking about how the Constitution bears on regulation of broadcasting, we might therefore distinguish among four possibilities. First, the market may be exposing people to public issues and diverse views, and if so it is entirely consistent with the First Amendment. It is important in this connection that the market is content-neutral. The rules that underlie markets are law, but they do not depend on the content of speech, much less on the viewpoint of the speaker. It is important as well that a market will make it unnecessary for government officials to oversee the content of material in order to assess whether it has value, or whether it deserves to be heard. The fact that a market removes official oversight surely counts strongly in its favor. If the market is promoting Madisonian goals, the rules that underlie it should not be held unconstitutional.

This is one possibility, but there are others. The second is that some of the rules that underlie the market might be unconstitutional *if* it could be shown that the existing system of property rights produces little political discussion or excludes the range of views necessary to offer diversity. The use of the law to exclude people who want to speak on a certain topic might therefore be **constitutionally** invalid. Courts should be extremely cautious before reaching this conclusion, in large part because the issue turns on complex factual and managerial issues not easily within judicial competence. Judicial oversight of the regulatory system for speech—and judicial comparison of the various alternatives— are especially ill-suited to judicial capacities. It follows that if the democratic process has selected a market system, courts should be reluctant to intervene.

Third, government interference with the current market might well be upheld, as against a constitutional challenge, if the legislature has made a considered judgment, based on a factual record, that the particular regulation will promote First Amendment goals. Those goals would be understood in Madisonian terms. The question would be whether the regulation at issue promotes attention to public issues and diversity of view without seriously compromising other First Amendment principles. A fairness doctrine, or some such regulation, should therefore be found constitutional if the legislature can make a reasonable factual argument on its behalf.

Fourth, government regulation of the market should be invalidated under either of two circumstances: (1) if it discriminates on the basis of viewpoint; or (2) if it can be shown that the regulation actually diminishes attention to public affairs and diversity of view. Viewpoint discrimination is constitutionally unacceptable, since it is likely to reflect an illegitimate reason for regulation and also to skew the public's deliberative processes in unacceptable ways (see chapter 6). For example, we should not allow government to say that pro-Republican speech will be favored in the market, or that special provision must be made for people who favor abortion rights.[4] Similarly, we should not allow government to use regulation to *lower* the amount of attention to public issues and the total level of diversity. On this latter, highly factual question, however, the legislature is entitled to a presumption of constitutionality.

So much for the four basic possibilities. How should we assess a free market in communications? In principle, it does seem clear that such a market could generate a range of serious problems. Imagine, for example, if someone in a new country—perhaps one of the emerging democracies of Eastern Europe—proposed the following explicit rule: *The right to speak will be allocated to those people to whom other people are willing to pay enough to entitle them to be heard.* Suppose, in other words, that the allocation of speech rights was decided through an ordinary pricing system, like the allocation of soap, or cars, or candy. It would follow that people would be prevented from speaking, or from having significant access to listeners, if other people were not willing to pay enough to entitle them to do so. Thus speaker Jones, favoring one cause or simply offering ethnic jokes, might have access to the media if people would pay $2000 to hear him, whereas speaker Smith, favoring another cause, might be excluded if he could draw only $100. People would be heard if and only if they could draw sufficient money to justify allowing them access to the airwaves.

Surely this would be a bizarre parody of democratic aspirations—the stuff of science fiction rather than self-government. Such a system would be especially perverse insofar as it would ensure that dissident speech—which is expression for which people are often unwilling to pay—would be foreclosed.[5] In a Madisonian regime, dissenting views are to be encouraged even if many people would prefer not to hear them. The hypothesized system of allocation, based on private willingness to pay, would conspicuously violate the norm of political equality, which is built into the American tradition of freedom of speech. It would significantly endanger political deliberation.

Now here is the oddity: In many respects, this parody of democratic aspirations is precisely the system we now have. Broadcasting access is the practical equivalent of the right to speak, and it is allocated very much on the basis of private willingness to pay. Although viewers and listeners do not pay cash to broadcasters, each station takes account of the revenue likely to be generated by different programs, and the revenue is in large part a function of the existing audience "demand" for programming.

In one respect our system is even worse than this. Programming content is produced not merely by audience demand, but also by the desires of advertisers. Viewers are in this way the product as well as its users; they are what advertisers are buying when they purchase commercial time. Viewers are commodities as well as consumers. For example, advertisers like to buy the viewing attention of children, and when they purchase that attention, they treat children as a potential source of revenues rather than as people deserving high-quality fare. As we will soon see, the role of advertisers introduces some large additional distortions. In any case, the First Amendment issues must depend in part on the details. A large gap in the theory and practice of free expression is an understanding of the actual operation of the speech market. It is especially important to bring some such understanding to bear on the legal and political disputes.

Some Facts

I now briefly outline some of our current knowledge with respect to the broadcasting market, with occasional reference to newspapers as well. My particular interest is the depth and breadth of attention to public issues and the degree of diversity of view, the Madisonian criteria for evaluating the system of free expression.

Local and network "news."   Much information has now been compiled on local news, which at its inception resulted, incidentally, as a direct response to the FCC's fairness doctrine.[6] Although local news was originally intended to ensure attention to public issues, surprisingly little of local news is now devoted to such issues. Instead it deals largely with stories about local crime, movies, entertainers, television, and sensationalized disasters.[7] "The search for emotion-packed reports with mass appeal has led local television news to give extensive coverage to tragedies like murders, deaths in fires, or plane crashes, in which they often interview survivors of victims about 'how they feel.'"[8]

During a half-hour of local news, no more than eight to twelve minutes involves news at all. Each story that does involve news typically ranges from twenty to thirty seconds. Even the news stories tend not to involve issues of government and policy, but instead focus on fires, accidents, and crimes. Government stories are de-emphasized even more during the more popular evening news slots.

Even coverage of government tends to describe not the content and consequences of relevant policies, but instead to focus on sensational and often misleading "human impact" anecdotes. People harmed or at risk are frequently asked "how they feel." The general purposes and general effects are usually not explored at all, and almost never in any depth. In addition, there has been greater emphasis on "features"—dealing with popular actors, or entertainment shows, or even stories focusing on the movie immediately preceding the news.[9] Economic pressures seem to be pushing local news in this direction even when many reporters would prefer to deal with public issues in a more serious way.

With respect to network news, the pattern is similar, and in some ways even worse. Most such news is anecdotal and fragmentary.[10] Networks seem to place a premium on striking visual imagery and highly personalized stories. This is so even if those stories are not representative and indeed turn out to be misleading.[11] Evocative pictures and strange examples apparently work better in capturing an audience and in shaping views and impressions than does more systematic and reliable evidence, including statistics and reasoned argument.[12]

Social psychologists have shown an important related point: in processing information, people tend to use certain standard heuristic devices, some of which may lead to systemic errors. One of the most crucial of these devices is the "availability" heuristic, by which people tend to think that an event is more likely if they can readily call an illustration to mind.[13] The point suggests that the use of vivid anecdotes in network news is likely to have a substantial effect on public perceptions of substantive issues. The anecdote can be easily recalled, and it may suggest, for example, that certain risks—of nuclear power accidents or airplane crashes—are far higher than they are in fact. There is systematic public misunderstanding of risk levels,[14] and this misunderstanding may well be in part a function of the media's focus on visible and dramatic anecdotes. The likely consequence is highly misinformed policies to protect the environment and other sources of risk.[15]

In covering campaigns, the networks often deal with the question of who is ahead and why, or with largely irrelevant scandals, and much less with substantive issues and disagreements. Often the question is whether some candidate or official is "riding in limousines," or whether he is truly "an outsider." The increasing focus has been on political strategy, with candidates being treated as actors or athletes with certain goals of self-presentation, such as "appearing presidential," "showing compassion," or "not seeming rattled or shrill." In these circumstances, members of the news media sometimes operate like movie critics.[16] When the relevant issues are ones of strategy, the public becomes a spectator to events rather than an active participant in public decisions. Education about issues, through exposure to the candidates and their claims, is often put to one side. Moreover, reasoned argument about policy choices becomes exceedingly rare. The latest polls turn into the principal subject to be covered.

In 1988, for example, almost 60 percent of the national campaign coverage involved "horse race" issues—who was winning, who has momentum —- while about 30 percent involved issues and qualifications. In the crucial period from January to June

1988, there were about 450 minutes of network campaign coverage, of which no less than 308 minutes dealt with the "horse race" issues.[17] An examination of broadcasting coverage of the "Super Tuesday" primaries in 1988 found that 75 percent of CBS stories dealt with these issues; 77 percent of local news followed suit.[18] Even the excerpted "sound bites" dealt disproportionately with horse race issues. Only 9 percent of excerpted comments had substantive content. According to one careful study of the 1988 election, only 9.7 percent of 7574 broadcast and print stories dealt with policy issues; 19.2 percent discussed candidate qualifications; and 36.1 percent assessed the "horse race."[19] Only about one story in six contained any discussion of a substantive issue. By contrast, about a third of all news election stories included the results of public opinion polls.[20]

It is notable in this regard that for presidential candidates, the average block of uninterrupted speech fell from 42.3 seconds in 1968 to only 9.8 seconds in 1988.[21] A statement of more than 10 seconds is therefore unlikely to find its way onto the major networks. Presidential campaign ads diminished in length from thirty minutes in 1952 to thirty seconds in 1988.[22] After an initial period in which news coverage attempted to offer longer excerpts, the 1992 campaign actually saw "soundbites" that were further reduced to about eight seconds. In these circumstances, speeches themselves become advertisements. The same is often true of interviews, news conference answers, and answers during debates.

On the national networks, there has been an increase as well in stories about television shows and movies, and a decrease in attention to public questions.[23] In 1988, there was an average of thirty-eight minutes per month of coverage of arts and entertainment news; in the first half of 1990, the average was sixty-eight minutes per month.[24] According to one person involved in the industry, "By the necessity of shrinking ratings, the network news departments have had to, if not formally then informally, redefine what is news."[25] According to the Executive Producer of NBC's Nightly News, "A lot of what we used to do is report on the back and forth of where we stood against the Russians. But there is no back and forth anymore. I mean nobody is talking about the bomb, so you have to fill the time with the things people *are* talking about."[26] (Note the circularity here: What people are talking about is in part of function of what sorts of things are presented on the popular media.)

There has also been a large increase in "infotainment" on the network news, in which journalists cover such issues as a baseball player's travels with his mistress and other sex-related scandals. These stories are characteristic of "tabloid television," which has become popular daytime and early evening fare, and which seems to be influencing the news itself and even the print media.[27] By contrast, public television stations have 46 percent more public affairs programming than do their commercial counterparts.[28]

There is now a great deal of evidence that the broadcasting media do affect public opinion.[29] Of special importance is the phenomenon of "agenda-setting": the issues that are covered on the news are the issues that are thought to be especially important. This is so not merely in the sense that people report stronger feelings about the covered issues, but also in the sense that they say that government should do more to respond to those issues. The network's selection of the lead story has especially important effects on people's perception of what matters. If the news gives the public a sense of relative priorities, and if the public's understanding of priorities affects legislative and bureaucratic behavior, a presidential program can be materially assisted or impaired by news presentations. Of course such presentations can influence the outcome of elections, especially by determining the grounds on which campaigns are conducted. Often television news tends to protect traditional institutions and practices.[30]

The influence of advertisers.   Advertisers influence the content of programming.[31] No conspiracy theory will have plausibility; but much of the existing picture is disturbing. In an important and detailed essay, C. Edwin Baker has shown that regulation of speech through advertising has significantly and adversely affected the diversity, the nature, and the performance of the media in America.[32] I summarize Baker's findings here, with occasional reference to additional sources.

First, the increasing importance of advertising appears to have diminished market competition, at least in the print media. It is clear that advertisers have been responsible for an increasingly large proportion of newspaper revenues. A consequence of this change is the emergence of a single newspaper in town, usually with a "centrist" position.[33] Baker shows that both theory and real-world evidence support the conclusion that diminished competition is partly a result of the mounting importance of advertising to newspaper budgets. The same may ultimately prove true for the broadcasting media.

Second, and more important for present purposes, advertising imposes a set of direct and indirect controls on the content of programming. Sometimes the media is quite naturally led to be generous to the advertiser's products and to the advertiser's more general economic interests. This is a perfectly predictable consequence of the broadcaster's economic self-interest. Sometimes the media seeks to create a broader "buying mood," since this will promote favorable attention to advertisements. Sometimes the media seeks to decrease the partisan content of its own presentations and to diminish controversy, so as to avoid giving offense to advertisers and their customers. Sometimes the media is led to seek to attract certain audiences—say, upper-income people between the ages of twenty-five and forty-five—precisely because these are the groups to which advertisers seek most to appeal. When the media is led in this direction, it is also led to ignore or downplay other demographic groups, even if those groups are numerous. It should not be controversial to suggest that all of these consequences are troubling from the Madisonian point of view.

It is especially disturbing if the independence of the press is compromised through advertising pressures that affect programming content. There are reports, for example, that advertisers are having a significant impact on programs that bear directly on products. This is clear for local news programs, especially with respect to consumer reports, which bear on both public and private choices. In Minneapolis, a local car dealer responded to a story involving consumer problems with his company by pulling almost one million dollars in advertisements. He said: "We vote with our dollars. If I'm out trying to tell a good story and paying $3,000 for 30 seconds, and someone's calling me names, I'm not going to be happy." Consumer reporters have increasingly pointed to a need for self-censorship. According to one, "We don't even bother with most auto-related stories anymore." According to another, "I won't do the car repair story, or the lemon story. . . . It's not worth the hassle."[34] There are many examples of car stories being eliminated because of advertiser pressures.[35]

Illustrations abound in other areas. "After '60 Minutes' discussed the health hazards of Alar, a chemical used on apples, the Washington State Fruit Commission, a trade association, withdrew $71,300 worth of advertising for cherries from three CBS affiliates in protest."[36] Procter & Gamble, real estate companies, and others have withdrawn advertisements as a way of protesting stories. In a similar vein, certain sections of the newspapers, involving food, real estate, and travel, seem to be a product of a desire to help advertisers by promoting attention to their commercial interests. Indeed, these sections were created largely as an effort to please advertisers.[37] There are analogies in the broadcasting area, where certain forms of programming, on the news and elsewhere, are an effort to promote sales.

An even more troublesome problem consists of deterrent effects on programming content, not because of criticism of advertisers and products in particular, but because the presentation is likely to be controversial or partisan. A revealing episode involved the effort by Turner Broadcasting Systems (TBS) and the Audubon Society to produce a program dealing with the "spotted owl" controversy between loggers and environmentalists in the Pacific Northwest. Believing that the program was biased, members of the logging community did not want it to be aired. All of the eight advertisers (including Ford, Citicorp, Exxon, and Sears) pulled their sponsorship of the program. TBS aired the program in any event, but it was forced to lose all of the $100,000 spent on production.[38] It is doubtful that this event will be irrelevant to future programming decisions.

Similarly, Coca-Cola tried unsuccessfully to persuade NBC to change a documentary depicting unfair treatment of migrant workers by Coca-Cola and others. When its efforts at persuasion failed, Coca-Cola withdrew all of its billings from NBC, in the amount of several million dollars. It did so even though the President of Coca-Cola acknowledged in later congressional testimony that the documentary had accurately depicted housing and worker conditions, and that as a result the company would change the situation. In the next eight years, NBC did not air any documentary on any controversial issue involving an important advertiser.[39]

In a similar vein, NBC had severe difficulties in finding sponsors for its television movie, "Roe v. Wade." Fearful of boycotts by religious groups, hundreds of sponsors solicited by NBC refused to participate.[40] It seems highly unlikely that advertisers could be found for any program adopting a "pro-life" or "pro-choice" perspective, or taking a controversial stand on homosexuality. Advertiser pressures of this kind create a strong general deterrent to any controversial programming.[41]

Advertisers can also affect programming content by seeking the appropriate general background against which to sell products. Television coverage of the 1991 war with Iraq did not attract many advertisers, on the explicitly articulated ground that "Commercials need to be seen in the right environment. A war is just not an upbeat environment."[42] The low volume of advertiser interest significantly affected programming decisions by making war specials economically disastrous. Quite outside of the context of war, an ABC vice-president for programming said that television shows should "attract mass audiences without unduly offending these audiences or too deeply moving them emotionally" because this would "interfere with their ability to receive, recall, and respond to the commercial messages."[43] Withdrawal of advertising from controversial or "depressing" programs has happened on a number of occasions.[44]

We might look as well at the relationship between advertising and children's television. Educational programming for children has a hard time in acquiring sponsors. Good programming for children can be found mostly on PBS.[45] On ordinary commercial networks, high-quality television for children has been practically unavailable. Instead children's television has been designed largely to capture their short-term attention, often through eye-catching, violent shows, and especially important, to sell products.

In the 1960s, the FCC attempted to respond to the situation. It issued recommendations and policy statements calling for "programming in the interest of the public" rather than "programming in the interest of salability." In 1974, it concluded that "broadcasters have a special obligation to serve children," and thus pressured the industry to adopt codes calling for educational and informational programs. In 1981, the new FCC Chair, Mark Fowler, vigorously rejected this approach. Shortly thereafter, network programming for children dramatically decreased, and programs based on products took its place. Thus it is that children's television became "a listless by-product of an extraordinary explosion of entrepreneurial life forces taking place elsewhere— in the business of creating and marketing toys."[46] In 1983, cartoons based on licensed characters accounted for fourteen programs. By 1985, the number rose to over forty. It has stayed about the same since that time. As a result, there is little high-quality programming for children. The Children's Television Act of 1990, a mild response to the situation, has met largely with network evasion and administrative inaction.

Violence and discrimination.   Much of children's television is quite violent, and the violence increased in the period after deregulation. Purely quantitative measures will of course be inadequate, but it is at least suggestive that before 1980, there were 18.6 violent acts per hour for children's programs, whereas after 1980, the number increased to about 26 acts per hour, with a peak of 30 to 32 such acts in 1981 and 1982. Children's daytime weekend programs have been consistently more violent than prime-time shows. By the time of graduation from elementary school, most children will have seen at least 8,000 murders and at least 100,000 other violent acts.[47] Children see over 20 acts of violence during every hour of television on Saturday and Sunday mornings. By the age of eighteen, many young people will have seen as many as 18,000 murders on television, and 800 suicides.[48] Few of these shows have anything like educational content.

Violence on children's television probably has social consequences. It has been found to increase children's fear and also to contribute to their own aggression. There is thus a plausible correlation between exposure to television violence in broadcasting and aggressive behavior. Some studies suggest that exposure to television violence can have a lasting effect on individual behavior patterns.[49]

More generally, there is a high level of violence on television.[50]

In most years, seven of ten prime-time programs depict violence. During prime time in 1980, there was an average of between 5 and 6 violent acts per hour. By 1989, the number increased to 9.5 acts per hour. In 1980, ten shows depicted an average of more than 10 acts of violence per hour; by 1989, the number was 16. A relatively recent high mark was in 1985, with 29 such shows. It seems clear that the level of violence increased in the aftermath of deregulation.

Empirical studies also show that news and entertainment programming sometimes reflects significant if unintended discrimination on the basis of sex. In the news, women are most frequently depicted as falling in the category "family members, that is, they were the mothers or other relatives of hostages, gunmen, spies, afflicted children and the like."[51] Next most frequent is the appearance of women as victims, including battered women, stabbing victims, and residents of areas affected by earthquakes and toxic waste sites. When women are used as speaking subjects on some public issue, it is often to speak against some position traditionally associated with women. Thus Christie Hefner, speaking on behalf of *Playboy Magazine*, was used as a prominent critic of an antipornography report, and a woman doctor was used to defend a company policy of transferring women out of jobs dealing with hazardous chemicals.

Children's programming frequently consists exclusively of male characters. When a female character is added "a group of male buddies will be accented by a lone female, stereotypically defined."[52] On this pattern, "the female is usually a little-sister type," or "functions as a girl Friday to ... male superheroes." Thus "[g]irls exist only in relation to boys."[53] Of dramatic characters in one survey, women made up only 16 percent, and "females were portrayed as younger than males, more likely to be married, less active and with lower self esteem."[54]

Potential Correctives and The First Amendment

Regulatory strategies cannot solve all of these problems; legal reforms should not be expected to bring about a Madisonian utopia. But they could help. Surely they could promote Madisonian goals far more successfully than does the current system. Some such strategies, I suggest, should not be treated as unconstitutional abridgments of the freedom of speech.

Free choice, the rise of all-news stations, and the large number of options.   Some people might argue that in an era of cable television and numerous radio stations, all or most of our problems disappear. If people are unhappy with what they see or hear, they can always change the channel. Some stations even provide news and public affairs broadcasting around the clock. CNN and C-Span offer detailed coverage of public issues; all-news stations are available on the radio in many markets. In some ways, the available broadcasting options are better and more numerous than ever. Perhaps we should celebrate the resulting system. Perhaps criticism of existing fare is simply a way for well-educated elitists to carp about the actual choices of real people.

An initial problem, for those who make this claim, is that only about half of the country is now wired for cable television. Even worse, the households and the children that are probably most in need of high-quality programming are least able to afford it. For these reasons, it seems overstated to say that people can see whatever they want. Nonetheless, it does seem clear that to an increasing degree, both attention to public issues and diversity can be found in light of the dazzling array of options made available by modern technology. In this light, a concern about the current market in broadcasting might seem to amount to a puzzling, even bizarre rejection of freedom of choice. Should we not rest content with that form of freedom, even if Madisonian goals are taken as primary? There are several answers.

Economic problems: Information as a public good.   First, freedom of choice, understood in market terms, is an incomplete solution when we are dealing with a public good, like national defense or clean air. Information about public issues has some of the characteristics of a public good, even in an era with diverse options.[55] Government regulation may be justified on conventional economic grounds, without rejecting private preferences in principle. The explanation of this point is a bit technical, but it is also quite straightforward.

It is well known that if we rely entirely on free markets, we will not have enough national defense and our air will be excessively dirty. The underlying problem is that it is not feasible to provide defense or clean air to one person without simultaneously providing it to many people or to everyone. The difficulty with this state of affairs is that because of this fact of "nonexcludability," each person has an inadequate incentive to seek, or to pay for, the right level of national defense or clean air. Each person might well think: Why should I pay for national defense, when I could instead take a free ride on the efforts of others? The tragedy of this state of affairs is that acting individually, many people will indeed reason in this way. As a result, no producer will have the appropriate incentive to produce national defense or clean air. The result will be unacceptably low levels of the relevant goods.

Much the same is true of information, especially with respect to public affairs. There are several points here. Society receives many benefits from a broad public debate, yielding large quantities of information through coverage of public issues, disclosure of new facts and perspectives, and diversity of view. But these benefits tend to accrue simultaneously to many people or to everyone. Once information is provided to one person, or to some people, it is also provided to many others too, or it can be so provided at trivial cost, especially when it is broadcast. The production of information for one person, or a few, thus produces large external benefits for many other people as well. But— and this is the key point—a free market in speech provides no adequate mechanism to ensure that these benefits will be adequately taken into account by those who produce the information, in this case the broadcasting industry.

The benefits of informing one person—of making him an effective citizen—may ultimately accrue to many other people as well, through that person's contribution to many conversations and to political processes in general. This is an important part of conversation in a democracy. But these external benefits of becoming informed will usually not be taken into account in each person's individual consumption choices. Freedom of choice will therefore fail to capture the important external and systemic benefits of learning about public issues.

In addition, each person, acting individually, cannot receive the full benefits of exposure to public information unless other people are similarly exposed. If I watch a show that deals seriously with public issues, I may obtain large benefits if, but only if, many friends watch the same show. A discussion cannot start unless we have something in common to talk about. A flourishing public debate, in which many people are focused on public problems, requires a degree of common exposure. In a deregulated market, it is therefore possible that each person will make a consumption choice that will fail to bring about the optimal outcome. In a free market for information, each person is in something of a prisoner's dilemma, in which rational individual action leads to collective or social harm.[56]

These various points allow us to reach a general conclusion. Because of the "public good" features of information, no single person has a sufficient incentive to pay for the benefits that he receives. The result is simple and clear: The market will produce too little information. Reliance on markets and "free choice" in expression will therefore have some of the same problems as reliance on markets for national defense or environmental protection. For this reason, some kind of regulatory solution, solving this problem, is justified in principle. Of course we should not compel people to watch public-affairs programs. But we might attempt a system of subsidies and incentives to try to respond to the situation; I offer details below.

It might be thought that the distinctive characteristics of the broadcasting market offer a solution. Because advertisers try to get a large audience, viewers are "commodities"—they are what is being bought—as much as they are consumers. In these circumstances, it is not right to think that individual people are purchasing individual pieces of information. Instead, advertisers are aggregating individual preferences in seeking especially popular programming. In that sense, they should be helping to overcome the public good problem.

The problem with this response is that the advertisers' desire to attract large audiences does not adequately serve the goal of overcoming the problem of inadequate information about public affairs. A program with a large audience may not be providing information at all; consider much of network television. Note too that documentary movies hardly ever appear on the list of the most popular shows. As we have seen, advertisers may even be hostile to the provision of public information. Their economic interests often argue against sponsorship of public service or controversial programming, especially if the audience is relatively small, but sometimes even if it is large.

My conclusion is that the large external benefits of widely-diffused information about politics are not captured in a broadcasting market. The peculiarities of the broadcasting market do overcome a kind of public good problem, by providing a system for aggregating preferences; but they do not overcome the crucial difficulty of ensuring adequate provision of information. Thus far, then, it seems plain that the broadcasting market will produce insufficient exposure to information about public issues.

Advertisers and consumer choice. Suppose that we want a system of broadcasting in which viewing options are perfectly tailored to the choices of the viewing public. This is a reasonably unambitious goal; it would not call for initiatives designed to promote Madisonian aspirations. From what has been said thus far, it should be clear that even in a period with many outlets, there will be a difference between what is provided and what viewers want to see. Certain demographic groups are likely to be disproportionately favored, simply because they are peculiarly likely to want the relevant products. Shows that create an unfavorable mood, or that are controversial or depressing, may not appear because of advertisers' wishes. This is so even though many viewers may want to see them.

A large number of outlets will reduce this problem, but it will not eliminate it. Certain regulatory strategies, discussed below, could bring about a tighter connection between viewing choices and viewing options, precisely by reducing the control of advertisers over programming content.

Madison vs. consumer sovereignty. The third and perhaps most fundamental problem with reliance on the large number of outlets is that sheer numbers do not explain why there is a constitutional objection to democratic efforts to increase quality and diversity by ensuring better programming on individual stations. Even with a large number of stations, there is far less quality and diversity than there should be. Perhaps people can bring about a partial solution by changing the channel. But this option may not be good enough for a democracy. Even without a public good problem, the unanswered question remains: Why should the Constitution be thought to prevent citizens from experimenting with new methods for achieving their Madisonian goals?

A large point underlies this question. Thus far I have argued that even if we respect the viewing and listening choices of consumers, there are reasons for government to restructure the speech market. But we can go further. There is reason to be extremely cautious about the use, for constitutional and political purposes, of the notion of "consumer sovereignty"—the notion that underlies the claim that freedom of choice amidst a large number of stations solves the free speech problem. Consumer sovereignty is the standard economic term for the virtues of a free market, in which goods are allocated through consumer choices, as these are measured through the criterion of private willingness to pay. People who invoke the notion of free choice in markets are really insisting on consumer sovereignty. But for purposes of assessing the system of free expression, Madison's conception of sovereignty is the governing one. That conception has an altogether different character.

On the Madisonian view, genuine sovereignty entails respect not for private consumption choices as reflected in market decisions, but for the considered judgments of a democratic polity. These judgments should be reached after a period of discussion that meets the appropriate conditions for democratic choice. Those conditions include a norm of political equality, adequate information, respect for the facts, a commitment to reasoned argument, and an effort to reach collectively beneficial outcomes rather than to behave manipulatively, strategically, or in a narrowly self-interested manner. In a democracy, our laws at least sometimes do reflect those considered judgments, or what might be described as the aspirations of the public. Those aspirations can and often do call for markets themselves. But they might also diverge from markets and consumption choices—a familiar phenomenon in such areas as environmental law, protection of endangered species, social security, and antidiscrimination law. In all these areas, laws often reflect not an aggregation of market choices, but the outcomes of a deliberative process in which the public expresses social aspirations based on reasons. This goal is part of the original Madisonian conception of a system of free expression.

No one should deny the obvious and pervasive influence of well-organized private groups seeking to satisfy their self-interested desires. No one should decide that venality and partiality, let alone unjustified disparities in power, play a large role in politics. But democratic aspirations should not be disparaged. Democratic liberty should not be identified with "consumer sovereignty." And in the context at hand, the people, acting through their elected representatives, might well decide that democratic liberty is more valuable than consumer sovereignty. People might well choose to view a silly situation comedy at night, while also enthusiastically supporting a requirement of media attention to public affairs. Their support of that requirement, operating through democratic channels, could reflect a reasoned judgment about what they value for the polity of which they are a part, not a consumption choice about what they want for their private enjoyment. That judgment should be respected.[57]

In the area of broadcasting regulation, the point has special force. In their capacity as citizens, many people seem to dislike the current system, largely on the theory that there is too little attention to public issues and to substance. People's consumption patterns in television-watching do suggest a more favorable attitude toward existing practices. But when these are in conflict, the democratic judgments should prevail, so long as they do not intrude on anything that is properly characterized as a right. It is incorrect to say that the consumption choices are more authentic or more real than the democratic judgments.[58] Nothing I have said here argues in favor of imposition of regulatory requirements that the democratic public has rejected after considered debate. If, after consideration, the public prefers unrestricted markets in communication, that is a permissible choice, at least in general. But the choice would be unfortunate, and if the public favors instead requirements designed to promote Madisonian goals, the First Amendment of the Constitution should not stand in the way.

Problems with "preferences." Finally, private broadcasting selections are a product of preferences that are partly a result of the existing broadcasting system and not entirely independent of it. In a world that provides the existing fare, it would be not at all unsurprising if people generally preferred to see exactly what they are accustomed to seeing. They have not been provided with the opportunities offered by a better system. When this is so, the broadcasting status quo cannot, without circularity, be justified on the basis of the preferences.[59] Preferences that have adapted to an objectionable system cannot justify that system. If better options were put more regularly in view, it might well be expected that at least some people would be educated as a result, and be more favorably disposed toward programming dealing with public issues in a serious way.

It is tempting but inadequate to object that this is a form of "paternalism" unjustifiably overriding private choice. The concept of paternalism is notoriously underanalyzed, and it has special problems in this setting. Because of the preference-shaping effects of current legal and social practices, respect for private choices is not always appropriate, even if freedom or autonomy is our ultimate criterion (see the discussion of autonomy in chapter 5). Autonomy should not be identified with respect for private choice, independent of the content or origin of that choice, and of the reasons that might be offered on its behalf. When private choice is a product of existing options, and in that sense a product of law, the inclusion of better options, through new law, does not displace a freely produced desire. At least this is so if the new law has a democratic pedigree and if the old choices are a product of an inadequate system of options. In such a case, the people, acting in their capacity as citizens, are attempting to implement aspirations that diverge from their consumption choices. If more and better choices are made available, the outcome may well be to promote autonomy, rightly understood.

Precommitment strategies and the Constitution.   For people who are skeptical about such arguments, it may be useful to note that many familiar democratic initiatives are justified on precisely these grounds. The Constitution forbids the President from serving more than two terms. It is hardly a decisive objection that voters can reject the two-term president in individual cases if they so choose. The same point applies to the proposed term limits for members of Congress.[60] The entire point of the rule is to reflect a kind of "precommitment strategy" in which people commit themselves to a certain set of results or processes. Through this sort of strategy, citizens can accomplish a number of goals. They can overcome their own short-sightedness or absence of deliberation. They can counteract collective action or public good problems, providing a kind of coercion—voluntarily and openly agreed upon—from which all or most people will benefit. Most generally, they can appeal to their broader aspirations, aspirations which they know that they will fail to promote in practice.

This is a familiar aspect of constitutionalism, much of which can be understood as a precommitment strategy designed to overcome public good problems. And to those who continue to be skeptical, it is worthwhile to emphasize that the American Constitution is itself a precommitment strategy, persistently foreclosing choices in individual cases. Indeed, the First Amendment reflects a social commitment to a certain form of governance, and it forecloses popular majorities from rejecting the commitment in particular cases. The First Amendment can even be understood as an effort to overcome public good problems with respect to information. Many regulatory strategies for speech, designed to promote democratic aspirations, have the same form. They should not be thought to violate the First Amendment without a close look at their purposes and effects.

Some general conclusions follow from these points. As I have noted, many people think that the only possible problem with a system of free expression is one of monopoly—that if we had robust competition among many sources of speech, all our difficulties would be solved. This is false. To be sure, a system of monopoly is on most counts far worse than a system of competition, and precisely because of the lower level of diversity that it entails. A system of government monopoly is worst of all, as experiences in Eastern Europe and China have made clear. But a system of free competition among stations and newspapers is no panacea for democratic ills. Indeed, it may well disserve the Madisonian goals of attention to public issues and exposure to diverse views. We have seen much evidence to this effect.

A thought experiment may make the point more vivid. Imagine a regime in which there was extraordinary competition with respect to broadcasting—such robust competition as to ensure 10,000, or 100,000, or 250 million separate stations. (The example may not be utterly fantastic; technological changes may make hundreds of stations available before long.) In the last of these cases, each person might even be allowed to see or hear a station all her own. If technology progressed this far, and if the marketplace worked perfectly to satisfy consumer tastes, would our problems be solved? Certainly not. A system of this kind would not be anything to celebrate. It could well entail the elimination of a shared civic culture, which contemplates a degree of commonality among the citizenry. It could fail on economic grounds, because no person would be adequately motivated to choose public affairs programming if she is not assured that other people will make a similar choice. Even more important, it could fail to promote Madisonian goals. Everything depends on the relationship between the robust marketplace and those goals. This issue cannot be resolved on an a priori basis, or through axioms.

In thinking about reform strategies for broadcasting, we should emphasize that people are not machines to be molded for Madisonian purposes. People face significant limits on their information-processing capacities. They cannot process endless details. Moreover, they want to think about things other than politics, and they are certainly entitled to do exactly that. No regulatory system should attempt to ensure that broadcasting stations subject everyone to discussion of public issues on a continuous basis. If we adopted such a system, we might see not merely a mass audience refusal to watch broadcasting stations, but also a kind of information overload, ensuring that the benefits of the system are very low.

Any regulatory strategies must take account both of the inevitable information-processing limits of human beings and of the risk that any such strategies may simply make the audience refuse to watch—especially because the latter risk may result in a diminished private incentive to provide information at all. But through our current system, we have hardly approached people's information-processing limits. Moreover, most of the relevant risks can be addressed through careful judgments at the level of implementation. We need to ensure that any new initiatives do not make people turn off the television (though this would not necessarily be bad); our strategies should try diminish the risk that they will be futile or counterproductive.

How Other Countries Do It: Comparative Notes

Ideas of this general sort have played a large role in other nations. Before discussing some possible reforms, it will be useful to look very briefly at experiences elsewhere.

A comparative survey shows that the identification of unregulated markets with free speech principles is hardly a necessary one. Indeed, the United States is unusual in its largely unqualified commitment to markets in broadcasting, in its reliance on advertising revenues for stations, and in its conception of television as purely commercial. Other countries tend to see television as a medium principally for education and information, and to view its entertainment role as merely one among others.[61] Many countries see the risks in unregulated markets. Many countries make efforts to increase attention to public issues, high-quality programming, and diversity of view.

The German experience is especially revealing. Remarkably, an unregulated market in broadcasting has been said to be fatally inconsistent with the German free speech guarantee. The German Constitutional Court has explicitly opposed free markets to democratic principles—or Holmes to Brandeis—and opted in favor of the latter. The relevant provision of the German Constitution, Article 5(1), guarantees to "everyone" the right "to express and disseminate his opinion by speech, writing, and pictures" and "to inform himself from generally accessible sources." In 1961, the central government attempted to create a new broadcasting network. The German Constitutional Court concluded that this effort was unconstitutional insofar as the new network did not reflect sufficient diversity of view:

Art. 5 of the Basic Law contains more than the citizen's individual basic right to a sphere of freedom within which he can express his opinion without state interference. . . . Art. 5 requires in any event that this modern instrument of public opinion not be placed in the hands either of the state or of any particular social group. *Broadcasting institutions must therefore be organized in such a way that all relevant interests have the opportunity to exert influence on their governing bodies and to express themselves in the overall program.*[62]

Thus the German Court concluded that the government is under a constitutional duty to ensure that a broad array of opinion is presented to the viewing public. The Court went well beyond the American *Red Lion* case (see chapter 2) to the extent that it made clear, as the American Court did not, that the government was not merely permitted to produce diversity, but constitutionally obliged to do so. To be sure, the German Court stressed the scarcity of broadcasting stations, and scarcity is now a far less plausible basis for regulation in either Germany or the United States. But very recent German decisions have rejected pure marketplace thinking even under contemporary technological conditions. In the 1970s and 1980s, some German lawyers urged that without serious scarcity, free markets in broadcasting would be constitutionally adequate. The German Constitutional Court emphatically disagreed.

In one of the key cases, the Court said that the Constitution "requires the state to regulate private broadcasting. Such regulation is needed to guarantee broadcasting freedom."[63] The goal of regulation is to ensure "the free formation of opinions." To achieve this goal, freedom from government domination is necessary but not sufficient. Government must also attempt "to ensure that the diversity of existing opinions finds its greatest possible breadth and completeness through broadcasting and that, as a consequence, comprehensive information will be offered to the public." This requirement calls for mandatory legislation, even if the scarcity problem "no longer exists." The Court said:

[T]here would be no certainty that the unwritten laws of the marketplace would produce a selection of programs which would live up to the standards of broadcasting freedom. . . . [We] must confront the danger that [private broadcasters] might exclude opinions deserving of dissemination from the public opinion-making process and that opinion holders in possession of broadcast frequencies and financial resources might exert a dominant influence on the public opinion-making process.

Thus the Court held that private stations cannot by themselves ensure the variety that is required by Art. 5, since expensive cultural programs, not appealing to a mass audience, cannot be expected to be provided by the advertisers on whom private owners must rely.[64] So too, the Court has concluded that private broadcasters may not be allowed to give any single person or group excessive influence over the formation of public opinion.[65] The state is also under a constitutional duty to control the power of advertisers over the content of private programming.[66]

From the German cases, then, we see an understanding of the free speech principle that overlaps a great deal with the Madisonian view. Germany of course has a relatively well-functioning democratic system, one that is especially alert to the risks of tyranny in the wake of the Nazi experience. In these circumstances, it is highly revealing to see that the German Constitutional Court has understood its own free speech guarantee to require democratic principles and to repudiate marketplace thinking.

The Italian Court has reached broadly similar conclusions. In an early case, the Court concluded that the government must limit the aggregate amount of advertising expended on broadcasting.[67] It reasoned that limitations were necessary in order to ensure against private domination of programming content. The Court also concluded that at least under conditions of scarcity, provision must be made to ensure access for political, religious, and cultural groups, representing a diverse cross-section of opinion. Finally, a right of reply would be required for individuals. More recently, the Italian Court has said that public and private networks must serve complementary functions. It appears to have rejected the view that market competition is sufficient to promote the goals of a system of free expression.[68]

In Denmark, Sweden, and Norway, there is no advertising on television, and a major emphasis is placed on informational and educational programming.[69] The same is largely true in Finland.

Many countries, including Austria, Italy, and Switzerland, attempt to ensure that morning broadcasts contain educational programs. They also limit the dependence of broadcasters on advertising revenue. The use of government funds reduces the authority of advertisers over programming content.

Many countries—including Canada, England, France, Australia, New Zealand, and Belgium—have tried to reduce the level of violence on television. In some countries, there are limited periods in which violent programming may be shown. In other countries, warnings must be given before and during the relevant programming, in the particular interest of protecting children against exposure. Some countries require or encourage codes of programming designed to limit time periods containing violence, to reduce the combination of violence and sexuality, and to stop the gratuitous display of violence. England and New Zealand have taken steps in this direction.

In England and France, national and state governments use strategies of regulation and subsidization in order to promote high-quality broadcasting. In France, there are two public television stations, including a national public service channel. French law authorizes substantial limits on product advertising on both radio and television. The French regulatory body attempts to control advertiser power over programming content. Government's authority over licensing ensures an opportunity to control some of the adverse effects of market pressures (though it may carry with it dangers of content discrimination as well). There is a legal restriction on the publication of poll results or advertisements shortly before elections. Televised campaign advertisements are banned in that period as well. (Note that Australia goes so far as to forbid all television advertising by candidates.)

The picture is broadly similar in England, where two public channels attempt to promote quality on television. The 1990 Radio Act requires the Radio Authority to promote diversity in programming. Quality plays a substantial role in licensing decisions, so that the highest bidder for licenses is not necessarily the successful applicant.

It is important to note that England has no constitutional protection of free speech, and the constitutional protection in France is quite limited. Because of the absence of constitutional safeguards, both countries are inadequate models for the United States. For present purposes, what is most revealing is that in many industrialized democracies, the interests in broadcaster autonomy and in responses to market pressures are not decisive for government policy. Instead they are merely part of a complex set of considerations, all of which must be weighed in the balance. It is especially revealing that almost all such countries explicitly recognize a tension between a well-functioning system of free speech and unrestricted economic markets. They take steps to promote the former when it is disserved by the latter.

Reform Strategies

What specific strategies for reform might emerge in the United States? The most important point is that the First Amendment should not operate as a talismanic or reflexive obstacle to our efforts to experiment with different strategies for achieving free speech goals. We should look carefully at the real-world consequences of various regulatory approaches, without thinking that any intrusion on broadcasters' choice of programming is automatically unacceptable.

Most generally, it follows from what has been said thus far that there should be a substantial change in the self-conception of both the broadcasting media and the Federal Communications Commission. The media's obligation is to provide accurate and diverse information about public issues, not merely to respond to existing economic demand. Journalists should not perceive themselves as members of an ordinary business. They should try to promote a well-functioning democratic process, even if that aspiration is not always consistent with the economic self-interest of their employers.

Undoubtedly many members of the media understand things in just this way. The outcry over "soundbite" coverage of the 1988 elections probably helped spur somewhat greater attention to substance in 1992. But it would be good to try to inculcate more general professional norms of this sort.[70] Even without government policing, for example, the networks might agree to provide free air time for public debates and public discussion. Broadcast journalists might decide to devote less attention to the issue of "who is winning?" or "how will you win?" and to ask fewer questions about the polls or about imagined inconsistencies or scandals. They might focus instead on substantive disagreements among candidates. They might ask not only what the policy conclusion is, but also about the reasoning that led the candidate to reach that conclusion. They might initiate creative methods for eliciting discussion of issues, as, for example, through the "town meeting" format used so successfully in the second debate of the 1992 presidential campaign. An insistence by broadcast journalists on their Madisonian duties might by itself go a long way toward solving current problems. Much could happen without new regulatory activity.

So too, the FCC should return to its earlier goals of promoting high-quality programming, attention to public issues, and diversity of view. At a minimum, it should issue guidelines or policy recommendations designed to bring about these goals. Guidelines and recommendations are not technically binding; they are not coercive. But they have had an important educative role in the past, and they can help shape both public perceptions of appropriate fare and the self-image of various people in the media. A reinvigorated FCC should not believe (as did the Chairman of the FCC in 1980s) that televisions are simply another commodity, like toasters. It should attempt self-consciously to promote Madisonian goals through its recommendations and through its general, nonmandatory guidelines.

The FCC might, for example, recommend that candidates for office should deliver substantial speeches on national and local television shortly before the election, and that candidates should participate in a set number of debates on issues determined by independent citizens.[71] An especially promising format is one in which undecided voters ask candidates about issues that concern them. This format seems to encourage far more attention to issues and far less attention to the matters of strategy, scandal, and public impression that seem of great interest to many professional journalists.

But recommendations and guidelines are not enough. In designing more intrusive strategies, our presumption should be in favor of incentive-based, market-oriented efforts. We should avoid rigid government restrictions in the form of the command-

and-control regulation so popular in America in the 1960s and 1970s. In many areas of regulatory law, the former set of strategies has been far more successful than the latter, and they are receiving an enormous amount of current attention. Incentive-based strategies do not displace the market entirely. They leave a large room for individual choice. But they do increase the price of socially undesirable goods and lower the price of socially desirable ones, and in that way, they can work as efficient and effective mechanisms for bringing about important public goals. In the environmental area, for example, the best remedy is usually to force polluters to pay for the harms they cause, rather than to dictate that polluters follow governmentally specified technological mandates.[72]

We can build on this model in designing new approaches for improving communications and broadcasting. Indeed, the relative rigidity of the fairness doctrine was part of the reason it failed in practice, largely as a result of government nonenforcement. The fairness doctrine should therefore be seen as one of a series of command-and-control restrictions characteristic of certain periods in American government—restrictions that were at best partly successful. The doctrine is especially ill-suited to the current era, in which so many stations are available. A rigid, uniform requirement is unlikely to be fruitful or otherwise to make much sense.

A promising alternative model is provided by an innovative measure enacted through the initiative of Senator Paul Simon in 1990.[73] Senator Simon's statute exempts from the antitrust laws any effort by the television networks to reduce violence on television. This measure does not require any agreement among the networks. It does not censor any speech. But it does say that an agreed-upon set of principles will not violate the antitrust laws. In this way, it encourages networks to reach agreements that would otherwise be unlawful. The Simon initiative is especially valuable insofar as it recognizes that competition for viewers can lead to an undesirable state of affairs, one in which there is an increasing incidence of violence. In late 1992, the networks did indeed reach a shared set of principles. The agreement should significantly affect programming in 1993 and after. Among other things, the new principles say that programs should not depict violence as glamorous or as an acceptable solution to human conflict; should avoid gratuitous or redundant violence; and should avoid mixtures of sex and violence. These principles may well do considerable good. Other possibilities being considered include full lists of violent programming, violence ratings, warnings, and computer chips permitting parents to block out violent programming.

Our task for the future, I suggest, is to adopt creative, incentive-based strategies that move the broadcasting media in directions more likely to fit with Madisonian aspirations. This is not the place for a systematic survey of possible reforms. My concern is to suggest possibilities that should be thought consistent with the First Amendment, not to defend an entirely new regulatory system.

Children's programming.   Begin with the issue of programming for children. Here our system is clearly unsuccessful in terms of both quality and quantity. There is a strong case for government efforts to promote high-quality programming for children and for incentives or obligations, imposed by government, to offer such programming.[74]

I propose the following reforms. First, government should increase funding for high-quality children's programming on PBS. The reduction of government contributions in the 1980s has had a harmful effect on such programming. In the same vein, government should make substantial subsidies to private groups that are willing to produce high-quality children's programming for commercial television. Education for young children is an especially high priority for government, and there can be no doubt that television can be an important educator. Federal policy should reflect this fact.

Second, the FCC should more aggressively enforce current legislation designed to reduce advertising time on programming for children, to limit or eliminate programs that amount to fulllength commercials, and to increase the amount of educational or informational programming. The Children's Television Act has been systematically violated by the networks. The principal network response to this important legislation has consisted of astonishing efforts to claim that conventional low-quality fare (old reruns from the 1950s, violent cartoons in which the "evil toads" are dispatched by the hero) in fact qualify as educational programming. The FCC should ensure against evasion of the current requirement that networks provide educational shows for children.

Third, government should take new steps to use its regulatory powers to encourage better programming for children. Government might require advertisers on commercial programming for children to subsidize the production of high-quality shows. It might award "points" to broadcast applicants who promise to provide high-quality programming for children even if this is not as profitable as other programming. Finally, government should take seriously the provision of the Children's Television Act requiring each licensee to demonstrate that it has provided programming to meet the educational needs of children and young people. (It is notable that in Australia, for example, the government requires all stations to devote a daily time slot to informative programs for children.) Initiatives of this kind should not be thought inconsistent with the First Amendment.

Elections. We could do a lot to improve coverage of electoral campaigns. Most important, government should ensure free media time for candidates. Almost all European nations make such provision; the United States does not. Perhaps government should pay for such time on its own. Perhaps broadcasters should have to offer it as a condition for receiving a license. Perhaps a commitment to provide free time would count in favor of the grant of a license in the first instance. Steps of this sort would simultaneously promote attention to public affairs and greater diversity of view. They would also help overcome the distorting effects of "soundbites" and the corrosive financial pressures faced by candidates in seeking time on the media.

So too, some regulatory restrictions on campaign coverage and influence might promote democratic processes. Thus, for example, government might impose a ban on national projection of winners in certain states, if it could be shown that the projection would compromise the electoral process in states in which voting continues. Certainly electoral outcomes should not be affected by projected outcomes in states in which the polling booths have closed. The point suggests that other restrictions might also make sense; consider a ban on electioneering within 100 feet of the polling booths. In chapter 4, I will deal with the free speech issues raised by campaign finance laws.

Decreasing the influence of advertisers.   Many steps might be taken to reduce the effects of advertising on program content.[75] Suppose that our goals are to decrease those effects and to increase the influence of the listening (or reading) audience. Here we would seek modestly to ensure that programming accords with current audience desires—hardly a controversial goal—rather than to change those desires and to promote greater attention to public issues and diversity of view. Here regulatory efforts do not displace consumption choices, but simply attempt to ensure that broadcasters respond to those choices.

If these are our goals, we might at a minimum exempt from the antitrust laws any effort by the media to reach a "code of competition" designed to prevent advertisers from controlling programming content. Through such a code, stations could ensure that advertisers would not be allowed to choose programs, or to withdraw from programs, on the basis of their views about appropriate content. Instead, advertising might be made a function of time of day or aggregate size of audience. There is considerable precedent for approaches of this kind.[76]

A more aggressive strategy would be to impose a tax on advertising proceeds from the newspaper or broadcasting industry as a whole and to use the proceeds to subsidize programming. The distinguished economist Nicholas Kaldor offered a recommendation of this kind to the British Royal Commission on the Press.[77] In the newspaper context, our goal might be to decrease the proportion of revenue coming from advertising and to increase the proportion coming from readership. The consequence would be to decrease the newspaper's incentive to respond to advertising desires and to increase its responsiveness to readers. As a result, we would diminish the advertisers' power to influence stories and also increase attention to controversial issues. Media options would be brought more closely into line with consumer choices.

A similar strategy would make sense in the broadcasting context. We might impose a tax on advertising proceeds in the industry as a whole and return the recovered amounts to particular broadcasters in proportion with aggregate audience size. This step could avoid the problem, highly visible during the Gulf War, of audience demand for shows that advertisers will not support. It could also counteract the problem produced by the fact that advertisers may skew programming content in the direction of predictable, affluent viewers, and offer fewer and worse choices to groups that are less likely to buy products. Through this route, we would decrease dependence on advertiser desires and increase the autonomy of the broadcasting industry, while at the same time placing a premium on viewer demand.

There are other possibilities as well. A simple tax on advertising would accomplish some of these same goals. Sweden has a slightly more complex system: It taxes advertising in newspapers and redirects the revenue to the industry in the form of a "production subsidy." In order to be eligible, the newspaper must carry general news and information. Moreover, the subsidy is proportional to the amount of newsprint used for editorial copy.[78] This plan has stopped the decline in newspaper competition in Sweden; it appears to have been a substantial success. Alternatively, the law could forbid an advertiser from attempting to influence a station or network not to show a program that it would otherwise present. A threat of withdrawal of support in retaliation for programming content might be prohibited.

All of these proposals raise hard issues. I do not discuss them in detail here. I suggest only that they deserve serious consideration and that the First Amendment objections should not foreclose that process.

Promoting Madisonian goals. We might take some general steps to promote Madisonian goals and to overcome some of the adverse effects of consumer sovereignty. Here as elsewhere, let us begin with flexible, market-oriented reform instruments and avoid command-and-control strategies. It is notable that the American government already grants licenses to broadcasters on the basis of certain enumerated criteria, including attention to local issues and minority ownership. The connection between minority ownership and diverse programming is indirect and (to say the least) controversial. Many people reasonably oppose the use of minority ownership as a factor counting toward grant of a license. It is far from clear that a black-owned firm will provide programming to the black community. The government might also (or instead) award "points" to license applicants who promise to deal with serious questions, to provide public affairs broadcasting even if it is unsupported by market demand, or to furnish services to groups inadequately served by the market.

Government might also use direct financial incentives to accomplish Madisonian goals. It might require purely commercial stations to provide financial subsidies either to public television or to commercial stations that agree to offer less profitable but high-quality programming. Government might offer financial resources to promote such programming, especially if it deals with public issues. The FCC might be authorized to subsidize high-quality production so long as it does so on a viewpoint-neutral basis. It is worthwhile to consider more dramatic approaches as well—such as rights of reply for both candidates and commentators, reductions in advertising on children's television, content review of children's television by nonpartisan experts, or guidelines in the form of recommendations to encourage attention to public issues and diversity of view.[79]

Objections: Official Abuse, Private Adaptation, Elitism

Of course there will be room for discretion, and abuse, in entitling government to make decisions about quality and public affairs. Any governmental intrusion or supervision of the sort I have outlined could pose risks more severe than those of the current system. The market, surrounded by existing property rights, may restrict speech. But it does not entail the sort of substantive approval or disapproval, or overview of speech content, that would be involved in my suggested free speech New Deal. It might seem reasonable to respond that the relative neutrality of the market minimizes the role of public officials in a way that makes it the best of the various alternatives.

Some of the proposals I have described might be abused in practice by self-interested government officials. Moreover, private groups frequently distort apparently public-interested regulatory programs in order to serve their own selfish interests. In the environmental area, this is a common phenomenon. Would it not be especially likely, and especially dangerous, in the context of speech, where selfish or partisan interests would predictably seek to capture government power to promote their goals?

There are two responses. The first is that the current system itself creates serious obstacles to a well-functioning system of free expression. The absence of continuous government supervision should not obscure the point. With respect to attention to public issues and diversity of view, the present system badly disserves Madisonian goals.

The second point is that it does seem plausible to think that government decisions can be made in a relatively nonpartisan way. Some regulatory policies have helped greatly in the past. Consider just four examples. First, government was responsible for the very creation of local news in the first instance. Whatever the failures of existing fare, the institution of local news was a major advance. Second, government has helped increase the quality of children's television, at least when it sought to do so. Third, government efforts to promote more cultural and public affairs programming helped produce excellent documentaries in the early 1960s. Finally, public television, which contains a wide range of diverse and high-quality fare, owes its existence to governmental involvement. We have no basis for doubting that much larger improvements could be brought about in the future. Nor is there any reason grounded in evidence—as opposed to market theology—to think that a regulatory solution of this sort would inevitably be inferior to the current system.

It might be objected that some of these strategies will merely get people to change the channel, to turn off the television. or to turn to other kinds of entertainment. This risk is especially severe for regulatory strategies that attempt to counter current audience desires for entertainment. A requirement of one hour of public affairs programming per night, for example, would probably produce a large diminution in the audience. This is of course a real possibility, and any regulatory efforts must be attentive to the risk. But it is hardly clear that a decision to turn off the television would be genuinely harmful for individuals or for society, at least if the relevant programming is low quality and does not contribute to Madisonian or other social goals. In any case, the possibility is just that—a possibility—and it should not close off discussion before we have even tried. Even with a significant decrease in audience size, millions of people would probably watch the new and better shows; a diminished audience would still be huge. Moreover, a greater taste for public affairs programming may eventually develop as a result of higher-quality fare.

There is reason to believe that viewing habits, like many other customs and cultural practices, are extremely vulnerable to large-scale shifts on the basis of relatively mild government interventions. Sometimes the practice of many people is dependent on what other people do. Once some people change their practices, a wide range of others change as well. Thus it has been shown that "mass behavior is often fragile in the sense that small shocks can frequently lead to large shifts in behavior."[80] This is so especially in view of the fact that the modest changes sometimes have a large signaling effect for other people. If new programming is offered, and if some viewers like it, there may be a massive shift in its direction. In any case there is no good basis for supposing that current tastes and habits are rigidly fixed.

Of course regulators should be flexible and attentive to consequences. If a particular strategy fails, it should be abandoned. In any case it is important to recall that several of the proposals I have set out—especially those designed to counteract advertiser pressure—do not depend on countering the existing consumption choices of audiences. The strategies that do depend on this goal must be monitored closely for their real-world effects.

Reform strategies designed to increase quality programming, or to promote attention to public issues, are sometimes criticized as "elitist." The criticism is rooted in the perception that high-quality fare is appreciated most by the highly educated, who are (not incidentally) the most wealthy. What some people think to be sensationalistic anecdotes, or low-quality fare, represents the basic entertainment choices of many Americans. Why should a self-appointed regulatory elite be permitted to use the power of government to impose its parochial preferences on the rest of us? Isn't it especially troublesome if the elite is trying to overcome the choices of people who are not highly educated? There are lurking issues of class bias here. Finally, the First Amendment protects the freedom of speech, not merely political discussion. Is it not unacceptably partisan for government to attempt to further one kind of speech and in the process to disfavor others?

The answer to these questions should now be clear. Madisonian goals are not mere preferences. They lie at the heart of our democratic aspirations. As we will see in chapter 5, the First Amendment is best understood principally (though not exclusively) by reference to democratic goals. If government favors political over nonpolitical speech, it may well be promoting the purposes of the free speech guarantee, at least if it is acting in a viewpoint-neutral way and if it can show that a system of unrestricted markets genuinely disfavors Madisonian goals.

It is not unacceptably elitist to favor a system of free expression that promotes attention to public issues and diversity of view. Of course it is possible or even likely that the well-educated will disproportionately enjoy high-quality broadcasting. But this is precisely because they have been educated to do so, and high-quality education is not something to be disparaged. It has a point. Indeed, we should think of the broadcasting media as part of a system of public education designed to serve all those who need it; and there is nothing elitist about that. Even if higher-quality broadcasting is seen disproportionately by the well-educated, its benefits will hardly be restricted to people who are already informed. Many people who are not college graduates should benefit a great deal from such programming. Indeed, they may receive disproportionately high benefits. And insofar as the consequence is to promote public deliberation, and to improve political outcomes (see chapter 8), there should be very general benefits to the public as a whole. In view of the general benefits of having a civic culture, government efforts to promote attention to public issues—or for that matter the arts (see chapter 7)—should not be considered unacceptably elitist or sectarian.[81]

Law. How might these possibilities bear on the constitutional question? It seems quite possible that laws that contained these various reforms could promote rather than undermine "the freedom of speech," at least if we understand that phrase in light of the distinctive American contribution to the theory of sovereignty, that is, an approach that located sovereignty in the people rather than in the King. The current system does not plausibly promote that understanding, but instead disserves, and sometimes even stifles, citizenship.[82]

I do not contend that government should be free to regulate broadcasting however it chooses. Regulation designed to excise a particular viewpoint would of course be out of bounds. Indeed, viewpoint discrimination would almost always be forbidden (see chapter 6). Some subject matter restrictions would be illegitimate, because they would suggest lurking viewpoint discrimination. Consider a requirement that government deal with feminism, national defense, or abortion; courts should strike down anything of this sort. More severe controls than those I have described—for example, a requirement of public affairs broadcasting around the clock—would raise quite serious questions. But at the very least, legislative initiatives of the sort discussed here should pose no serious doubts.[83]

I believe that legislative or administrative efforts to restructure the marketplace should even be seen as the discharge of the legislature's constitutional duty—a duty that courts are reluctant, for good institutional reasons, fully to enforce. We might understand the courts' unwillingness to require rights of access to the media, or better and more diverse programming, to be a result of the judiciary's lack of a democratic pedigree, limited fact-finding competence, and inadequate managerial and remedial authority. A legislature faces no such institutional limits. If it is promoting Madisonian goals, its actions can therefore be treated as a response to genuine, though judicially underenforced, constitutional obligations.[84]

A legislative effort to regulate broadcasting in the interest of democratic principles should not be seen as an abridgment of the free speech guarantee. On the contrary, such an effort would respond to the powerful threats to democratic principles that come from the current marketplace for speech. I conclude that a New Deal for broadcasting could serve Madisonian aspirations without compromising any of the purposes of the system of free expression.

Chapter 4

Does the First Amendment Undermine Democracy?

DOES THE FIRST AMENDMENT prohibit government from restricting multimillion dollar expenditures on campaigns? From controlling political action committees? What if one candidate has many millions, and another candidate has practically nothing? Or suppose that the government wants to keep important information to itself. During a war, does the public have a right to receive information that government wants to keep secret, perhaps to avoid embarrassment? There is often a conflict between interests in security, order, and aesthetics, and interests in allowing open places for expressive activity. When must the government keep areas free for speech?

In this chapter I describe a number of places in which free speech law has lost sight of Madisonian aspirations. I deal particularly with campaign finance laws, with the provision of places for public access, with the rights and duties of newspapers, with government secrecy, and with the use of government funds to pressure the exercise of the free speech right. My special concern is that the First Amendment is sometimes used to undermine democracy. It is invoked as if it were a purposeless abstraction unrelated to democratic or indeed to any other public goals.

Campaign Financing: Money as Speech

The question whether government should restrict expenditures on campaigns has received enormous attention in the last generation. It may receive even more attention in the next decade. Such restrictions might well reduce political corruption—contributions to candidates in return for special favors. The reality and appearance of corruption are a major reason for campaign finance laws. But such laws are often justified as an effort to promote both political deliberation and political equality, by reducing the distorting effects on elections of disparities in wealth. Indeed, many justifications for campaign finance reform are distinctly Madisonian. Some people who favor such reform say that the political process should be a system of deliberation among political equals, and that domination by wealthy interests is inconsistent with the democratic ideal.

It should not be controversial to say that an expenditure of money on behalf of a candidate or a cause qualifies as speech for First Amendment purposes. Such an expenditure is intended and received as a contribution to social deliberation. At the very least, an expenditure of money is an important means by which people communicate ideas, and the First Amendment requires a strong justification for any government regulation of an important means of communication. We might therefore think of campaign finance laws as content-neutral restrictions on important speech. The restrictions are content-neutral because the content of the speech is irrelevant to whether the restriction attaches. The area is especially difficult because while these restrictions can be severe, the government can point to strong reasons in their support.

By far the most important campaign finance case is *Buckley v. Valeo*.[1] In that case, the Supreme Court invalidated restrictions on campaign expenditures. The government attempted to limit the amount of money that people could spend on candidates or on themselves (Ross Perot would therefore have been in big trouble if the Court had upheld the law). There was a $25,000–$50,000 limit on total individual expenditures and a $1000 limit on expenditures for any single candidate. According to the Court, such restrictions are a kind of First Amendment "taking" from rich speakers for the benefit of poor ones. In the key sentence, the Court pronounced that "the concept that government may restrict the speech of some elements of our society in order to enhance the relative voice of others is wholly foreign to the First Amendment." If the purpose of such laws was to increase political equality, they were constitutionally unacceptable. The goal of political equality could not be invoked to stop people from spending money on themselves or on candidates of their choice. Redistributive arguments for campaign finance laws are therefore impermissible.

The Court did not say that the First Amendment would forbid all campaign finance laws. Reasonable limits on campaign *contributions* are acceptable. According to the Court, those limits could be justified not on the objectionable ground of political equality (restricting the speech of some to enhance the relative voice of others), but as an entirely legitimate attempt to combat both the appearance and reality of corruption in the form of political favors in return for cash. These are very different justifications from that of political equality. In any case, the Court said, limits on campaign contributions are a minor restriction of speech, since they do not affect other possible uses of people's resources to express their political views. Even with contribution limits, people can make unlimited expenditures on behalf of favored candidates. Government may therefore restrict the amount of money that people can give to candidates for elective office.

By contrast, limits on campaign *expenditures* are indeed impermissible, since those limits are not easily justified by the anticorruption rationale. The key point is that someone who is spending money on her own campaign, or advertising explicitly on her own for a candidate, is not giving money to a candidate. The reality and appearance of corruption are therefore minimized. According to the Court, limits on expenditures are really an effort to prevent spending by people with a substantial amount of money. Since corruption is not at issue, these limits are illegitimate. Moreover, limits on expenditures are far more intrusive than limits on contributions, since expenditure limits do not leave people free to express their views through other means. The Court rejected the view that limits on expenditures were necessary to prevent evasion of the limits on contributions. It did not believe that people would form tacit but mutually understood arrangements with candidates to spend money in excess of allowable contributions.

The post-*Buckley* cases reveal that there are enormous complexities in holding the line between regulation of contributions and regulation of expenditures.[2] First, it is not clear that this distinction is relevant, for expenditures on behalf of a candidate can create some of the dangers of contributions. A limit on expenditures may be necessary to prevent evasion of the limit on contributions. Candidates often know who spends money on their behalf, and an expenditure may in some contexts give rise to the same reality and appearance of corruption. Second, the distinction is not crisp even if it is relevant. This is so especially in light of the dramatic rise of political action committees (PACs). Oddly, the rise of PACs is partly an unfortunate consequence of the *Buckley* decision. By upholding contribution limits and invalidating expenditure limits, the Court encouraged a large-scale shift away from direct contributions. The extraordinary proliferation of PACs is the result.

Many PACs are created precisely in order to exert political influence as a result of financial contributions. Is a grant of money to a PAC a contribution, or is it an expenditure? It might be thought to be an expenditure in the sense that it usually does not involve the award of money to a particular candidate; many PACs are devoted to numerous candidates and to general causes. The grant of money to a PAC may thus not involve the risk of "corruption" in the simple sense of an exchange of money for political favors. On the other hand, the PAC could spend a great deal of money on behalf of one candidate; it could be organized by a close friend or ally of the candidate. Indeed, in practice it could be nearly indistinguishable from the candidate herself. It is easy for candidates to find out who has given money to PACs, and to reward contributors accordingly. PACs often have unusual access to candidates, and if we are concerned about disproportionate access based on financial contributions, we might well be concerned about PACs.

Moreover, people usually know that contributions to PACs will go to certain candidates and not to others, and there is thus some risk of corruption here as well. A limit on contributions to PACs is far less intrusive than a limit on all expenditures; it does leave the individual with the option of making ordinary expenditures on his own. Finally, PACs are often said to have unusual political influence and for this reason to be a distinctive threat to political equality and political deliberation,[3] our Madisonian goals. For all these reasons, a limit on contributions to PACs—or on expenditures by PACs—should probably be thought very different from an expenditure by a candidate on her own behalf, or by an ordinary citizen purchasing an advertisement on her own behalf to help someone she likes.

The Supreme Court has not clearly resolved the resulting conundrums. In two key cases, it has given conflicting signals. First, it has invalidated a $1,000 limit on the amount of money that a PAC can give to promote the election of a candidate.[4] In the Court's view, the PAC expenditure is core political speech, and because the money does not go directly to the candidate, the risk and reality of corruption are not at stake. After all, PAC expenditures are not coordinated with the campaign and are in that sense independent. On the other hand, in the second case the Court upheld a $5,000 limit on the amount of money an individual or group can give to any PAC.[5] The Court said that this limit does not affect a wide range of other possible expenditures designed to advocate political views, and that Congress could reasonably decide that the limit was necessary to prevent evasion of the limits on direct contributions. The two cases are in obvious tension, and it is therefore unclear whether and how Congress may constitutionally limit contributions to or by PACs. This is an especially important question in light of the large and sometimes corrosive effects of PACs on the political process.

Let us put these various complexities to one side and deal with the fundamental issue of political equality. This issue is raised by a legal prohibition on financial expenditures when we know that we are dealing with simple expenditures. In *Buckley*, the Supreme Court prohibited government from imposing controls in such cases. In rejecting the claim that these controls could be justified as a means of promoting political equality, *Buckley* seems to reflect pre–New Deal understandings. Indeed it might well be seen as the modern-day analogue of the infamous and discredited case of *Lochner v. New York*,[6] in which the Court invalidated maximum hour laws. Both cases accepted existing distributions of resources as prepolitical and just, and both cases invalidated democratic efforts at reform.

On the view reflected in both *Buckley* and *Lochner*, reliance on free markets *is* governmental neutrality. In *Buckley* in particular, the use of existing distributions for political expenditures marks out government inaction. But from what has been said thus far, it should be clear that elections based on those distributions are actually a regulatory system, made possible and constituted through law. That regulatory system is not obviously neutral or just. On the contrary, it seems to be neither. The real problem is that *Buckley* removes many difficult issues of campaign finance reform from the democratic process and resolves them through judicial fiat. The Court did not explain why it was constitutionally illegitimate for Congress to say that economic inequalities could not be translated into political inequalities in the form of wide disparities in political expenditures.

Because it involves speech, *Buckley* is in one sense even more striking than *Lochner*. Efforts to redress economic inequalities, or to ensure that they are not turned into political inequalities, should not be seen as impermissible redistribution, or as the introduction of government regulation into a place where it did not exist before. Campaign finance laws should be evaluated not through axioms, but pragmatically in terms of their consequences for the system of free expression.

Consider John Rawls' remarks:

> [T]he Court fails to recognize the essential point that the fair-value of the political liberties is required for a just political procedure, and that to insure their fair-value it is necessary to prevent those with greater property and wealth, and the greater skills of organization which accompany them, from controlling the electoral process to their advantage. . . . On this view, democracy is a kind of regulated rivalry between economic classes and interest groups in which the outcome should properly depend on the ability and willingness of each to use its financial resources and skills, admittedly very unequal, to make its desires felt.[7]

In this light, a system of unlimited expenditures should be seen as a regulatory decision to allow disparities in resources to be turned into disparities in political influence. Why is it unconstitutional for government to attempt to replace this system with a better alternative? The Court offered no answer. Its analysis was startlingly cavalier.

There are some hard questions of policy here and perhaps some constitutional obstacles as well. The case for legal controls on campaign expenditures is plausible, but hardly clear-cut, and the effectiveness and even the constitutional legitimacy of any such controls will depend on the details. In purpose and in effect, some expenditure controls might operate as incumbent protection measures, insulating insiders and making it impossible for new candidates to have a legitimate chance at victory.[8] Some such controls might also diminish the total level of political discussion, and more equality is not necessarily good if it means much less speech. The system invalidated in *Buckley* was hardly a model of sensible reform; it had some of the crude features of the command-and-control regulation characteristic of American law in the 1960s and 1970s.

We can approach some of these issues with a glance at the role of Ross Perot in the 1992 presidential election. It seems clear that Perot's astonishing success was attributable in large part to his extraordinary wealth, which enabled him to deluge the media with advertisements in his favor. The Perot candidacy offers some mixed lessons. It is disturbing to see that someone may become a serious candidate largely because he can purchase his way into public consciousness. But it is hardly disturbing—indeed it is extremely healthy—to allow insurgent candidates to pressure the two parties. Perhaps campaign finance limits would prevent this salutary outcome, because a lot of money is a prerequisite for political success by an unknown. In any case, there is no evidence that a rich person can actually buy office. Perot ended up with only 19 percent of the vote, and with an arguably beneficial effect on the election. These points count against some kinds of campaign finance laws.

On the other hand, a campaign finance law might turn out actually to help insurgents. It is often incumbents who have the best access to resources. It is often most difficult for challengers to combat the financial imbalance. Perhaps certain campaign finance schemes could redress this problem.

Moreover, even if we suppose that political equality is a legitimate goal, the government could have promoted that goal through means less restrictive than those in *Buckley*. Instead of imposing a flat ban on expenditures, the government could, for example, adopt a system for public financing, accompanied by (1) a promise not to accept or to use private money as a condition for public funds and (2) a regime in which public subsidies are provided to help candidates match their privately financed opponents.[9] Under (2), a candidate could elect to use private resources, but the government would ensure that his opponent would not be at a substantial disadvantage. This system would promote many of the goals of the system in *Buckley* without intruding so deeply into expression.

Alternatively, Bruce Ackerman has argued on behalf of an innovative voucher system, in which voters would be given a special card—citizen vouchers in the form of red, white, and blue money—to be used to finance political campaigns.[10] Under this system, regular money could not be employed at all. Candidates could attract citizen vouchers, but they could not use cash. The advantage of this system is that it would avoid many of the problems posed by centralized, bureaucratic control of finances in elections, while at the same time promoting political equality, and without threatening to diminish aggregate levels of political discussion.

I cannot discuss these alternatives in detail here. Certainly we should look closely at the benefits and risks created by the various possibilities. But an inquiry into these considerations would raise issues quite different from those invoked by the *Buckley* Court. It would mean that an assessment of campaign finance restrictions would depend on a detailed inquiry into their effects, not on axioms about "redistribution." It would call for a large degree of democratic experimentation.

The alternatives should be explored on their merits and usually without constitutional barriers. Here, as in the broadcasting context, market theology is operating to bar a serious look at the democratic effects of different regulatory systems. We should be entitled to examine such alternatives as full, or fuller, public financing; a promise not to accept private money as a condition for receiving public funds; various voucher systems; public funding to put candidates on an even basis with opponents who have been benefited by private or PAC money; flat caps on donations to campaigns; and sharper curbs on contributions to or expenditures by political action committees. These and other options raise serious issues about the nature of our commitment to political equality, indeed about our self-definition as a democratic system. They should not be foreclosed by the Constitution.

Public Forums: The Need for Available Outlets

The campaign finance laws attempt to ensure equal access to the political arena by limiting the effects of wealth. The Supreme Court has faced similar issues when people claim that certain places are "public forums," in the sense that they must generally remain open to the public. The Court has often agreed with this claim. In so doing, the Court's goal has been to provide a sufficient range of outlets for expression. For a dictator, a tempting solution to political disagreement is to close off the streets and parks, so that political protests cannot be seen. Communicative processes can wither simply for lack of arenas. The Supreme Court has tried to ensure against this possibility.

Current law appears to take the following form.[11] The state may not close off streets, parks, and others areas held open to the public "from time immemorial." Here the public has earned a kind of First Amendment "easement"—a right to use property that government owns. Reasonable, content-neutral regulations will be upheld, but government cannot eliminate the basic right of access. For example, government may stop people from making loud noises in the streets and parks, and it may impose time, place, and manner restrictions on access to these places. But it must ensure that both streets and parks are generally open to the public.

The same rules apply to other areas if they have been "dedicated" to the public. Areas count as "dedicated" if the state has generally opened them for expressive activities. A train station, for example, is not a traditional public forum, since it is not so treated as an historical matter; but it may become a public forum if the government opens it to expression. If it is a public forum, government may impose reasonable time, place, and manner restrictions on communication, but it must generally allow access.

On the other hand, areas other than streets and parks—and this is a very large category—need not be open at all. Any restrictions on expression in these areas will be upheld so long as they are minimally "rational." In practice, this principle means that government has extremely broad power to restrict speech on government property, even if its justification for eliminating speech is weak in the particular case. Viewpoint-based restrictions are of course invalid. Government may not say that only Republicans have access to the grounds surrounding the post office. Moreover, content-based restrictions will be viewed with skepticism. The Court would not allow the government to say that the grounds surrounding the post office are open for all speech except that relating to AIDS. But generally, the government has a great deal of discretion to close areas off to the public. Courts will uphold even severe content-neutral restrictions on access to areas that the government owns.

So much for the basic law. One of its most remarkable features is that the Supreme Court decides whether an area is a "public forum" by examining nineteenth-century common law rules. Usually the Court does not undertake any assessment of the importance of the area to public expression or of the weight of the government's reasons for limiting speech. It gives access if and only if the area has been "dedicated" by tradition or practice for public access. This test is based on whether, at common law, the area in question was held open.[12]

Long ago, and in a period in which streets and parks were the principal places for communicative activity, this historical test was eminently sensible. It nicely served the goal of the public forum doctrine, which was the creation of access rights to places where those rights were most effective and most crucial. At its origin, the historical test preserved the system of free expression by ensuring that important areas were available for expressive activity.

But this test is now an anachronism. In the modern era, the streets and parks no longer carry out their common law roles. They are not the only or even the most important places for communicative activity. Other areas—perhaps mailboxes, probably railroad stations and airports, certainly broadcasting stations—are the modern equivalents of streets and parks. It is here that current law is most ill-suited to current needs. To keep the streets and parks open is surely important. But this is far from enough if we are to allow broadly diverse views to reach the public. The Court should abandon the common law test and look instead at whether the government has sufficiently strong and neutral reasons for foreclosing access to the property.[13] On this test, certainly airports and train stations should be open to the public whether or not the government has "designated" them as public forums.

The Supreme Court was therefore wrong when it ruled, by a 5–4 vote, that airports are not public forums for First Amendment purposes.[14] This important ruling means that government can close off airports to expressive activity so long as it does so on a content-neutral basis. As Justices Kennedy and Souter emphasized in dissent, it is absurd to say that only "traditional" public forums will qualify as such. For contemporary Americans, new arenas, unknown to the framers or to the common law, have assumed the role of those traditional forums. If the government has broad discretion to close off the areas where most people meet and congregate, it has broad discretion to undermine the system of free expression. In Justice Kennedy's words, "public forum doctrine ought not to . . . convert what was once an analysis protective of expression into one which grants the government authority to restrict speech by fiat."

Access as a Constitutional Right?

The public forum doctrine is an effort to ensure access to places where communication is most crucial. Under similar logic, a private right of access to the media might turn out to be constitutionally compelled. The notion that access will be a product of market pressures seems constitutionally troublesome.

I have suggested that it would make a mockery of the democratic ideal for government to allow people to speak in accordance with the amount of money that other people were willing to pay in order to hear them. But we have seen that in practice, our current system has many of these features. Suppose, for example, that a group objecting to a war, or to the practice of abortion, seeks to buy advertising time to set out its view. Suppose too that the purchase is refused because the networks want to avoid controversy, or because they or their advertisers object to the message. Is it so implausible to suggest that the refusal, to the extent that it is backed up by the law, violates the First Amendment, at least if other outlets are unavailable or far less effective?

I propose that the use of property law to exclude speakers should be reviewed under the standards applied to content-neutral classifications. I discuss these standards in some detail in chapter 6. For the moment, it is necessary only to say that some form of balancing should be applied to the use of property law to exclude people from places that are plausibly indispensable for free and open discussion. Government should have to show that the harmful consequences on the exercise of rights of free speech are justified by important governmental interests.

Under these standards, courts should probably deny a right of access to the media. The underlying factual questions are quite complex here, and courts should be reluctant to resolve them on their own. The government might plausibly claim that market forces already assure a fair degree of diversity, and that any intrusion on such forces would call for a form of objectionable content-based review. I have suggested that these claims are not ultimately persuasive; but whether or not this is so, they should not readily be rejected by judges. The role of the courts in American government is properly modest, and the creation of an access right would call for an unusually intrusive judicial role. If courts were to recognize such a right, they would have to engage in a high degree of managerial activity, assuming some of the functions of the FCC. This is a role for which courts are extremely ill-suited. They lack the appropriate fact-finding and policy-making tools.

For all these reasons, I do not believe that courts should create a right of access to the broadcasting media. But if we attempted a balancing test for content-neutral restrictions on speech, we would take a new look at the Supreme Court's famous "shopping center" cases.[15] In these cases, people tried to use the grounds of the shopping center in order to engage in political protest. They claimed that access to those grounds was indispensable if the public was to be presented with a certain point of view. Their claim was not very different from that which underlies the notion (accepted by the Court) that the state may not ban leafletting or door-to-door solicitation.[16] Nonetheless, the Supreme Court has flatly denied access rights to shopping centers and indeed to all privately owned property.

In view of the pivotal role of the shopping center in many areas

of the country, a right of access seems fully justified. Such a right creates no real intrusion into the legitimate interests of the shopping center owners. Shopping centers are open to the public in any case. No serious privacy rights are at stake (as there would be if courts created a right to access to people's living rooms). Moreover, the relevant rights can be recognized in a content-neutral way. At a minimum, state legislatures and state courts should be encouraged to create such a right.

May Government Withhold Information From the Public?

Suppose that the government wants to keep information secret. The information may bear on what is happening during a war, on a past or pending criminal investigation, or on the life of the President. Does the First Amendment bear on this question? As the law stands, it does not. The government is under absolutely no obligation to make information available to the public. This is so even if the information is extremely important to political judgments, and even if the government has no good reason for maintaining secrecy. In a cliché: The First Amendment is not a Freedom of Information Act.[17] The Constitution bans government from regulating speech containing information that private people have, but it does not require government to disclose information that it has. Or so the Supreme Court has held.

On the Madisonian view, the Court's understanding to this effect should be approached with great skepticism. Government can compromise public deliberation at least as effectively through secrecy as through censorship. At first glance, secrecy seems highly destructive to the system of free expression. The Court has justified its refusal to recognize rights of access to information held by government in part by referring to the text of the First Amendment.[18] Surely—we might conclude—it is not an "abridgment" of "the freedom of speech" for government merely to withhold information. We might think that the text of the Constitution simply does not reach this problem.

It is certainly customary to read the text in this way. But I do not believe that the words themselves are so clear. If we understand "the freedom of speech" to entail a certain form of self-government, it may well be an abridgment of that freedom if

government maintains secrecy without adequate justification. Suppose, for example, that the *New York Times* seeks information about the government's conduct of a war. Is it textually implausible to say that the government's refusal to disclose is an abridgment of the freedom of speech?

Alexander Bickel, a celebrated teacher of constitutional law, attempted to defend the government's power to withhold information not by reference to the constitutional text, but by reference to the salutary "equilibrium" that, in his view, follows from constant competition between the press and the government. In Bickel's view, "If we should let the government censor as well as withhold, that would be too much dangerous power, and too much privacy. If we should allow the government neither to censor nor to withhold, that would provide for too little privacy of decision-making and too much power in the press."[19] Bickel believed that we could achieve the right balance by allowing government to withhold but not to censor. The institutional competition between the government and the press would ensure good outcomes.

Bickel's theory is elegant, but I wonder whether it is much more than that. In the end his claims are based on empirical judgments that lack evidence. We have no reason to believe that any particular equilibrium in any particular period will be adequate for our purposes. In some periods, the government will have excessive power to withhold information that is indispensable to democratic processes; consider the Vietnam War era. In other periods, the press will disclose information that does not bear on those processes but that compromises important interests; consider disclosure of the names of rape victims. Bickel's theory depends on claims about the facts—about press and government incentives and about their relative power—that seem both unsupported and unlikely.

In light of these considerations, it might seem to make sense to urge the Supreme Court to hold that the government may not maintain secrecy unless there is a good reason for it. Perhaps this would be a superior understanding of the First Amendment. As in the context of access rights in general, the principal obstacle to this conclusion is that courts have singularly poor tools for deciding when secrecy is appropriate. A right of access to information

would require judges to develop a complex catalogue of exceptions—for national security, for privacy, for pending investiga-
tions, and for much more. It is unlikely in the extreme that courts
could adequately perform this quasi-legislative task. For this reason, it seems right for courts to have denied a judicially vindicated right of access to withheld information.

It is important to emphasize, however, that this conclusion follows from the limited institutional capacities of courts, not from
the substance of the First Amendment. Legislators and members
of the executive branch, not burdened by these institutional limits, might therefore be encouraged to work against secrecy, and
precisely in the interest of First Amendment principles. We might
conclude that the current Freedom of Information Act is a reasonable response to the (judicially underenforced) constitutional
obligations of government. We might also conclude that there is
indeed a constitutional problem whenever government denies
information that bears on public issues, unless it has a good and
sufficiently neutral reason for doing so. This conclusion holds
even if courts do, and should, refuse to intervene.

Ownership Rights as a Free Speech Problem—Newspapers

Can the government regulate newspapers in the interest of
achieving Madisonian goals? From what has been said thus far, it
follows that insofar as newspapers invoke the civil and criminal
law to prevent people from reaching the public, they too might be
subject to mild forms of regulation without abridging the freedom
of speech.[20]

To reach this conclusion, we might build on the discussion of
broadcasting in chapter 3. If the government seeks to promote
quality and diversity in the newspapers, some modest regulatory
efforts should be upheld, especially in view of the fact that many
newspapers operate as de facto monopolies. Consider, for example, the following possibilities: government imposition of a right
of reply; a system designed to diminish the power of advertisers
over the content of newspapers, as adopted in Sweden; a tax on
advertising proceeds; and government subsidies, on a viewpoint-
neutral basis, to newspapers that agree to cover substantive issues
in a serious way. These proposals would build on the judgment

that government has a legitimate role to play in encouraging the creation of a civic culture.

Some such proposals might be applied not merely to broadcasters, but to newspapers as well. Of course we would continue to impose the stringent limits that apply to any government controls. They must be viewpoint-neutral; any content restrictions must be persuasively justified. Under the approach I suggest, moreover, we would be committed to undertaking a continuing, pragmatic, experimental inquiry into the effects of different regulatory regimes. Here as elsewhere, the First Amendment should not operate axiomatically as an obstacle to experimentation of this kind. Regulation at the state level should be preferred to national controls, in the interest of the greater room for experimentation that is afforded by federalism.

In fact one of the major puzzles in free speech law involves the dramatic differences between legal treatment of the print media and legal treatment of broadcasting. Under current law, government has little power to regulate the print media, whereas the Court allows a range of restrictions on broadcasters. A fairness doctrine has been upheld as applied to broadcasting; it was struck down as applied to newspapers. Profane words can be regulated on the radio; the Court would not allow this in magazines. In a number of cases the Court has drawn a sharp distinction between the broadcasting and the print media.[21]

How might this be explained? There are five possibilities. I discuss them here because the asymmetry between the broadcasting and print media raises important questions about the theory and practice of free expression.

1. *Government gives out broadcasting licenses.* It might be thought that government has special authority over broadcasters because it "licenses" them, whereas it has no authority over newspapers because it does not "license" them. This is a tempting but, I think, an unhelpful claim.

The first problem is that there is nothing inevitable about a system in which government explicitly licenses broadcasters. If it wanted to, the American government could give out explicit property rights to broadcasters, rather than license them in individual cases. Under such a system, broadcasters would be offered "title" to certain stations, and ownership rights could be traded on a market, just like all other ownership rights. If government did this, we might no longer say that it licensed broadcasters at all; but would government thereby lose its current regulatory powers? This would be very surprising. The mere decision to create a genuine property regime should not eliminate authority that would exist otherwise. And if government would not lose its regulatory authority under a system of property rights, it is hard to see how it gains such authority by adopting the current system. In other words, the fact that it chooses to allocate licenses as it does, rather than through ordinary markets, ought not to give it power that it would not otherwise have.

There is a second problem. Despite appearances, the line between explicit property rights and the current system of broadcasting is extremely thin in principle. A broadcast license is no more and no less than a kind of property right, enabling owners to exclude others. There is nothing mystical about a property right; it consists simply of a right to do some things, but not others, with something that government has entitled you to "own." A license to broadcast is precisely this. Our current licensing system is indeed one of property rights. Its difference from ordinary property rights is that government plays a somewhat more constraining role over those who are allowed ownership. Thus far, then, there seems to be no substantial difference between the broadcast and print media.

In any case—and this is a third point—newspapers are now "licensed" in a largely equivalent but simply less visible way. Newpapers are given explicit, exclusive property rights by government, and it is these exclusive rights that enable newspapers to exclude other people. The *New York Times* is able to exclude others only because of the law. Without the law of trespass, the right of exclusion would be much less effective. This is very much like the grant of a "license" to the *New York Times*. The grant of "licenses" of this kind may be conspicuous only in the broadcasting context, but that is just because property law tends to be invisible as law. There is no respect in which the exclusive rights of broadcasters are more "governmentally conferred" than the exclusive rights of newspapers. Government confers the relevant rights in both cases.

I reiterate that this does not mean that property rights are bad or that we should restrict them. But it does mean that any distinction between broadcasters and newspapers cannot be justified on the ground that broadcasters are the recipient of government licenses. Both broadcasters and newspapers have been allocated some rights, but not others, by government. Nothing in the original allocation of rights justifies a greater role for government over broadcasters or a lesser role for government over newspapers.

2. *Scarcity.*   It might be thought that the real distinction lies in the fact that broadcasting licenses are technologically scarce, whereas technology allows the creation of a market bearing an infinite number of newspapers. The Supreme Court relied on this point in *Red Lion*. Perhaps the scarcity of broadcasting outlets allows government to engage in greater regulation of that media.

At one stage, this argument may have been plausible. Because of technological limits, some or all areas in the United States could have only a few radio or television stations. If we have just one, two, or three stations, it may well make sense to allow government to regulate programming content, so as to ensure diversity of material and point of view. Under conditions of station scarcity, we may be able to satisfy private tastes better with regulation than without—a conventional point among economists.[22] But as I have noted, there is no longer much scarcity in the current broadcasting arena, at least in most places in America. Technological change, cable television, and the proliferation of radio stations have ensured a vast array of programming options.

Indeed, only one or two regular newspapers can be found in many cities, whereas there are many broadcasters. It is true that the limitation on newspapers may be purely economic, whereas the limitation in broadcasting is a combination of technology and economics. But it is not clear that this distinction should make the slightest difference.[23] I conclude that the scarcity idea fails to explain the difference between broadcasters and print journalists.

3. *The best of both worlds; two competing, mutually constraining systems.*   Dean Lee Bollinger has come up with a creative and appealing justification for the asymmetry.[24] On Bollinger's view, there is no real difference between the print and broadcast media. If we look for one, we will be chasing ghosts. The key point is

instead that there are two appealing but distinct conceptions of the First Amendment: the first, with roots in Holmes, embodies a kind of free speech laissez-faire; the second, with roots in Brandeis, reflects a commitment to a kind of deliberative process, one that calls for government protection of public discourse and government encouragement of diversity of view. In the terminology used here, the first conception is based on the marketplace, whereas the second is civic.

Bollinger contends that if either one of these conceptions prevailed over both the print and the broadcasting media, there would be unacceptable risks. Self-conscious government protection of the deliberative process, if adopted as a universal strategy, would threaten the autonomy of journalists and to that extent would endanger a form of liberty. It would also introduce serious risks of bias. But laissez-faire would also pose dangers. It would threaten our public aspirations; it would sacrifice public deliberation through economic pressures. It is here that the dissimilar treatment of the two media turns out to make surprising sense. For Bollinger, the asymmetry in treatment may be intellectually messy, but it turns out to provide us with excellent and simultaneous insurance against both kinds of risk. It ensures that the print media will be immune from threats of governmental control, while also ensuring that the broadcast media will not be subject to the great dangers of reliance on markets alone. The happy result is two competing, mutually constraining systems, reflecting two plausible but incomplete conceptions of the First Amendment.

The argument has a great deal of appeal; but it is hard to evaluate in a factual vacuum. The problem, I think, is that Bollinger's claim is too abstract, too speculative, insufficiently empirical. It may well be that with enough facts, we would see that either the laissez-faire conception or the "government protection" model is extremely ill-adapted to the print media, the broadcast media, or both. If laissez-faire produces grave Madisonian harms in both contexts, then controls on advertiser authority, rights of reply, subsidies, and incentives, or even some kind of fairness doctrine should probably be acceptable as applied to both. If efforts to promote Madisonian goals turn out to create serious threats of bias and abuse, any such efforts should be abandoned, again as applied to both.

Indeed, it would be possible to think that the media, print and broadcast, should be evaluated as a whole. If the entire package is sufficient to provide exposure to public issues and diversity of view, perhaps the system is satisfactory, even if one or another source is inadequate standing by itself. On this view, regulation of broadcasting is not justified, and precisely because the print media pick up the Madisonian slack. I do not believe that this view is persuasive. Even if taken as a whole, the current media package does not adequately serve Madisonian goals. Moreover, the uniquely pervasive and influential character of the broadcast media justifies particular concern if its performance is inadequate. But Bollinger's claims would be more persuasive if he took account of the possibility that the media, taken as a whole, promote all of the various purposes of the system of free expression. In the end this, too, is in large part an empirical question.

Bollinger's proposal is appealing, even ingenious. But it may well provide excessive comfort with a difficult situation, rather than fully grappling with some hard factual, predictive, and theoretical issues. At most, we might conclude that if we are really in a factual vacuum about the relevant risks, or if knowledge of the facts leaves us quite uncertain, the asymmetry is a plausible method for avoiding all relevant risks.

4. *The print media are substantively better.*   Perhaps the asymmetry can be justified on the simple ground that content regulation of some kind is necessary for broadcasters but unnecessary for the print media. I have argued on behalf of an intensely pragmatic and factual inquiry. Under that inquiry, it may be right to think that there is simply no need for government regulation of the print media, because newspapers are basically fulfilling their Madisonian responsibilities. Among the best-selling newspapers are the *New York Times*, the *Washington Post*, and the *Los Angeles Times*. All of them provide a good deal of information bearing on public debate. With the broadcasting system, by contrast, experience has shown a range of Madisonian failures. If this is indeed the case, the asymmetry makes sense for good practical reasons.

A good deal of empirical work would be necessary to evaluate this suggestion. It is far from entirely implausible. Many newspapers do provide a kind of detail, depth, and substance that are lacking in the broadcast media. But there can be no doubt, too, that the work of the print media might be substantially improved. It is at least possible that something like a right of reply, combined with an incentive to attend to controversial questions, would be an improvement on the current situation even for newspapers. It is even more likely that legal controls on the influence of advertisers would help promote Madisonian goals.[25]

5. *The broadcast media are uniquely pervasive and intrusive.* The Supreme Court has sometimes justified regulation of the broadcast media on the ground that they are distinctly pervasive and intrusive.[26] Children, for example, might be exposed to obscenity simply by turning a switch. Moreover, television seems to be especially immediate, vivid, sometimes even assaultive.[27] What one reads on the page may be more distant, more mediated by complex cognitive capacities.

This is a controversial characterization of the situation, and it may not be right. But even if taken for all that it might be worth, the point does not get us very far; certainly it does not justify a large-scale difference between the broadcasting and print media. Perhaps the point would allow the government somewhat more leeway to protect children through regulation of the broadcasting media. Perhaps violent and obscene material should be more regulable on broadcasting than in the print media. But these would be relatively minor differences. They would not amount to an enormous asymmetry.

Any general conclusion about appropriate controls on newspapers should be tentative. If we are focusing on the need for attention to public issues and diversity of view, certainly the first priority is the broadcast media. It is here that the status quo is especially bad, and it is here that the bad consequences of the existing system are especially well-documented. Restrictions on the print media should be approached far more cautiously. In the absence of much more information about the existing system and the effects of alternative approaches, the Bollinger solution has much to recommend it. A system in which government tries to promote democratic goals through broadcasting regulation, but relies on the market for newspapers, seems generally appropriate. On the other hand, narrow regulatory initiatives—including controls on advertisers and right to reply laws—might well be upheld as applied to newspapers, even though the Constitution does not require them.

Unconstitutional Conditions and the Problem of Government Funding

May the government affect speech through the use of government funds? May it fund its favorite causes? This is one of the most important and sharply disputed problems in all of modern free speech law. It has sparked a great deal of public attention, especially in connection with limits on government funding of the arts and with restrictions on abortion-related expression from federally funded medical care. Should government withhold funding of sexually explicit art? May government stop federally funded clinics from discussing abortion?

Many people are puzzled by the idea that the First Amendment has any role to play in this setting. They do not believe that the Constitution should stop the taxpayers from using their own money as they choose. Other people think that the First Amendment applies to funding decisions "in the same way" that it applies to criminalization. In both settings, it is said, government cannot play favorites.

On the legal issue, the Supreme Court's cases fall under the rubric of the complicated "unconstitutional conditions" doctrine. This doctrine sets out the legal standards governing conditions placed on government grants in a way that might compromise constitutional rights. The cases are a bit hard to unpack. We might distinguish among several different principles. In concert, these principles reflect the Supreme Court's understanding of current law.[28]

1. Government is under no obligation to *subsidize* speech. It can refuse to fund any and all speech-related activities. If it does not want to fund expression at all, it is free to do so. In this sense, it can remain entirely out of the speech market.

2. Government may speak however it wishes. Public officials can say what they want. There is no free speech issue if officials exercise their own free speech rights. Speech of this kind abridges the speech of no one else.

3. Government may not "coerce" people by fining or impris-

oning them if they exercise their First Amendment rights. Fines and imprisonment are the most conventional examples of free speech violations. They do not raise "unconstitutional conditions" issues at all.

4. Government may not use its power over funds or other benefits so as to pressure people to relinquish rights that they "otherwise" have. This is an obscure idea in the abstract, but it can be clarified through some examples. Government cannot say that as a condition for receiving welfare, poor people must vote for a certain political party. It cannot tell you that if you want a driver's license, you must agree not to criticize the President. It cannot say that to receive social security, you must promise to speak out against racism. In all these cases, government is making funding decisions in a way that deprives people of rights of expressive liberty that they otherwise have.

It is tempting to say that the "greater power" to abolish the program includes the "lesser power" to impose the condition, or that the would-be speaker has waived her right and therefore cannot be heard to complain. On these views, government should be able to impose whatever conditions it chooses. But this response is inadequate. The First Amendment limits the reasons why government may act and the effects of its actions. If the government is attempting to stop or reduce the expression of a point of view, its action is unconstitutional for that very reason. Moreover, the First Amendment has the structural goal of promoting a certain kind of deliberative process. Citizens may often find it in their interest to give up the right to free speech in return for government benefits. But if government is permitted to obtain a number of enforceable waivers of the free speech right, the aggregate effect may be substantial, and the deliberative processes of the public will be skewed. This skewing effect is intolerable even if individual citizens voluntarily agree to waive their rights.

But—and this is an important qualification—government may indeed "condition" the receipt of funds, or other benefits, on some limitation on rights of free speech, if the condition is reasonably related to a neutral, noncensorial interest. For example, the government can say that it will not allow you to work for the CIA unless you agree not to write about your CIA-related activities. An appropriate price for CIA employment is an agreement to maintain secrecy.[29] Government may even say that you may not engage in partisan political campaigning if you work for the federal government. In both cases, government has legitimate, neutral justifications for restricting speech. The limitation on expression by CIA employees is designed to ensure the successful operation of the CIA, which entails a measure of secrecy. The limitation on speech by government employees is designed to ensure that partisan political campaigning does not compromise basic government functions. Of course this principle will create some difficult line-drawing problems.

5. The hardest and perhaps most sharply disputed proposition on this list is that government may subsidize speech selectively. It may apparently be selective in its funding choices in the sense that it may direct its resources however it chooses, so long as it does not run afoul of principles (3) and (4) above. What this means, again apparently, is that *government may give funding only to those projects, including those speaking projects, of which it approves.* If this is so, the government may apparently fund art, or literature, or legal and medical care, and impose any and all speech-related limits on what the grantees may do with the money. The taxpayers are in this sense free to say what may be done with government funds.

Rust v. Sullivan,[30] an especially controversial Supreme Court decision involving the abortion "gag rule," is the source of this last proposition. The "gag rule" prevented clinics receiving federal money from using the funds for abortion-related services. The clinics argued that the rule was impermissible viewpoint discrimination. The Court responded that so long as the government is using its own money, and not affecting "private" expression, it can channel its funds however it wishes. In the key passage, the Court explained why the government could forbid clinics receiving federal funds from offering counseling services with respect to abortion: "The Government can, without violating the Constitution, selectively fund a program to encourage certain activities it believes to be in the public interest, without at the same time funding an alternate program which seeks to deal with the problem in another way. In so doing, the Government has not discriminated on the basis of viewpoint; it has merely chosen to fund one activity to the exclusion of the other."[31] In this way, the Court seemed to establish the important principle that government can allocate funds to private people to establish "a pro-gram" that accords with the government's preferred point of view. In this area, even viewpoint discrimination is permitted.

On its particular facts, the outcome in *Rust* was not unreasonable. The case did not involve public advocacy.[32] Moreover, the government will likely affect speech whenever it funds clinics that provide services relating to reproduction. Speech is part of most medical services, and whether the government requires funded clinics to provide abortion or forbids them from doing so, it will affect doctors' liberty of expression. This effect need not be invalid, for any effect on expression is ancillary to the provision of medical services. *Rust* can be understood as a case involving private speech, or speech that is part of a medical service, rather than communication about a public issue. The "gag rule" was quite different from (say) a governmental program stipulating that funds will go to pro-choice speakers rather than pro-life speakers, or vice versa.

Notwithstanding the plausibility of the particular outcome in *Rust*, the Court's broad principle is striking, even alarming. It seems to suggest that government can allocate funds to Democrats but not Republicans, or to anyone who agrees to speak for causes that government favors. What underlies this idea? In fact, the Court seems to make a sharp distinction between government "coercion"—entry into the private realm of markets and private interactions—on the one hand and funding decisions on the other. Coercion is objectionable. Selective funding is not.

So made, this distinction is based on pre–New Deal understandings. It sees funding decisions as unproblematic because they do not interfere with the voluntary or private sphere. But if the New Dealers were correct, this view is inadequate. There are no such fundamental distinctions among the law that underlies markets, the law that represents disruption of markets, and the law that calls for funding decisions. All of these are law. All of them must be assessed in terms of their purposes and effects. All laws, including funding decisions, should be invalidated if they are unsupportable by reference to a legitimate, neutral purpose, or if they have unacceptable skewing effects on the system of free expression.

To make the point a bit more sharply: It turns out that all constitutional cases are really unconstitutional conditions cases. Whenever the government penalizes speech, it is conditioning a right that it has granted. When the government says that someone will be fined for speaking—our category 2 above—it is in effect imposing an unconstitutional condition. It is saying that your property—which is, simply as a matter of fact, governmentally conferred—may be held only on condition that you refrain from speaking. To be sure, courts do not see cases of this sort as involving unconstitutional conditions at all. But this is only because existing holdings of property are seen, wrongly, as prepolitical and prelegal.

If we were to try to make sense out of current law, it would be far more precise to say that a condition is usually unconstitutional when government is using its power over property (which it has created through law) to deprive you of something to which you are "otherwise" entitled—and you are always otherwise entitled to property that you now own. If we said this, we would begin to place funding cases and other cases on the same basic ground. The sharp split drawn in *Rust*—between restrictions on funding and other kinds of restrictions—is misconceived. At its foundations, it depends on pre–New Deal distinctions between government intrusion on existing rights and government funding.

I do not claim that funding decisions affecting speech should be treated the same as other sorts of government decisions that affect speech. The development of constitutional limits on funding that interferes with expression raises complex issues, and I take these up in detail in chapter 7. But for now we have reason to doubt whether the Court would really insist on proposition 5 above. Can it be seriously argued that the government could fund the Democratic Convention but refuse to fund the Republican Convention? Is it even possible that government could give grants only to academic projects reflecting governmentally preferred viewpoints? Surely the government must show a justification of sufficient generality and neutrality, even if it is engaging in selective funding.

The proposition that government may allocate funds however it chooses is rooted in anachronistic ideas about the relationship between the citizen and the state. It poses a genuine threat to free speech under modern conditions.

Conclusion: A New Deal for Speech

I have argued in favor of a reformulation of First Amendment law. The overriding goal of the reformulation is to reinvigorate processes of democratic deliberation, by ensuring greater attention to public issues and greater diversity of view. The First Amendment should not stand as an obstacle to democratic efforts to accomplish these goals. A New Deal for speech would draw on Madison's conception of sovereignty and on Justice Brandeis' insistence on the role of free speech in promoting political deliberation and citizenship. It would reject Justice Holmes' "marketplace" conception of free speech, a conception that disserves the aspirations of those who wrote America's founding document.

It is important to emphasize that a system of free markets in speech does have major advantages over other forms of regulation. Free markets are content-neutral, at least on their face. This is an important point, above all because in markets, no government official is authorized to decide who will be allowed to speak. There is no need to emphasize the risk of bias when government decides that issue. In addition, markets are highly decentralized. With respect to both the print and electronic media, there are numerous outlets. Someone unable to find space in the *New York Times* or CBS may well be able to find space elsewhere. A great advantage of a market system is that other outlets generally remain available. At least some other forms of regulation do not have this salutary characteristic. In any case it is important to ensure that any regulation does not foreclose certain points of view.

But our current system of free expression does not serve the Madisonian ideal. Free markets in expression are incompletely adapted to the American conception of sovereignty and to the commitment to government by discussion. If we are to promote our founding ideals, we need to rethink our free speech principles.[33]

Chapter 5

Political Speech and the Two-Tier First Amendment

I HAVE ARGUED THAT there is a difference between a system of democratic deliberation and free markets in communication. It is now time to explore whether the foundations of the free speech principle do lie in democracy, or whether other ideas give content and shape to that principle.

Every democrat places free expression at the center of the catalogue of legally protected rights. It is for this reason that we should reject the odd but pervasive view that democracy is incompatible with the protection of individual rights. The right to free speech is hardly in tension with democracy; it is a precondition for it. But if we think of the free speech principle through a democratic lens, we will make some controversial claims about the scope and nature of that principle. If we understand the free speech principle largely in democratic terms, we will give less than complete protection to nonpolitical speech.

Absolutism, Madisonianism

Some people purport to be free speech "absolutists," advocating constitutional protection for every form of speech; but no one really thinks this way. The government can prevent many forms

121

of speech, including perjury, attempted bribes, threats, private libel, false advertising, unlicensed medical and legal advice, conspiracies, and criminal solicitation. It can do this even if the only target of regulation is "speech" rather than conduct. Free speech absolutism is at most a theology, and it has no real followers. But is there a unifying principle to explain what speech is protected and what speech is not? Can we develop a framework to account for either our convictions or our law?

If we start with the Madisonian ideal, we will insist on the traditional but now disputed idea that the First Amendment is focused first and foremost on political deliberation. I suggest that "political speech" lies at the heart of constitutional concern. Such speech is securely protected against government; when the state tries to ban political speech, it is subject to the strongest presumption of unconstitutionality. Without a showing of likely, immediate, and grave harm, government cannot regulate political speech. This conclusion has broad and dramatic implications. It suggests, for example, that government may rarely regulate speech critical of its own performance during wartime; that claims for the violent overthrow of government are usually protected; and even that racist and sexist speech usually falls within the free speech "core."

But nonpolitical speech—which I define below—receives less stringent protection. A view of this general sort, asserted most vigorously in the work of the philosopher Alexander Meiklejohn,[1] would help solve many of our current controversies. It would do so while maintaining our focus on deliberative democracy, and without sacrificing the basic features of free speech law as it now stands.

On the Madisonian view, ours is a "two-tier" First Amendment.[2] The two tiers are defined in terms of constitutional value. Constitutional value is measured by reference to the animating purposes of the free speech guarantee. This is not a matter of uncovering some preexisting fact; with respect to constitutional purposes, there is no such thing. Instead we try to give the best constructive interpretation to the constitutional provision. In this process, we accord weight to structure and history, but acknowledge that these sources of meaning do not afford complete guidance. And in working toward a general interpretation of the First Amendment, we look at what approach best fits our considered judgments about particular free speech cases, and also at what approach is best matched both to counteracting governmental bias and to safeguarding political processes against intolerable self-insulation.

For Madisonians, political speech is firmly protected; it may be regulated only on the basis of the strongest showing of harm. But much speech does not fall in this category. Attempted bribery, criminal solicitation, threats, conspiracies, unlicensed medical or legal advice, perjury—all these are words, to be sure, but they are not by virtue of that fact entitled to the highest level of constitutional protection.

This proposition leaves open an important question: the standard of protection to be given to lower-tier speech. Here as elsewhere, no general formulation will resolve contested cases. For the moment, I suggest that diverse and plural values are served by the principle of free expression, and that nonpolitical speech is indeed entitled to a degree of protection. Such speech may be regulated only on the basis of a persuasive demonstration that a strong and legitimate government interest is promoted by the regulation at issue. On this view, many common reasons for legal controls on speech should be considered illegitimate; consider the effort to regulate ideas because they are offensive or likely to be influential.

This general standard, drawing on the Court's commercial speech cases, is far from a carte blanche for government. But the required demonstration is less than is necessary for regulation of political speech. On the approach I suggest, the government should be permitted to regulate false or misleading commercial speech, scientific speech with potential military applications, and violent pornography—even though these forms of speech could not be regulated under the stringent standards applied to regulation of "top-tier" speech.

In short, many forms of regulable expression are not entirely without constitutional protection. They do count as "speech." They are safeguarded for important reasons. But they do not lie within the core of the free speech guarantee.

I claim that much of free speech law should have a simple structure. The first question is: Does the speech at issue fall inside the constitutional core? If so, it can be regulated only on the gravest showing of harm. A protest against a war cannot be stopped unless the protest is nearly certain to cause immediate and serious harm. If not, it can be regulated by an invocation of legitimate, sufficiently weighty reasons. (I am putting to one side the issues raised by content-neutral restrictions, discussed in chapter 6.) Particular results will depend on the details. But the basic framework is important, and it is not complex. I suggest that this approach helps give order to most (though not all) of existing law, and that it makes good sense out of current practice without disturbing the most attractive features of free speech doctrine as it now stands.

The Two-Tier First Amendment

The idea that some forms of speech are less valued than others is frequently met with considerable alarm. The alarm is easy to understand. Does this mean that literature is unprotected? What about art? Who will make these decisions? Why should we trust anyone to make such controversial judgments? Shouldn't we look only at the question of whether the speech causes harm, and avoid the inquiry into value altogether?

In order to defend my proposal, it is useful to begin with this last question and to suspend the question whether we should accept the Madisonian view. Let us, then, explore the more general issue whether speech should be assessed by reference to value at all. Notwithstanding its controversial character, the view that value is relevant receives strong support from current law. Indeed, every justice on the Supreme Court has expressed some such view within the last two generations. Under current law, it is clear that some speech may be regulated not merely because it is harmful, but also because the government need not, for that category of expression, meet the ordinary, highly protective standards for regulating speech.

For example, the Supreme Court gives less than complete protection to commercial speech. It excludes obscenity from First Amendment protection altogether. It treats libel of private persons quite differently from libel of people who are public figures.[3] The absence of constitutional protection for criminal conspiracies, purely verbal workplace harassment of individuals on the basis of race and sex, unlicensed medical and legal advice, extortion, attempted bribery, and threats owes at least something to the common-sense judgment that different values are placed on different categories of speech. Suppose, for example, that the government seeks to ban a deceptive advertisement for lawyers' services. Under current law, the advertisement may be regulated without the least offense to the Constitution—and this is so even though we would not permit government to ban deceptive speech in the context of a political campaign.

To be sure, the Court has yet to offer anything like a clear principle to unify the categories of speech that it treats as "low value." The apparent absence of a unifying principle is a source of continuing frustration to people who try to make sense of free speech law. But the existence of a two-tier First Amendment is hard to deny; and the tiers are defined by reference to value, not simply by reference to harm.

It is tempting to resist this conclusion by proposing that the speech that is unprotected is really not speech at all, but merely action. When someone attempts to bribe a government official, perhaps he is "acting," or perhaps the regulation of criminal solicitation is "ancillary" or "incidental" to the regulation of conduct. But as stated, I think that this suggestion is unhelpful. Criminal solicitation and attempted bribes are speech, not action. They may lead to action; but by themselves they are simply words. If I tell you that I want you to help me to commit an assault, I have spoken words; if I say that I will give you $10,000 if you vote for me, I have merely talked; if I say "Kill!" to a trained attack dog, I have done something regulable, but I have still just spoken. If these things are to be treated as action—that is, if they are not to be protected as speech—it is because of their distinctive features. This is what must be discussed. The word "action" is simply a placeholder for that unprovided discussion.

In beginning that discussion, perhaps we can make some progress by suggesting that some words actually amount to a way of performing independently illegal acts. If someone writes a letter saying, "You're fired, because I won't let blacks work here," we can properly categorize the letter as a form of action. The letter amounts to the commission of an illegal act, that of racially discriminatory discharge. If government can punish that act, surely it can punish the speech that *is* that act. The letter is simply evidence of what is unlawful, a discharge based on discrimination. Use of the letter to prove discriminatory motive is hardly unconstitutional even if the letter is speech.

Something of this kind might also be said of a conspiracy to set prices, a threat, an attempted bribe, or a purely verbal act of sexual harassment. If an employer tells an employee, "I will fire you unless you sleep with me," the statement is the act of harassment; we would not say that the statement "causes" or "leads to" harassment. Through a route of this kind, it might be possible to say that some things that look like speech can be treated as conduct, and properly banned, because they amount to the commission of unlawful acts.[4] But even if we carry out this task, the category of regulable second-tier speech would be very narrow. It would not include all of the speech that is now treated as low-value. It would probably have to exclude, for example, both obscenity and false or misleading commercial speech; and libel will be difficult to handle. In any case, I think that it is best to be able to justify the regulation of speech by reference to considerations of value and harm even in cases in which the speech is plausibly characterized as action. The speech/action distinction is not enough (see chapter 6.)

Thus far, then, we see that the Supreme Court understands the First Amendment to have two tiers, and that the speech-action distinction is an inadequate way to make sense of the situation. But is a two-tier First Amendment inevitable or desirable? Surely there are many problems with any sort of two-tier system, and I will discuss them in some detail below. But it does seem likely that any well-functioning system of free expression must ultimately distinguish between different kinds of speech by reference to their centrality to the First Amendment guarantee.[5]

Begin with a truly absolutist position: Anyone may say anything at any time. By now it should be clear that this position could not be seriously maintained. It would not make sense to forbid government from regulating—our now-familiar catalogue—perjury, bribes, threats, unlicensed medical and legal advice, willfully false advertising, and many other forms of expression. Realistically speaking, our choices are a range of non-absolutist approaches.

The only nonabsolutist alternative to an approach that looks at free speech "value" would be this: All speech stands on basically the same footing. We will not look at value at all. The only relevant issue is one of *harm*. Speech may be regulated if government can make a demonstration that the speech at issue will produce sufficiently bad consequences. This is the only question for the Court. Would it not be possible, and desirable, to have a "single-tier" First Amendment, in the sense that all speech is presumed protected, but we allow government to regulate speech in those rare cases where the harm is very great?

On reflection, this position does indeed seem unacceptable. If it were the law, the same standards of harm would be applied to all speech. This would mean that regulation of (for example) campaign speeches must be tested under the same standards applied to regulation of false commercial speech, child pornography, conspiracies, libel of private persons, and threats. If the same standards were applied, one of two results would follow; and both seem to face decisive objections.

The first possible result of a test based solely on harm is that the burden of justification imposed on government—the required showing of harm—would have to be *lowered* as a whole, so as to allow for regulation of false commercial speech, private libel, unlicensed medical and legal advice, and so forth. Under such a system, we know that value would not matter. The only question would be the government's justification, which would, by hypothesis, have to meet the same standard in all cases. But if the consequence of this system were to lower the government's burden—so as to permit regulation of false commercial speech, private libel, and the rest—there would seem to be an unacceptably high threat of censorship of many other forms of speech, including political expression. A system in which political speech receives the same relatively low level of protection now given to commercial speech would produce serious risks to democratic self-governance.

Such a system might well, for example, allow government to regulate political speech when it is misleading or false. This approach would provide far too little breathing space for important speech. Misleading and even false political speech is part and parcel of vigorous political debate.[6] So too, severe risks would be produced by a system in which libel of government officials received no more protection than libel of ordinary citizens. Such a system would deter criticism of government, and criticism of government is indispensable to democracy. But a framework looking only at harm would put libel of government officials on the same ground as libel of private citizens,[7] and if the current, relatively lenient standards for private libel are to be applied generally, we would endanger democratic processes.

The second possible outcome of an exclusive focus on harm would be that the burden of justification imposed on government would be *raised* as a whole. Thus the properly stringent standards applied to government efforts to regulate political speech would also be applied to efforts to regulate false commercial speech, private libel, unlicensed medical or legal advice, and child pornography. The same very high burden would be placed on all government efforts to regulate speech. This approach would have the large advantage of removing possible risks to political speech. But it would also ensure that government controls could not be applied to speech that in all probability should be regulable.

To be more concrete: A system in which the most stringent standards were applied across the board would probably ensure that government could not regulate (among other things) criminal solicitation, child pornography, private libel, and false or misleading commercial speech. The harms that justify such regulation are of course real. But if we are to be honest, we will have to conclude that those harms are insufficient to permit government controls under the extremely high standards applied to regulation of political speech. For example, child pornography causes harm to children, but a speech-protective approach to the problem of child pornography would probably not be legal controls on the speech, but only legal controls on the production of the material.[8] Similarly, a speech-protective approach would mean that we could no longer regulate all attempted bribes, criminal solicitation, and conspiracy, but only when these forms of speech threaten clear and immediate harm. Many attempted bribes, solicitations, and conspiracies are doomed to failure from the start; they do not cause harm in the world. If they are to be treated as core speech for constitutional purposes, they cannot be regulated when the harm is not likely to occur.

These would be the appropriate conclusions if we impose, in all these cases, the burden applied to "core" speech. An insistence that "all speech is speech," and that value is irrelevant, would mean that many currently unobjectionable controls would have to be eliminated—or more likely that judgments about value, because unavoidable, would continue to be made, but covertly.

I conclude that the alternatives to the two-tier First Amendment, or to some system that looks at the "value" side of the First Amendment judgment, will meet decisive objections. An inquiry into harm alone would do violence to many of our considered judgments about particular free speech cases. As we will soon see, a system that does violence to those judgments is not likely to deserve support.

The Plurality of Free Speech Values

We should acknowledge that free speech values are likely to be plural and diverse rather than unitary. This is true for most constitutional rights, which serve a range of purposes. The protection of property rights, for example, helps to promote economic prosperity by creating appropriate incentives for productive activity. But it also safeguards individual security—an important noneconomic value—and by limiting government discretion over our holdings, it serves democratic goals as well. Plural values are promoted by other constitutional rights too. Consider the hearing rights guaranteed by the due process clause, the protection against unreasonable searches and seizures under the Fourth Amendment, the barrier to cruel and unusual punishment provided by the Eighth Amendment. The problem with unitary or monistic theories of constitutional value is that they are obtuse. They fail to perceive the multiple interests served by constitutional guarantees.[9]

It would be especially obtuse to suggest that the free speech principle serves only political values. As everyone who consults personal experience is aware, a system of free communication yields a wide variety of diverse social goods. As we will see, significant autonomy interests, quite independent of democracy, help justify the protection of free speech. There is also an important connection between free speech and individual self-development. The opportunity to create art or literature, like the opportunity to read the products of other minds, is crucial to the development of human capacities. Sexually explicit speech, for example, often deserves protection for this reason; it should not be ruled outside of the First Amendment altogether. Scientific progress is also a goal of most societies, and a vigorous free speech principle can be important in securing that goal. Free communication is also indispensable to economic development.

Those who believe in a two-tier First Amendment, or who insist on the primacy of political speech, do not deny the plurality and diversity of free speech values. Instead they seek to design a system of free expression that can be both substantively acceptable and judicially administrable, and that is also highly attuned to the strengths and weaknesses of all our governmental institutions. If a Madisonian understanding of free speech turns out to be acceptable, it still remains possible to insist that nonpolitical values are often at stake in free speech cases, and that courts should be careful to protect those values. Let us now turn, then, to the reasons for offering special protection to political speech.

The Primacy of Politics: The Basic Case

I have suggested that a two-tier First Amendment will be superior to the alternatives. It remains, however, to explain by what standard courts should distinguish between low-value and high-value speech. From what has been said thus far, we can envision many possible standards. We might emphasize autonomy, self-development, or the many other social goals likely to be promoted by the free speech guarantee. But of all the possible standards for distinguishing between forms of speech, I suggest that an emphasis on democracy and politics is best. To support this argument, it is of course necessary to begin by defining the category of political speech.

For present purposes I mean to treat speech as political *when it is both intended and received as a contribution to public deliberation about some issue.* This is a broad standard. It categorizes all speech that bears on potentially public issues as falling within the free speech core. It is unnecessary to show that the relevant speech specifically calls for some change in the law, or tells government to do something. Public deliberation can deal with social norms as well as with legal requirements. An attack on private discrimination against homosexuals, a complaint about inequality between men and women with respect to childcare, or a plea for voluntary protection of unborn life ("adoption not abortion"), falls comfortably within the free speech core. This is so even if it does not bear explicitly on what government should do.

But the standard does contain limits. Both intent and receipt must be shown. It seems implausible to say that words warrant the highest form of protection if the speaker does not even intend to communicate a message. The First Amendment should not be taken to put gibberish at the core even if it is taken, by some in the audience, to mean something. By requiring intent, however, I do not mean to require individual trials on subjective motivation. Generally this issue should be resolved by making reasonable inferences from the speech at issue. Almost all cases will be easy on this score.

By requiring that the speech be received as political, I do not mean that all listeners or readers must see the political content. It is sufficient if a few do. Many people of course miss the political message in speech that should qualify as political, especially in art or literature. Here too most cases will be easy. But if no one sees the political content—if all we have is the artist's claim that in putting a hundred indecipherable marks on the page, he was really speaking about the President—it is hard to understand why the speech should qualify for special protection. Despite the relevance of intention, however, the definition of the political is free-standing and independent of how the particular writer or artist understands the notion of "politics." A work of literature that is intended and received as a contribution to social deliberation about some issue counts as political speech even if the artist or writer denies its political character. Of course the speaker's denial that the speech was intended as a contribution to social deliberation about some issue would count strongly against constitutional protection.

Finally, both requirements must be met, though in almost all cases, speech that is intended as political will be seen by some people as such. Under the test I propose, the mere fact that a speech is seen by some as political is insufficient if we assume that it is not so intended. Consider, for example, commercial speech, obscenity, private libel, or a rock formation. Some people understand commercial speech and obscenity to be "political"; and indeed it is plausible to think that almost all speech is political in the sense that it relates in some way to the existing social and political structure. Commercial speech and obscenity are examples. But if some people understand the speech in question to be political, it cannot follow that the speech qualifies as such for constitutional purposes, without treating almost all speech as political and therefore destroying the whole point of the two-tier system. Of course the definition I have offered leaves many questions unanswered, and there will be hard intermediate cases. I shall offer it as a starting point for an analysis of particular problems.

My approach is justified on four basic grounds. Here, then, is the affirmative case for the Madisonian conception of free speech.

1. The view that political speech belongs in the top tier receives firm support from history. By this I refer first to the founding generation's own theory of free expression. The role of framers' or ratifiers' "intent" in constitutional interpretation is of course extremely controversial, and I do not believe that the meaning of the First Amendment is limited to the original understanding.[10] It is a hard question at what level of generality to read that understanding; often we should read constitutional provisions as setting out general concepts, to be filled in over time, rather than particular conceptions, to be understood by reference to the specific views of those who wrote the provisions. All I mean to suggest is that in any legal system, it is surely relevant if those who are responsible for a constitutional provision understood it to mean adherence to a relatively well-defined, ascertainable principle. That principle is entitled to great respect from current interpreters.

The best view of the relevant history is that political speech was thought to form the core of the free speech principle.[11] This does not mean that all other speech was entirely excluded; but it does mean that the framers' principal fear was government censorship of political speech. There can be little doubt that suppression by the government of political ideas of which it disapproved, or which it found threatening, was the central motivation for the clause. There can be little doubt that to the founding generation the main examples of unacceptable censorship involved efforts by the government to shut off dissent or to insulate itself from criticism.

By history I do not mean only the framers' views. I refer as well to the development of the free speech principle through the long history of American law. The great free speech opinions from Justices Holmes and Brandeis, discussed in chapter 1, grew out of government suppression of political dissent. In most of the defining cases of the modern era, very much the same is true.[12] In *New York Times v. Sullivan*, for example, the law of libel was applied against an advertisement for the civil rights movement, an advertisement that served as a political protest. In *New York Times v. U.S.*, the government tried to stop the publication of the Pentagon Papers, which contained damaging material about the American government's performance during the Vietnam War. A look at the free speech tradition shows that a political conception of the First Amendment is firmly supported by judicial interpretations over the course of time. If we are seeking to retain continuity with our tradition, that conception deserves strong support.

2. A political conception has the large advantage of fitting relatively well with our provisional or considered judgments about particular free speech problems. Our approach to the First Amendment should take substantial account of those judgments and adjust itself accordingly. It should generate theories at least in part by close engagement with particular judgments. To the extent possible, the theory should be adjusted to conform to those judgments, and vice versa, until we reach a state of equilibrium.[13]

We may disagree about many free speech issues, but it seems clear that speech that bears on political life is entitled to the fullest protection of the free speech principle. No one denies that at a minimum, this principle includes all or almost all forms of political speech. By contrast, such forms of speech as perjury, attempted bribery, threats, misleading or false commercial advertising, unlicensed medical or legal advice, criminal solicitation, and libel of private persons—or at least most of these—are not entitled to the highest degree of constitutional protection.

It is a conspicuous fact that all such forms of speech are nonpolitical in the sense that I understand that term here. At least as a general rule, private libel is not intended to contribute to political deliberation. So too with a false advertisement, or unlicensed medical advice, or an attempted bribe. The political approach accounts surprisingly well for our considered judgments about all or most of these cases. As we will soon see, no other approach seems as well-suited to that task. At a minimum, the Madisonian principle seems to fit with our considered judgments about what is a *sufficient* condition for inclusion with the core of the free speech principle, and at least it helps explain why some speech is not so included, since the categories of "low-value" speech all seem to be nonpolitical in the relevant sense.

There are, however, some hard issues here with respect to art, literature, scientific speech, and perhaps even music. Many of our considered judgments are opposed to restrictions on these forms of speech, and these judgments seem to argue powerfully against a political conception of the First Amendment. I do not claim that the two-tier First Amendment, defined in terms of politics, corresponds perfectly with our considered judgments—certainly not until much more is said to explain what will happen to speech within the second tier. Moreover, we should not say that in a diverse society, there is a simple, single category called "our judgments." People sometimes disagree. But as I will soon suggest, there are ways of taking account of relevant disagreements, and of the substantial support for protection of nonpolitical speech, without endangering the political conception of the First Amendment. It is therefore possible to account for our considered judgments in favor of protection of art and literature without concluding that all speech of this kind must be placed in the free speech core, and without jeopardizing the Madisonian view.

3. An insistence that government's burden is greatest for regulating political speech is based on a sensible view of government's incentives. It is in this setting that government is most likely to be biased or to be acting on the basis of illegitimate, venal, or partial considerations.[14] Government is rightly distrusted when it is regulating speech that might harm its own interests; and when the speech at issue is political, its own interests are almost always at stake. It follows that the premise of distrust of government is strongest when politics is at issue. And when the premise of distrust is strongest, the burden of justification is highest.

The premise of distrust is weaker when government is regulating (say) commercial speech, attempted bribery, private libel, or obscenity. In such cases there is less reason to suppose that it is likely to be biased or partial, or to be insulating itself from criticism. Government regulation of commercial speech, private libel, or attempted bribery seems no more likely to be biased than government regulation of anything else.

To be sure, a good deal of work in public choice theory has shown that government will have bad incentives in many areas.[15] For example, restrictions on commercial advertising by pharmacists might well be not an effort to promote the public good, but a measure sought by a well-organized group of pharmacists to eliminate price competition. Many forms of regulation are attempts to stop marketplace competition, favored by self-interested groups and operating at the expense of the public at large. This is surely true for regulation of commercial speech as well as for regulation of commerce.

In the area of art and literature—on which I will say much more—there is a special fear. It is common to worry that moralistic people or religious groups will attempt to use the arm of the state in order to censor speech that threatens their particular, partial conception of the good.[16] But these kinds of threats, though real, do not distinguish regulation of speech from regulation of anything else; hence they provide us with no special reason to be suspicious of government regulation of speech. If courts are not especially suspicious of government regulation generally, they should not be especially suspicious of government regulation of nonpolitical speech.[17] Regulation of political speech, by contrast, raises the distinctive spectre of government censorship harmful to its own self-interest. A political conception of the two-tier First Amendment responds well to an understanding of where government is least trustworthy.

This point leads to an important conclusion. Even if we think that free speech serves a wide array of diverse human interests, we might conclude that the constitutional principle of free speech places political expression at the core. This is not because political speech is always more important than other speech; this would be an absurd conclusion. It is because constitutional protection against politics is peculiarly necessary when political speech is involved. A theory of the function of the Constitution must pay a great deal of attention to the contexts in which ordinary majoritarian politics is least trustworthy.[18]

4. An emphasis on politics protects speech not only when regulation is most likely to be biased, but also when it is most likely to be harmful to the democratic process. Restrictions on political speech have the distinctive feature of impairing the ordinary channels for political change. It is for this reason that such restrictions are especially dangerous.[19]

Suppose, for example, that the government imposes controls on commercial advertising. If so, it always remains possible to argue that such controls should be lifted. On the Madisonian view, this very argument is protected as "core" speech. If the government bans violent pornography, citizens can continue to argue against the ban on the ground that it is foolish or paternalistic, or invasive of liberty, rightly conceived. But if political discussion is foreclosed, the democratic corrective is unavailable, or less readily so. Suppose, for example, that government bans criticism of a war. That political criticism is shut out of the process of social discussion about how or whether to conduct the war effort. The result is an unacceptably corrosive effect on the public's deliberative processes.

Without a ban on criticism of bans, of course, it remains possible for people to criticize the very law that bans the criticism of the war, and in this sense there is a structural parallel among all the restrictions discussed in the previous paragraph. But there is a large difference between controls on political speech and other sorts of restrictions. While controls on commercial advertising do not have especially adverse effects on political deliberation about any political topic—including deliberation about the value of those controls, which is unquestionably political—controls on political speech have distinctly damaging effects on public debate. Those controls are distinctly damaging because they impair the processes of political deliberation that are a precondition for democratic legitimacy. Impairments of nonpolitical speech may undermine deliberative processes by removing vivid examples of the conduct whose illegality is at issue; but they do not have the special characteristic of preventing democratic debate.

I believe that, taken in concert, these considerations amply justify the view that government should be under a special burden of justification whenever it seeks to control speech that is intended and received as a contribution to social deliberation. A lesser burden should be imposed on regulation of other kinds of speech.

Autonomy and Free Speech

A political conception of the First Amendment is hardly the only candidate for understanding free speech "tiers." Before we accept that controversial conception, we should consider alternatives. An especially interesting nonpolitical conception of the free speech principle stresses the relationship between autonomy and free speech. There have been many distinguished efforts to understand the First Amendment largely or only as a protection of autonomy.[20] The term "autonomy" is of course sharply contested, and a few general remarks are therefore in order.

Some people think that government abridges autonomy if and only if it prevents people from doing what they wish to do.[21] But there are at least two problems with this formulation. First, any legal system will prevent people from doing what they wish to do. Even the rules of property and contract impose negative constraints on action; so too with rules of the road, antidiscrimination law, labor law, and much more. A conception of autonomy that endangers so much seems far too broad. Second, there is much ambiguity in the phrase "what they wish to do." People who are desperately poor, or who otherwise do not have an adequate range of options, might well be thought nonautonomous in the sense that they are subject to multiple constraints on their action. Indeed, preferences and beliefs themselves tend to adapt to existing opportunities, and we might well conclude that someone has been deprived of autonomy if her preferences and beliefs have been shaped by oppressive or unjust background conditions.[22]

From these objections we might be led to suggest that autonomy requires government not to allow everyone to do as she wishes, but instead to respect all conceptions of the good. We might adopt this understanding of autonomy not because we cannot assess which conceptions of the good are best, but because it is right—a recognition of individual dignity—to let people choose their own path.[23] This understanding of autonomy is much narrower than the first. It would allow the state to constrain people's liberty by, for example, creating property and contract law, imposing traffic rules, and redistributing wealth. But it too runs into serious difficulties. We may doubt whether we really respect autonomy by respecting all conceptions of the good, regardless of their origins and effects, and of the reasons that can be offered on their behalf. Even conceptions of the good may be a product of lack of information, desperation, or unjust background conditions. Suppose that someone appears to want to be a prostitute, or to continue as a drug addict, or to sleep at home in a bathrobe all day, or to watch cartoons every morning and afternoon. It is hardly clear that the interest in autonomy calls for respecting these "decisions," which may well be a product of social conditions that fail to allow for autonomy, rightly understood.

Of course there will be many problems if government tries to override people's choices about what course to pursue. Government efforts of this kind may simply breed resentment and frustration, and this is a reason for great caution. But if autonomy is really our goal, respect for all conceptions of the good does not seem the right path.

If this is correct, we might be lead to a third conception of autonomy. On this view, autonomy is a form of self-mastery, through which people are permitted to be, roughly speaking, authors of the narratives of their own lives.[24] This form of autonomy can be abridged not only by the obvious forms of government tyranny, but also by desperate need, lack of decent education, physical pain or poor health, insufficient opportunities in private and public life, exclusion from political processes, and even preferences, beliefs, or conceptions of the good that are produced by social deprivation. An understanding of this kind would require not government nonintervention—though nonintervention would indeed be required in many places—but a range of positive government acts designed to furnish the preconditions for autonomy, thus understood. Among these acts is the provision of diverse opportunities, of course a recurrent theme of this book.

We can see the outlines of this conception of autonomy in Justice Brandeis' *Whitney* opinion. Brandeis emphasized the kinds of characteristics that an autonomous citizenry must have; one of his special concerns is the threat to democracy created by "an inert people." Of course this third conception of autonomy raises many questions, and I cannot adequately defend it here. I describe it only to suggest some of the complex relations between the concept of autonomy and any particular role for government.

So much for autonomy in general. For purposes of speech, we should distinguish between *speaker autonomy* and *listener autonomy*. The two ideas raise quite different issues, and they should be discussed separately.

A principle of speaker autonomy might forbid government from imposing the distinctive invasion that occurs whenever public officials stop people from expressing themselves. It does seem especially troublesome when government prevents people from communicating, even if government is permitted to prevent people from doing other things that they want to do. It is not necessarily worse to be stopped from doing something than to be stopped from saying something. But there is a qualitatively distinctive invasion of individual freedom when government tells you not to speak. Consider, for example, a government refusal to permit communication among friends or lovers, or to allow the dissemination of art that we all agree does not qualify as political in the relevant sense. Even if we believe that government may often act paternalistically—as, for example, by requiring seatbelt use or banning the sale of drugs—we might disable government from interfering with one person's desire to communicate his thoughts and desires to someone else. An interference of this kind has some of the invasive characteristics of an intrusion on religious liberty. It is a similarly severe interference with rights of intimacy, association, and private conscience. The point is not that bans on speech are always worse than bans on acts; it is that there is a qualitative difference between the two. From this idea we might generally conclude that government should be presumed unable to stop people from expressing themselves, whether the issue involves politics or not.

A principle of listener autonomy, set out most prominently by

T. M. Scanlon, has a different form. This principle would protect listeners by forbidding government to regulate speech because listeners might be influenced by it.[25] On this view, government cannot insult the moral autonomy of its citizens by stopping them from hearing what other people have to say—especially if the reason that government acts is its fear that citizens will be influenced or persuaded by what is said. This is a unique invasion into each individual's moral and deliberative capacities. It is different in kind from more conventional restrictions on what people want to do. The principle of listener autonomy helps explain Justice Brandeis' insistence that the "fitting remedy" for harmful speech is "more speech, not enforced silence." More speech is the "fitting"—not necessarily the adequate—remedy precisely because it does not insult the moral autonomy of listeners.

It is more than plausible to think that autonomy, understood in these ways, helps explain why a democratic system protects speech. The notions of speaker and listener autonomy show why government interference with speech is especially disturbing. These notions also help account for the Court's protection of speech that is wholly nonpolitical. Thus a private conversation between friends, lovers, or associates, even if wholly unrelated to politics, deserves protection unless the government can come up with a good reason for regulation. Government should not be permitted to stop adults from hearing things simply because the government believes them to be wrong or dangerously influential. Most generally, a democratic government should not intrude on the individual's decision about what to say, what to hear, and what to believe. At least as a general rule, it should respect every person's capacity to make that choice for himself.

These ideas emphatically rule out certain common reasons for regulation of speech. They suggest that speech can rarely be regulated because government thinks that people will be persuaded or influenced by it. The autonomy principle also helps explain why art, literature, and even commercial speech are entitled to constitutional protection. There is a qualitatively distinctive invasion of speaker autonomy if government tells an artist that she may not produce a certain work. Moreover, there is an objectionable intrusion on listener autonomy if government censors truthful commercial speech on the ground that people will be persuaded if they hear it.

To this extent, principles of autonomy have an enduring and important role to play in the theory and practice of free expression. But it is unlikely that an autonomy principle will be able to account for all the features of a well-functioning system of free speech law. It is only part of the picture. To make sense of the First Amendment, we will have to speak of many things other than autonomy. In particular, I think that even if we emphasize, as we should, the interests in speaker and listener autonomy, we will have to introduce the Madisonian conception in order to account for our considered judgments about hard cases.

The basic problem with an autonomy-based account, if it is intended to be a full one, is that such an account will make it difficult or impossible to distinguish in the appropriate way among different categories of speech. Speaker autonomy, at first glance and taken in the abstract, seems to argue in favor of similar protection of all, or almost all, forms of speech. If we protect speech because people want to talk, it is not easy to come up with standards by which to distinguish among different kinds of talk. And if we cannot come up with such standards, an approach based on speaker autonomy will not be able to do what a theory of free speech is obliged to do, that is, to make distinctions among different kinds of speech. (Return to our familiar catalogue: bribes, threats, perjury, conspiracies, criminal solicitation, unlicensed medical and legal advice, false commercial speech.)

Perhaps advocates of speaker autonomy could respond to this challenge. Perhaps we will be able to say that the autonomy of speakers is genuinely expressed through art, literature, and politics, and far less so through commercial speech, unlicensed medical advice, perjury, and conspiracies to fix prices. Perhaps some or all of the latter should be described as "speech acts." Perhaps the interest in speaker autonomy does not really call for protection of much of what we now consider to be "low-value" speech.[26] Perhaps we will be able to say that some forms of speech actually serve speaker autonomy and that other forms are mere reflections of personal or economic self-interest.

In light of these possibilities, I do not deny that a suitably designed autonomy principle might ultimately be able to account for a two-tier First Amendment. But adjustments of this kind are likely to have a disturbingly ad hoc quality. It is doubtful that autonomy will be doing all of the relevant work. For this reason, I believe that the concept of speaker autonomy is unlikely to fit with our considered judgments about particular free speech cases. There are other problems as well. Its historical roots are relatively weak, and it does not build on an understanding of when governmental action is likely to be least reliable and most dangerous. Compared with an approach that is based on politics, it has other disadvantages too (see below).

Listener autonomy raises similar difficulties. In order to generate a two-tier system with listener autonomy at the forefront, we would have to distinguish among different government regulations in terms of their offense to listener autonomy. This will not be easy, but perhaps the task could ultimately be carried out. A restriction on factually false statements, for example, may seem not to offend the autonomy of listeners at all. Their autonomy may not require that they be subject to falsehoods, for there may be no offense to the moral independence of listeners if the government tells people not to lie.[27]

Perhaps the same can be said of most of our cases of low-value speech. Consider, for example, bribery, threats, unlicensed medical and legal advice, sexual harassment, and criminal solicitation; it is hardly clear that the interest in listener autonomy requires protection of these forms of speech. Someone who is susceptible to a bribe or threat could not reasonably complain that the government has invaded his autonomy by forbidding attempted bribes and threats. Someone who is subject to sexual harassment is not likely to think that the principle of listener autonomy stops the government from interfering with this form of speech. Through some such route, we may be able to develop a two-tier system of free expression through the lens of listener autonomy.

But there would be many difficulties here. If listener autonomy is the guiding idea, truthful commercial speech would probably have to be treated in the same way as truthful political speech; it would therefore seem necessary to strike down current restrictions on advertisements for liquor, cigarettes, and gambling. Even more dramatically, it might well be necessary to invalidate restrictions on advertisements for illegal products, like cocaine and heroin. So too, false political speech might have to be treated in the same way as false commercial speech; perhaps both could be banned. Restrictions on libel of government officials would probably be treated the same as restrictions on libel of private people uninvolved in public affairs.[28] We would therefore have to strike down the law allowing recovery for libel of private people. Does this really make sense?

Similarly, a principle of listener autonomy would seem to entail the odd and important conclusion that restrictions on scientific speech should be treated the same as restrictions on political campaigns. It would therefore appear necessary to invalidate current restrictions on the dissemination to foreign nations of scientific material with potential military applications. (There is, to be sure, a risk of harm here, but it is inevitably speculative, and the "clear and present danger" test properly applied to other government restrictions on speech could not be satisfied.) These various conclusions appear unacceptable. But they do seem to be entailed by the principle of listener autonomy, and this counts strongly against seeing that principle as the general key to hard free speech cases.

A final point is in order. I have suggested that autonomy, rightly understood, requires not respect for all choices, but instead for ensuring that people can have a large degree of mastery over the conduct of their own lives. In our world, many actual choices do not reflect this kind of mastery, and indeed reflect an absence of autonomy. People have insufficient options; their very desires are affected as a result. The point complicates arguments based on speaker and listener autonomy. The connection between any particular decision to speak and individual autonomy, rightly understood, will not always be clear. Some speech—consider certain forms of commercial advertising or racist hate speech—may not reflect speaker autonomy at all. Moreover, there are many real-world constraints on the autonomy of listeners, stemming from lack of sufficient education, information, and opportunities. In these circumstances, it is by no means clear that government respects listener autonomy by allowing all speech to be heard. Consider, for example, advertisements for cigarettes or alcohol; and note the large number of New Deal intrusions on speech plausibly in the interest of listener autonomy, including the regulations of the Food and Drug

Administration, the Securities and Exchange Commission, and the Federal Trade Commission. In these cases, restrictions on speech might reasonably be thought to promote listener autonomy. And if this is so, a vigorous free speech principle, based on listener autonomy, may be hard to justify.

The fact that speakers and listeners are not fully autonomous in the relevant sense should not be taken to license government to regulate speech whenever it likes. This would be a recipe for tyranny. Ad hoc governmental inquiries into whether people are really autonomous carry an obvious risk of abuse; we do not have good institutions for making such judgments. But the complexities in the notion of autonomy make it all the more difficult to generate an acceptable theory of free expression based on autonomy alone.

I do not claim to have settled the autonomy issue here. But what has been said is, I think, sufficient to show that it would be difficult to use notions of autonomy as the complete basis for a system of free expression.

Alternative Approaches

An autonomy-based conception of speech is not the only alternative to the political approach. There are many other possibilities. Perhaps we should hold speech to be entitled to special protection whenever it involves rational thought. An idea of this sort would extend well beyond the political to include not merely literary and artistic work, but commercial and scientific expression as well. It would draw the line between speech tiers by reference to whether the speech at issue appealed to "rationality." Because the connection between rationality and obscene speech is unclear, obscenity may well be bannable on this approach; so too with "fighting words" and racial epithets. Considerable work would have to be done to explain what is entailed by the complex notion of rationality. But perhaps this is something to which we should be devoting our attention.

Even if we could accomplish this task, the rationality idea seems like an unpromising start, at least as the foundation for a full system of free expression. Does it really seem right to think that (for example) technological data with potential military applications should be given the same degree of protection as political speech, merely because such data are rational? Do we really believe that misleading commercial speech deserves the same legal protection as misleading political speech, because the two cannot be distinguished on the level of rationality? An affirmative answer to these questions would make it difficult or impossible to justify the regulation of misleading advertising, or the export to unfriendly foreign countries of dangerous technological data. These seem to be jarring results. They suggest that the standard of rationality is unlikely to fit with our considered judgments about free speech cases.

As an alternative, we might reflect more broadly on the sorts of fundamental interests that are promoted by a system of free expression. I have emphasized that these interests extend beyond political deliberation; indeed, it would be an exceedingly strange account of free speech that reduced all expressive interests to the political. The core of the free speech principle might include any representation that reflects deliberation or imagination in a way that is relevant to the development of individual capacities.[29] Somewhat more broadly, an illuminating essay by Joshua Cohen argues that the relevant interests are indeed plural. They include expressive interests, deliberative interests (both political and non-political), and informational interests as well.[30]

Thus Cohen suggests that the catalogue of free speech interests must include the expressive desire to communicate thoughts and feelings and, through this route, to influence others. This desire extends protection to art, literature, even music and dance. It emphatically includes private communication as well as public speeches. We also have a general social interest in finding out what is best or most worthwhile. Free communication is indispensable to promote this deliberative interest, which extends far beyond the political as I have defined it here. When we deliberate about what is best, we are frequently not speaking of politics at all, even if this term is conceived broadly. Finally, scientific and commercial speech, among many others, conveys information that helps people to pursue their aims and aspirations. Important information is provided by much expression that does not relate to politics or social deliberation.

Cohen proposes that we think about free speech cases by (1)

cataloguing interests of this sort, (2) identifying the likely costs of unrestricted speech, and (3) assessing individual cases through frameworks developed on the basis of an expansive understanding of both free speech interests and free speech costs. An approach of this sort carries considerable promise. In particular, an emphasis on the relationship between free speech and a wide range of fundamental human interests helps reinforce the argument, stemming from narrower considerations of autonomy, that nearly all speech, and certainly much nonpolitical speech, deserves presumptive protection.

Much work remains to be done to evaluate approaches of this sort. But at first glance Cohen's own view, which is an exercise in political philosophy and not intended as an account of constitutional law, poses four risks for that latter discipline. Taken together, these risks suggest that a Madisonian approach is probably better for courts attempting to implement a free speech guarantee.

First, a broad inquiry into expressive interests may give insufficient weight to history. I have argued that the free speech principle should devote considerable attention to history, including the general understandings of those responsible for the First Amendment and the development of the free speech principle over time. If we look in these places, it is political speech that belongs at the First Amendment core.

Second, the system of free expression should be alert not only to the benefits and costs of expressive activity in particular cases, but also to the institutional biases of government and to the contexts in which those biases are likely to cause most harm. In the context of political speech, government is uniquely unreliable (which is not to say that it is fully reliable elsewhere). In the context of political speech, restrictions will be especially damaging, because they close off the ordinary processes through which public deliberation occurs.

Third, a general catalogue of free speech interests might well produce a body of legal doctrine that is too complex, ad hoc, and unruly. So broad a catalogue is hard to make into a judicially manageable framework. At least this is a large risk until we provide a wide range of workable, intermediate principles designed to simplify the judicial task (see also the discussion below of the problems with judicial balancing). A constitutional system of free expression should place a high premium on judicial administrability as well as on substantive plausibility. Any proposed framework must be usable in the real world, and it should attempt to counteract the possible bias of individual judges. Judge Learned Hand emphasized this point in favoring "a qualitative formula, hard, conventional, difficult to evade," because of the pervasive "herd instinct," from which judges are not immune.[31] We might therefore develop implementing principles that are a bit more crude and mechanical than we would like, simply because those principles limit discretion and abuse in the process of judicial administration.

Finally, Cohen's approach could make it hard to come up with necessary distinctions among the cases—necessary in the sense of having to be made in order to fit our considered judgments about free speech issues. On a capacious view of free speech "interests," it might, for example, become difficult to distinguish between scientific and political speech, and also difficult to regulate such materials as child pornography. Certainly scientific speech and child pornography serve some of the interests that Cohen catalogues. To make the appropriate distinctions, we would need to have a quite refined understanding of the weight to be given to the expressive, deliberative, and informational interests in different contexts. What if the informational interest is strong but the other interests are weak? What are the relevant principles of priority? Without answers to such questions, an approach to free speech rooted in a general catalogue of relevant interests might fail to match our judgments about particular cases.

Even if we reject this approach for purposes of constitutional law, it should be clear that there are good reasons to protect speech that does not involve politics at all. Such speech serves the interests of speaker and listener autonomy; certainly it can convey information; often it is relevant to the development of individual capacities. Those who emphasize the primacy of political deliberation ought not to disparage these considerations. The challenge for the Madisonian view is therefore to develop our second tier of speech, as established through the political conception, in such a way as to respond to the legitimate concerns of those who stress the relationship between free speech and a diverse array of human interests. I try to do this below. If it is possible to accomplish this task, a conception of free speech that places a special premium on political speech will probably seem most reasonable, even if its superiority cannot be established by anything like an algorithm.

Counterarguments and the Second Tier

The discussion of alternatives reveals that there are many difficulties with a political conception of the First Amendment. For one thing, we must try to separate the political from the nonpolitical. Once we try, we will have to face all of the questions that produce the current First Amendment preoccupation with line-drawing. How, for example, are we to treat the work of the controversial gay artist Robert Mapplethorpe, or rap music, or nude dancing? There is a hard problem of definition here. Both commercial speech and pornography are political in the crucial sense that they reflect and promote a point of view, broadly speaking ideological in character, about how important things in the world should be structured. The feminist attack on pornography has drawn close attention to the political character of such speech, and in this sense might be thought to invalidate any effort to regulate it.[32] In any case, the distinction between the political and the nonpolitical may be extremely difficult to draw.

So much for the problem of definition. We should also question the claim that apparently nonpolitical speech ought to be deprived of the highest level of protection. We now know that speech that has nothing to do with politics is entitled at least to a degree of First Amendment protection. But then how are we to treat music, or art, or science? Surely it is philistine, or worse, to say that the First Amendment protects only political platforms. There are four points here. First, many of the deepest political challenges to the existing order can be found in art, literature, music, or (perhaps especially) sexual expression. Second, such forms of speech may well be entitled to a high level of protection because of what they offer for the development of human capacities, even if they have absolutely nothing to do with politics, or if their connection with politics is only indirect. Justice Brandeis' civic conception of free speech stresses that expression is valued as an end as well as a means; the point suggests that a system of free expression can have salutary effects on the development of character, and these effects may ultimately prove beneficial or even crucial for politics. If so, should we not protect much non-political speech even if we put politics in the foreground?

Third, the real reason for regulation of apparently nonpolitical speech is often deeply political. Public officials know what threatens the existing order; they try to stop the threats. Attempts to regulate D. H. Lawrence, James Joyce, and the comedians Lenny Bruce and George Carlin are all examples. For this reason, a political conception of speech should be alert to the political purposes behind censorship of apparently nonpolitical speech. Finally, art, literature, and science—even music and dance—are central to what is most important to human lives, sometimes far more central than politics. Exactly how will a Madisonian approach treat these forms of expression?

These comments raise hard questions without simple solutions. I venture some remarks in response.

The aversion to line-drawing.   Some of the attack on a political conception of free speech stems from the aversion to line-drawing. Who, it is asked, will be drawing these lines? Line-drawing is subject to notorious abuses. Ought we not to avoid drawing lines entirely, and simply protect speech as such whenever we can?

Enough, I hope, has been said to show that these questions are unhelpful. There is no way to operate a system of free expression without drawing lines. Not everything that counts as words or pictures is entitled to full constitutional protection. Return yet again to our familiar catalogue: perjury, threats, bribes, unlicensed medical or legal advice, false advertising, child pornography, sexual harassment. The question is not whether to draw lines, but how to draw the right ones. For this reason, the existence of hard line-drawing problems should not be taken by itself to foreclose an attempt to distinguish between political and nonpolitical speech.

Perhaps the evident risks of bias are especially high for that particular distinction; if so, we have a reasonable argument against the Madisonian view. Perhaps the risks of bias in the area of free speech always argue in favor of protecting speech in expansive ways, even if the expansive protection would not be justified if we had perfect judges and could eliminate the risk of bias in administration. This point seems right; but some distinctions are inevitable. The first question for any system of free expression is whether the relevant distinction is plausible in principle and administrable in practice. The second is whether alternative systems are better. If the Madisonian conception does well on these counts, the inevitable difficulty of drawing lines is acceptable.

Balancing rather than tiers?   I have argued in favor of a two-tier First Amendment, understood by reference to Madisonian goals. But perhaps this approach is too rigid. Perhaps we should abandon a system of "tiers," and engage instead in a broader form of balancing, looking generally at all relevant factors. Justice Felix Frankfurter spoke eloquently on behalf of this approach in the last generation of constitutional law.[33] Justice Stevens sometimes speaks for this approach in the current period.[34] As we have seen, Joshua Cohen's approach is similar.

If everything could be properly balanced, we could not properly object to balancing. If all relevant factors could be taken into account, and given their appropriate weight, we would indeed have solved our First Amendment problems. Many apparent critics of balancing are really objecting to the excessive or inadequate weight placed on relevant factors, not to balancing itself. But in the real world, balancing has notorious problems. Ad hoc determinations of the harm from speech pose extremely high risks. Under the pressure of the moment, there will be temptations for judges to find the harms great (or small) in particular cases. Ad hoc determinations of free speech value may be even worse. Here the prejudices and myopia of particular judges, even judges operating in good faith, would produce unacceptable dangers. A large goal of constitutional law is to respond to the institutional risks of ad hockery. We do this through the development of categories that, though imperfect and perhaps excessively protective as a matter of pure principle, respond well enough to our thinking about particular cases.[35] There are many possible categories, and we should decide among them. In the real world, ad hoc balancing is likely to be inferior to many categorical approaches.

A broader point follows. Constitutional law is a peculiar mixture of substantive theory and institutional constraint. Suppose we developed a fully satisfactory substantive theory of freedom of speech. It would still be necessary to adjust the theory to conform to the institutional requirements of the courts. It is for this reason that constitutional law is not political philosophy,[36] and that some constitutional rights are "underenforced" through the judiciary. The appropriate limits of courts in promoting social reform[37] call for courts to truncate enforcement of the best substantive theory of, for example, equality on the basis of race and disability. On these matters, an aggressive judicial role in the service of the best theory would strain judicial competence and legitimacy. Some constitutional rights should instead be "overenforced," in the sense that judges should develop broad, institutionally workable rules that protect the right more firmly than would the best, more specifically tailored, substantive theory.

This point is buttressed by Vincent Blasi's valuable suggestion that courts should assume a "pathological perspective" on free speech problems,[38] preparing First Amendment law for the worst of times. Blasi's suggestion could push Madisonians to put much art and literature in the top tier, in order to counteract the possibility that judges will miss the political content in art and literature, partly because of their own biases.

Selective exclusions rather than tiers? It might be tempting to think that we should start with a broad presumption that speech is protected, and allow regulation if and only if government can marshall especially good reasons in the particular case. Instead of a two-tier First Amendment, we might offer a capacious, all-inclusive free speech principle, but recognize that in certain selective, narrow areas, the principle can be overridden by other important values. This approach could even claim to account for much of current law. Perhaps the exclusion of perjury, bribery, threats, and so forth can be understood as a recognition that speech is broadly protected, but that the case for regulation is strong in a few isolated cases.

There may be important strategic and institutional reasons to cultivate an understanding of this kind. If we say that the free speech principle is presumed to protect all expression, but recognize that there are some narrow exceptions, we might work against the likely abuse, in practice, of any principle that we can devise to distinguish among free speech tiers. But strategy to one side, I do not think that the "selective exclusion" idea can be justified as a matter of principle. The problem with this idea is that we need to explain why some exclusions, and not others, seem to make sense. Once we embark on that enterprise, we have to say something about the content of our theory of free expression— about autonomy, development of the capacities, rationality, democracy, or other values that are plausibly promoted by free speech. Once we do that, we will have started to develop principles explaining what characteristics entitle expression to special protection, and what harms allow regulation. And once we do that, we will be well on our way to something very different from an approach of selective exclusion—to a two-tier First Amendment, or to balancing, or to one of the various alternatives that I have already discussed.

The "selective exclusion" idea may have some psychological value, and it may help to overcome the omnipresent risk of censorship. But if we are really trying to understand the nature of the free speech principle, the notion of "selective exclusion" will be inadequate. It is not really an independent approach to the First Amendment. When we think it through, it will rapidly develop into a quite different and much fuller conception of the system of free expression.

What is political? The definition I have offered of "political speech" would encompass not simply political tracts, but all art and literature that have the characteristics of social commentary. Much fiction and poetry have these characteristics. They are intended and received as a contribution to social deliberation about public affairs. We might therefore conclude that art and literature often qualify for the top tier. This broad conception seems right, first, because such speech is often in fact self-consciously political in the relevant sense despite initial appearances, and, second, because it is important to create a large breathing space for political speech by protecting expression even if it does not explicitly and securely fall within that category. Though they are hardly political tracts, both *Ulysses* and *Bleak House* are political for First Amendment purposes. *Bleak House* contains a great deal of comment on the fate of poor people under conditions of industrial profit-seeking. *Ulysses* deals with the role of religion in society. The same conclusion follows for the work of the gay artist Robert Mapplethorpe, which (among many other things) attempts to draw into question current sexual norms and practices.

It is true that the self-consciously political element of great literature and art is often a small part of the work, or peripheral, or largely irrelevant. This may well be true of Wordsworth, for example; it is certainly true of the narrow and now-largely forgotten political import of some of Shakespeare's plays. In the context of great literature and art, the word "political" threatens to become hopelessly ambiguous or just philistine. If we reduce a work of literature, art, or music to its "political message," we will be badly disserving it. *Ulysses* and *Bleak House* are much more than political commentaries. Those who accept the Madisonian view of free speech do not claim that literature or art is valuable only for its political content, or that by identifying the political content of art, we are getting anything like a full picture of art. The Madisonian view is not that constitutional value and social value are the same. Its only claims are that speech belongs in the top tier if it has political content, that much art does have this content, and that it is for this reason that the material is especially protected from censorship. (There is protection as well for speech in the second tier, a subject I discuss below.)

All this does not mean that speech with broadly political consequences is by virtue of that fact "political" in the more specific constitutional sense. We should distinguish between speech that has political consequences and speech that is political for constitutional purposes. Obscenity is surely political in its consequences, for it has political effects; the same is true of commercial speech, perjury, and even threats and attempted bribery—certainly threats to and attempted bribery of public officials. An employer's purely verbal sexual or racial harassment of an employee surely has political effects, including the creation of a disincentive for women and blacks to go to that workplace at all. There is no doubting that this is a political consequence.

But these forms of speech are not entitled to the highest form of constitutional protection. If we said that speech is political for constitutional purposes because it has political causes and effects, we would be saying that nearly everything that amounts to words or pictures is immune from legal regulation. For reasons suggested above, that conclusion cannot be right. For purposes of the Constitution, the question is whether the speech is intended and received as a contribution to political deliberation, not whether it has political effects or sources. Thus, for example, there is a distinction between a misogynist tract, which is entitled to full protection, and many pornographic movies, which are not, but which are in essence masturbatory aids (see chapter 7). There is a difference between personal, face-to-face racial harassment by an employer of an employee, which is not entitled to full protection, and a racist speech to a crowd, which indeed falls within the core, and cannot be regulated in the absence of a clear and present danger. There is a difference between an essay about the value of unregulated markets in oil production and an advertisement for Exxon—even if both are written and published by the same oil company.

Too much censorship? Second-tier speech and impermissible justifications. My approach would exclude a good deal of speech from the category of high-value expression. For this reason, it might be thought to pose an unacceptable danger of censorship. If we say that the core of the First Amendment involves politics, we might seem to offer exceptionally fragile safeguards for art, music, literature, and perhaps commercial entertainment. A First Amendment that would offer such little protection to so much might be thought embarrassingly weak and thin. If the exclusion of such materials results from a theory of free speech that is not compelled by the Constitution's text, surely that theory should be repudiated.

As I have noted, it might even be thought that free speech doctrine should be devised substantially to "overprotect" speech, and for good institutional reasons. Just as a two-tier First Amendment is superior to balancing, because of the risks posed by judicial bias and discretion, so too very broad protection of speech might be preferable to a two-tier system, at least one that is defined in political terms. We might insist on protecting materials that would not, in the best world of perfect judges and costless administration, receive protection—simply because without such protection, people in positions of authority will, in our world, draw and implement lines in a way that is too threatening to the system of free expression.

In fact, however, the framework I propose would allow much room for powerful First Amendment challenges to most regulatory efforts aimed at speech, including those outside of the political setting. The central point here is that we would bring to bear on second-tier speech a category of *impermissible government justifications*.[39] Even speech within the second tier is protected if the reason for regulation is illegitimate. From the discussion of autonomy and development of capacities, we can start to identify a list of impermissible justifications. In general, government cannot regulate speech of any sort on the basis of (1) its own disagreement with the ideas that have been expressed, (2) its perception of the government's (as opposed to the public's) self-interest, (3) its fear that people will be persuaded or influenced by ideas, and (4) its desire to ensure that people are not offended by the ideas that speech contains.

It should be clear that the Madisonian conception itself bans official disagreement or self-interest as reasons for regulation of speech. Courts should develop legal doctrines to "flush out" these impermissible reasons even when they are disguised. Moreover, the principle of listener autonomy is an important component of a system of free expression. That principle usually forbids government from regulating speech because people will be persuaded or influenced by it. This is so even if the speech is entirely nonpolitical—a principle with many consequences. For example, government should be permitted to ban false commercial speech because of the harms it causes; but it should generally be required to permit truthful, nonmisleading commercial speech. So too, government cannot regulate child pornography on the ground that it will persuade people that child pornography is a good idea. But it may ban this form of pornography as a means of preventing the harms inevitably at work in its production.

I also suggest that the government should not be allowed to regulate speech because people are offended by the ideas that it contains. This suggestion raises some complexities. "Offense" is a complex and underanalyzed category. The term is sometimes taken to include an extraordinary diversity of things—for example, people's reactions to loud noises, to extreme political positions, to racial epithets, to pornography, and to grotesque art. Surely government can ban loud noises at night, even if it is concerned to prevent offense to listeners. It is at least plausible to think that the victim of a racial epithet suffers something other than mere offense (see chapter 6).

Offense at the content of ideas is the defining case of a prohibited use of the justification of "offense." Suppose, for example, that people are offended by speech that is politically extreme; this often happens when there is speech by radicals of the left or the right. I suggest that government cannot ban ideas that citizens find offensive. If it could, there would be an impermissible intrusion on the exchange of political ideas that lies at the heart of the Madisonian system. People find many ideas offensive because they are incompatible with existing practices or convictions, and the whole point of a Madisonian system is to ensure that social deliberation can draw on very different understandings of the right and the good. We should not forget that many of the most productive political discussions include ideas that people initially or even ultimately find offensive.

But Madisonianism is not the only interest at stake. The commitment to speaker autonomy, and the insistence on the importance of expressive interests, do not allow government to invoke offense as a reason for regulation of speech, and this prohibition is triggered whenever government is concerned that people will be offended by ideas. Of course it may be hard to apply the prohibition in cases in which people dispute whether the offense really involves an objection to ideas. Consider cases of profanity, racial epithets, sexually explicit speech, and grotesque art. In such cases, people may claim that their target is not offense at ideas but something different, perhaps because more analogous to what happens when people are subjected to loud or threatening noises at night.

We can imagine some hard cases along these lines. The government might ban the use of profanity on billboards; it might say that sexually explicit (not necessarily obscene) materials may not be sold in certain places. I cannot discuss all of these issues here, but *Cohen v. California*[40] sets out many of the key principles. There the Court concluded that a state could not criminalize Cohen's wearing of a jacket bearing the words "Fuck the Draft." According to the Court, the use of profanity was an inextricable part of the political message. "Darn the Draft" would not carry the same meaning. Moreover, the emotive and cognitive elements of Cohen's statement could not readily be separated. The Court said that the government could not rely on its desire to protect the sensibilities of those unwillingly exposed to profanity. In a system of free expression, it would be required to show that "substantial privacy interests are being invaded in an essentially intolerable manner." Under *Cohen*, the government is banned not only from invoking offense at the content of ideas, but also from claiming that it seeks merely to stop profanity as a way of preventing a particular means of expressing ideas, at least in the context of a political protest.

On the other hand, the Court has said that offense is a legitimate reason for zoning restrictions on adult theatres, in part because the regulation was not, in the Court's view, an attempt to censor ideas or to control political speech.[41] The Court's conclusion in this regard seems reasonable. Zoning restrictions on adult threatres do not aim at any particular point of view, and they can be supported by the interests in preventing the deterioration of the neighborhood, prostitution, and perhaps sexual assault or violence. Perhaps we can conclude from this that offense at the content of ideas is always unacceptable and that offense at the means of expressing ideas will be unacceptable (a) when the speech is political or (b) when there is some basis to believe that government is trying to suppress a viewpoint.

This proposition does not resolve the question of whether government can regulate profanity, sexually explicit, or otherwise offensive material at particular times or in particular places. In the key case, *FCC v. Pacifica Foundation*,[42] the Court upheld a civil prohibition on the use of profanity on the radio. The Court emphasized the especially invasive nature of broadcasting and the possibility that children will be exposed to profane language. The outcome in *Pacifica* is hardly a major threat to freedom of expression in America, but it is troublesome in light of the fact that the case involved the use of profanity as an inextricable part of the speaker's political protest—against the very FCC regulation at issue in the case! I take up some aspects of this controversial issue in chapters 6 and 7.

The most general principle here is that government may not regulate speech of any kind if the reason for regulation is that it disapproves of the message or disagrees with the idea that the speech expresses. Regulation can only be justified by reference to genuine harms, and the category of harms must be defined independently of categories (1) through (4) above. For example, an effort to regulate music because it stirs up passionate feeling would run afoul of the free speech clause, simply because the justification for regulation is constitutionally off-limits.

All this suggests that many quite conventional reasons for regulation are out of bounds, even if applied to speech that does not qualify for the top tier in the Madisonian system. Formidable barriers to censorship are contained in the simple notion that usually government cannot regulate speech merely because people will be persuaded or offended by it.[43] Even under a two-tier First Amendment, speech that falls within the second tier cannot be restricted without a substantial showing of harm.

In real-world cases, the actual reason for regulating speech is often illegitimate even if the speech is nonpolitical. The regulation will therefore be unconstitutional. For example, commercial speech can be regulated only when government can show both a good justification for the regulation and a solid connection between the particular means of regulation and the particular justification in question. This system does not allow government to regulate truthful commercial advertising except in the most unusual circumstances. It gives substantial protection to commercial speech.[44] The same should be true for scientific speech, art, and private libel. So too, regulation of sexually explicit material should not be permitted if the purpose of the regulation is to repress a message rather than to redress genuine harms.

Of course there will be hard cases in which it has to be decided whether a legitimate justification is at work. The resolution of these cases cannot be purely mechanical. But I hope that I have said enough to show that even if the First Amendment is understood as centrally concerned with political speech, there is little reason to fear a large increase in official censorship.

Counterarguments combined. The strongest general argument against the Madisonian view would bring together several of the points made thus far. It would stress the considerable difficulty of defining political speech. It would also insist that a political conception of the First Amendment, far from fitting our convictions about particular cases, does extreme violence to them.

With respect to the problems of definition, the claim is both conceptual and institutional. It is conceptual insofar as it stresses that if we try to work with the Madisonian framework, we will be unlikely to generate a definition that fully captures what we really believe. It is institutional insofar as it stresses that even a good working definition will be susceptible to misapplication by a diverse, decentralized, and sometimes biased judiciary. And with respect to our judgments about particular cases, the claim would be that art, literature, and science are simply at excessive risk in the system I propose.

I can offer no algorithm to respond to these concerns. But I do not believe that the definition of the political is beyond judicial capacities. Under the approach I recommend, art, science, and literature would not be at serious risk. To support these claims, I now turn to particular cases.

Practice

With respect to actual legal practice, the most important initial point is that a Madisonian approach would not require major changes in current law. Its chief advantage is that it would help us deal with the new controversies, not that it would unsettle resolution of the old ones. As we have seen, the Court has already created a series of categories of speech that are less protected or unprotected at all. What the Court has not done is to give a sense of the unifying factors that justify the creation of these categories. But it is highly revealing that political speech never falls within them and that all speech that does so is not political in the sense that I understand the term here.

Libel. There are, however, several important exceptions to my claim that the Madisonian view would not change current law. The Madisonian approach would significantly alter the law of libel. Under current constitutional law, celebrities—including famous movie stars and athletes—are treated as "public figures." As a result, they are sharply constrained from bringing libel actions against people who have lied about them. Astonishingly, celebrities are constrained in exactly the same way as government officials, and they cannot recover unless they can prove that the speaker acted with "actual malice." Actual malice is defined to mean knowledge of falsity, or reckless indifference to the matter of truth or falsity.[45] Carol Burnett, Mary Tyler Moore, Mike Tyson, Jack Nicholson, Michael Jordan, and Madonna, for example, face major constraints in recovering for libel.

The Supreme Court has not adequately explained this outcome. It has relied largely on the argument that by becoming famous, famous people "assume the risk" of being libeled. But Carol Burnett and Jack Nicholson did not voluntarily assume the risk of being lied about, any more than I voluntarily assume the risk of being mugged when I walk alone at night. If I am mugged, my assailant will not be heard to complain, when I sue him, that I assumed the risk. It is hard to see why the libel case is different on this score. The decision to become famous need not be taken as a decision to subject oneself to lies.

Moreover, celebrities cannot fairly be charged with knowingly assuming the risk of being libeled. What the risk is depends on the rules for libel, and this is the issue that we are discussing. The issue cannot be resolved by saying that the risk has been assumed, at least not until we have said what the law is. The Court's argument that celebrities have "assumed the risk" sounds like a mere description of voluntary behavior, but it is really a disguise for a complex argument to the effect that it is reasonable to subject celebrities to this risk.

The Court has yet to spell out this argument, and I cannot see how the argument might be made persuasive. The fact that famous people have relatively good access to the media, and thus can counter any libel, is hardly adequate. The truth rarely catches up with a lie. Outside of the context of political expression, it is hard to see why there is a special interest in protecting speech about movie stars and athletes.

Under my approach, libel of celebrities often does not involve politics, and states could protect these people without offense to the First Amendment. I believe that if the speech at issue is not political in the constitutional sense, celebrities should be able to bring suit for libel if they can show that the libelous speaker was merely negligent. If a newspaper falsely and negligently reports that a movie star was convicted of a crime, or engaged in some awful and bizarre activity, it should have to pay damages. If a newspaper falsely and negligently reports that an athlete uses cocaine, it should have to compensate the victim. It may even make sense to allow celebrities to recover under the traditional libel standard of "strict liability," which allows recovery simply by virtue of the fact that the speaker has spoken falsely. On my approach, libel of so-called public figures not involved in governmental affairs would not be subject to special constitutional disabilities. In this way, my approach would give less protection to some libelous speech.

But I suggest that this would be a major improvement. Is there is any special interest in protecting the "breathing space" of the press insofar as it is libeling athletes or movie stars? On what principle must a legal system provide special "breathing space" to falsehoods about famous people?[46] The test for special protection should be whether the speech is political in the relevant sense, not whether the plaintiff is famous. In some ways, this approach would afford more, not less, protection to the press. Under my approach, there would be special constitutional protection for libel of private people if and only if the speaker's claim is intended and received as a contribution to political deliberation about some issue. This could well be the case if, for example, a newspaper reports that a corporate president, or a low-level executive, has offered a bribe to the Defense Department.

On the Madisonian view, then, current law is both overprotective and underprotective. It is overprotective insofar as it imposes special disabilities on libels about celebrities. It is underprotective insofar as it fails to offer special protection to speech that involves people who are not famous but who are nonetheless engaged in matters of public concern. I will not suggest all the details of constitutional limits on libel law imposed by the Madisonian view. Probably the Court's real mistake has been to set out complex rules with respect to the issue of liability, rather than to control excessive damage awards, which are the real problem posed by libel law for the system of free expression. Probably we should experiment with a system in which the media is strictly liable for libelous falsehoods, in the sense that it must offer at least a retraction and, perhaps, modest damages limited to provable losses. This suggestion raises many complexities; but these brief remarks should indicate the general tendency of what I am suggesting—a more concrete focus on the effects of libel law on democratic processes.

Sexually explicit speech.   My approach would also change the treatment given to sexually explicit speech. Under current law, such speech usually receives strong protection, at least if it does not appeal to the prurient interest, is not patently offensive, or has significant social value, even if the value is scientific or literary rather than political. As this test is applied, the category of bannable "obscenity" is exceedingly small. Almost all sexually explicit speech is protected. The notorious prosecutions of a few artists and musicians—including the gay artist Robert Mapplethorpe and the rap group 2 Live Crew—should not obscure the extraordinary protectiveness of the basic test. It is exceedingly hard to win an obscenity prosecution before a jury, and most such victories will be overturned on appeal.

An emphasis on the political foundations of the First Amendment "core" appears to threaten this speech-protective idea. But under the approach I suggest, regulation of sexually explicit speech would also be invalid in many cases. Some such speech is indeed political in the relevant sense. Consider the work of Robert Mapplethorpe, which conspicuously relates to the social treatment of homosexuals, even if this is not its only point. Even when sexually explicit speech is not political in that sense, regulation of such speech would often be unsupportable by reference to a legitimate justification. Recall that on the Madisonian view, government cannot regulate speech because people would be persuaded by it or because they find its ideas offensive. These are illegitimate justifications for controls on expression. It would therefore be impermissible to ban sexually explicit speech to protect people from unacceptable ideas about sexuality.

In some ways, my approach would offer even greater protection to sexually explicit materials than does current law, which permits courts to consider whether the materials are "patently offensive." Under the Madisonian view, offensiveness is not a legitimate reason for regulatory controls. A narrow category of materials combining sex with violence or coercion would, however, be regulable (see chapter 7). There would therefore be a major and salutary shift from issues of offense to issues of harm. Regulation would be acceptable in some cases, but for new and different reasons.

Securities law, names of rape victims.   Under my approach, the securities laws would raise no serious question. Government would have broad power to ensure truth and fair-dealing in the sale of stocks. Indeed, many of the controversies now haunting the law of free speech could be resolved fairly automatically. For example, disclosure of the names of rape victims could be prevented. Such disclosure has no real political content. It is usually a way to exploit victims, or to titillate readers and viewers, and not part of political deliberation about some issue. Moreover, the ban on disclosure can easily be justified on neutral grounds. Unauthorized disclosure of names of rape victims is both a deterrent and a penalty to those who attempt to redress an especially underenforced crime.[47]

Hate speech.   A harder case here is so-called "hate speech." Such speech, including racist and sexist expression, quite plausibly has political content in the sense that it is a self-conscious statement about how current political controversies should be resolved. The analysis here should depend on the extent to which something labeled as "hate speech" is actually intended or received as a contribution to political thought about some issue. Most of the regulations of hate speech, on the campus and elsewhere, do in fact apply to speech that is political in this sense (see chapter 6). On the other hand, speech that amounts to simple epithets, showing visceral contempt, would fall within the lower tier, and could probably be regulated because of the presence of sufficient justifications. In an analogy to the obscene telephone call, a university can prevent students and teachers from using words in a way that is not plausibly part of democratic deliberation about an issue.

Science.   Under the Madisonian approach, some forms of scientific speech should be regulable. The government could, without constitutional offense, regulate the export to unfriendly nations of purely verbal technology with military applications. This is so even though the showing of harm is insufficient under the standards properly applied to political speech. Technological information is not entitled to the same level of protection. There is an important interest in avoiding the obvious danger of improving the military capability of other nations. This interest provides an adequate justification for restrictions.

Art, literature, dance. What of art and literature? As noted, these can be highly political, and when this is true they belong in the core of constitutional protection. Indeed, the fact that they are frequently political—combined with the severe difficulty of deciding about their political quality on an ad hoc basis—argues powerfully in favor of the view that art and literature should generally be taken as "core" speech. When government seeks to censor art or literature, it is often because of the political content. Any such censorship is impermissible. And even when art or literature stands outside the core, government cannot attempt to regulate because it disagrees with the message, or because it thinks that people will be persuaded, or because it believes that the speech is offensive. A legitimate justification is always required, and a legitimate justification is almost always lacking.

By contrast, government would have the power to regulate some forms of (for example) nude dancing. Such dancing does warrant at least a degree of First Amendment protection. It is both communicative and expressive. (On the speech-conduct issue, see the discussion of cross-burning in chapter 6.) But a state could plausibly decide that some kinds of nude dancing are associated with a range of serious real-world harms, including prostitution, criminal activity of various sorts, and sexual assault. At least this is so if government can muster evidence that the regulated form of nude dancing does produce these harms, which would be sufficient to justify regulation under the standards applied to lower-tier speech.[48] I conclude that the Supreme Court was probably correct to rule that the First Amendment did not protect nude dancing in the Kitty Kat Lounge. This is so even if the majority erred in emphasizing the state's moral reservations about public nudity rather than the existence of more tangible harms. Of course a quite different issue would be raised in a case in which nude dancing was part of a political protest, or if the particular acts could not plausibly be associated with real-world harms.

The Madisonian approach would solve most of our current First Amendment problems without making it necessary to enter into the complicated current debates about "power" and "powerlessness," or about the nature of neutrality in constitutional law. This approach would also have the advantages of drawing on history in America and elsewhere, on the best theories about the function of the free speech guarantee, and on a sensible understanding of when government is least likely to be trustworthy and most likely to be dangerous. It would offer considerable protection to second-tier speech, recognizing that such speech promotes a plurality of values and that government frequently lacks a legitimate or sufficiently weighty justification for regulation. I cannot claim to have offered anything like a mathematical proof that the Madisonian approach is best. But I do hope to have shown that it is very reasonable, and that when everything is taken into account, it promotes free speech principles more sensibly than the alternatives.

Chapter 6

Discrimination and Selectivity

Hard Cases, Especially Cross-burning
and Hate Speech

IN CHAPTER 1, WE SAW that free speech law distinguishes among three kinds of restrictions on speech. Courts are especially hostile to viewpoint discrimination. They are hostile as well to viewpoint-neutral forms of content discrimination, though somewhat less so. They are especially receptive to content-neutral restrictions. It is clear that the Court would forbid a viewpoint-based law preventing people from criticizing the President while showering between 1 A.M. and 1:15 A.M., even though the restriction on speech would be minimal. On the other hand, the Court would uphold—has upheld—a content-neutral ban on solicitation within airports, even though the restriction on speech is substantial.[1]

These examples show that viewpoint-based restrictions can be much less intrusive than content-neutral restrictions. Some people think that the Court therefore has it all wrong.[2] For the critics, the Court should look at the magnitude of the restriction, or engage in a form of balancing, rather than deciding whether the restriction is "neutral" or not. In this chapter, I discuss the issue of discrimination, or selectivity, in the law of free expression. I devote particular attention to controversial issues raised by regulation of hate crimes and hate speech.

167

Purposes, Effects, and the Tripartite System

The current approach might seem too mechanical, even misdirected. The tripartite system—involving viewpoint discrimination, content discrimination, and content neutrality—does not look broadly at the extent of the restriction on free expression or the justifications for the restriction in any particular case. But I think that the system has major advantages. It is probably superior to any possible alternative.[3]

In thinking about government intrusions on the system of free expression, we should emphasize two things: the legitimacy or illegitimacy of the government's reasons for intruding; and the nature and extent of the effects of the intrusion. It might be tempting to think that the government's reasons are irrelevant and that we should care only about effects. But this would be a mistake. Laws unsupported by legitimate reasons are invalid, whether or not the illegitimate reasons can be tied tightly to concrete effects in individual cases.[4] There is an analogy here in the Constitution's due process clause, which forbids a judge from deciding a case in which he has a personal interest. The due process clause forbids judicial bias even if the victim of the bias has a frivolous claim, or would ultimately lose on the merits. If the judge has accepted a bribe on behalf of Smith's adversary Jones, Smith has a right to complain, whether or not he would win before a neutral judge. The requirement of a legitimate reason for regulation of speech should be seen in similar terms. An illegitimate reason is enough to doom the regulation, even if the effect on free expression is small in the individual case. We are not concerned with consequences alone.

Let us begin, then, with reasons, and then turn to effects. If we are focusing on the legitimacy of the government's reasons for action, it appears that we should be most suspicious of viewpoint discrimination and least suspicious of content-neutral restrictions. There is no legitimate reason for government to say that people may not criticize the President while they are showering. The only possible reason is to insulate the President from criticism, and this is illegitimate. The restriction is therefore unconstitutional even if it is minor. Courts should not uphold a restriction on speech based only on illegitimate reasons.

Even if the example seems odd, it carries a general lesson. When government regulates on the basis of viewpoint, it will frequently be acting for objectionable reasons. In individual cases, we will sometimes have trouble in deciding whether such reasons are at work; but whenever there is viewpoint discrimination, we know enough to presume that objectionable reasons are operating. The presumptive invalidity of viewpoint-based restrictions can be understood as an effort to "filter out" illegitimate reasons. Most such restrictions are difficult to support on sufficiently neutral grounds.

By contrast, most content-neutral restrictions have at least plausibly acceptable justifications. If government bans solicitation in airports, it may be trying to reduce unwanted intrusions on people's time and attention. Perhaps it wants to reduce congestion in a crowded place. Perhaps it wants to manage security at the airport; perhaps solicitations endanger that worthwhile goal, even if in a minor way. This example also carries a general lesson. When government regulates without regard to content, it will frequently be able to invoke legitimate, neutral justifications.

If we continue to look at reasons, content-based restrictions that are viewpoint-neutral appear to occupy a place between viewpoint-based and content-neutral restrictions. Suppose, for example, that the government forbids all discussion of racial issues on a racially integrated beach. The government has foreclosed no particular point of view, so we might think that it is not trying to entrench any orthodoxy. But what is the neutral justification for the restriction? Perhaps government wants to produce racial harmony. But is it really legitimate for government to say that it will produce racial harmony by preventing people from discussing racial issues? Shouldn't government be required to demonstrate at a minimum that the free discussion of racial issues will imminently and certainly produce violence? If government cannot make such a demonstration, shouldn't we be concerned that its real reason lies elsewhere?

When government regulates content, there is a large risk that the restriction really stems from something illegitimate: an effort to foreclose a controversial viewpoint, to stop people from being offended by certain topics and views, or to prevent people from being persuaded by what others have to say. There are large differences among various kinds of content-based restrictions, as I will soon explain. But if we are focusing on whether there are legitimate reasons for regulation, many such restrictions should be analyzed in the same basic way.

Now let us turn to effects. On this score, there are also important differences among the three different kinds of restrictions. A viewpoint-based restriction may not be "more" intrusive than one that is content-neutral; but it is intrusive in a much different and less acceptable way. If government disallows speech that is unfavorable to the President, it is badly skewing the system of free expression, by removing one side in a debate. This skewing effect is a distinct harm to deliberative processes.

By contrast, if government says that no one may speak on billboards—whatever the speaker's views—it leaves existing debate as it was, and does not push it in one direction rather than another. Significantly, there are usually strong political safeguards to protect against biased or misguided content-neutral restrictions. Both sides, or all sides, should try to prevent such restrictions; the size and generality of the burdened group means that we can rely on the political remedy. In the billboard case, for example, ordinary democratic channels may be trusted to say whether aesthetic and environmental goals justify a foreclosure of one avenue of political discussion. By contrast, viewpoint-based restrictions tend to reflect the mobilized political force of one position or of one faction. To be sure, the skewing effect of some viewpoint-based restrictions is small. But it is very hard to draw lines in individual cases between small and large effects, and in any case the impermissible motive should be sufficient by itself to doom viewpoint-based restrictions.

In this basic framework, content-based restrictions again occupy an intermediate position. Such restrictions may well have viewpoint-based effects. Consider a ban on discussion of AIDS or of sex equality. It is very plausible to think that such a ban will help one or another side. Moreover, content-based restrictions always skew debate in accordance with content, and hence can distort the system of democratic deliberation.

Provisionally, then, we might well endorse the tripartite scheme reflected in current law. It seems to make a good deal of sense. This does not mean that every content-based restriction is unacceptable or that every content-neutral restriction is fine. On the contrary, certain well-defined categories of speech are generally relegated to an intermediate level of protection. Consider commercial speech, private libel, obscenity. We cannot decide what these categories are, or whether certain speech falls within them, without taking a close look at content. It is for this reason quite wrong to say that courts do not allow content-based restrictions on speech. Indeed, it would be impossible to run a system of free expression without making some content-based restrictions, if only to decide whether speech may be regulated when the need is obviously compelling. In any case, some content-based restrictions are perfectly acceptable. The tripartite framework should not make us lose sight of this fact.

Moreover, some content-neutral restrictions should be struck down. Such restrictions may foreclose important expressive outlets and have profound content-differential effects; consider a ban on door-to-door solicitation. For this reason, such restrictions can be invalid. But they should be viewed more hospitably than content-based restrictions.

Qualifications, Provisional Conclusions, Puzzles

This account may be attractive, and in most ways it captures current law; but it is a bit too simple. The first puzzle is that even within the category of unprotected or low-value speech, such as libel and commercial speech, it seems clear that government may not be unacceptably selective. Some regulations of unprotected or low-value speech should therefore be invalidated.

For example, we know that threats and libel are sometimes unprotected. But suppose that a government said that threats against Democrats will be punished more severely than threats against Republicans, or that libel of liberal public officials will be punished more harshly than libel of conservative public officials. Laws of this kind could not possibly be upheld. This is an important manifestation of the principle that government may not carve out, from the category of regulable expression, speech that is chosen for regulation on the basis of its viewpoint.[5] It is therefore incomplete to say that speech either "is" or "is not" protected by the First Amendment. Some speech that "is not" protected cannot be controlled on the basis of unacceptable justifications, or through impermissibly selective regulations. This, then, is a important refinement of the general framework.

The framework also leaves it uncertain how we should handle content-based regulations. It is tempting to think that aside from the well-established categories of unprotected or "second-tier" speech, content-based restrictions should always be invalidated. This approach would introduce a good deal of simplicity and certainty into the law. But some content-based restrictions turn out to be justified even if we are not dealing with unprotected or "second-tier" speech. Imagine, for example, that a public school requires its science teachers to teach science rather than literature. This is a content-based distinction; but is it invalid? Surely a science teacher could not argue that her constitutional rights had been violated. Or suppose that the government is funding artistic projects related to the Civil War, and refuses to fund projects that deal with World War II. Surely this content-based restriction is permissible.

Perhaps these kinds of restrictions fall within a narrow category of regulations that have nothing to do with censorship at all, and everything to do with government's ability to undertake legitimate responsibilities that cannot be carried out without some restrictions on speech. Education and promotion of the arts are necessarily replete with content-based distinctions. But even if we can deal with some cases in this way, it is notable that the Supreme Court has upheld other content-based restrictions not involving "second-tier" speech. For example, it has allowed a ban on partisan political speech at army bases.[6] It has also permitted government to ban political advertising in buses.[7]

The Court may have been wrong in so holding. These were hard cases. But whether right or wrong, the cases show that even outside of the category of second-tier speech, sometimes government has neutral, harm-based restrictions for regulating speech on the basis of content. In the army base case, the government could claim to be preventing the reality and the appearance of political partisanship within the military (imagine if a commanding officer took, or was seen to take, a position for or against an incumbent President). A viewpoint-neutral ban on partisan political speech could be thought to promote the legitimate interest in military neutrality and preparedness. In the bus case, the ban could be understood to be a means of preventing what would be a disturbing form of government selectivity in choosing among advertisements. A flat ban avoids some of the difficulties that would be involved in almost all systems of selection. It seems, then, that there is no escape from the conclusion that content-based restrictions will be upheld not only for "second tier" speech, but also in a range of other settings.

From the discussion thus far, we might offer the following provisional conclusions:

1. Viewpoint restrictions will be subject to a very strong presumption of unconstitutionality.

2. Content-based restrictions will face a presumption of invalidity. They will be permitted only if (1) they involve a category of unprotected or "low-value" speech *or* (2) they can be tightly connected to a sufficiently general and neutral justification *and* they do not involve viewpoint discrimination or any other form of impermissible selectivity.

3. Content-neutral restrictions will be assessed through a form of balancing. In the process of balancing, courts will look at a number of factors: the extent of the intrusion on speech, the strength and legitimacy of the reasons for the restriction, the availability of good alternative places to get across the message, the existence of content-differential effects on speech, and the consequences of the restriction for poorly financed causes.[8] This is of course a relatively unstructured inquiry, and there is an inevitable degree of uncertainty in the cases. But the sheer number of cases involving content-neutral restrictions have made for a relatively predictable body of law.

We could do far worse than to use these three principles to govern our system of free expression. This is so especially if intrusive content-neutral restrictions are approached with at least a degree of skepticism. As generalizations, the provisional conclusions seem correct, and any qualifications are, I think, relatively unimportant.

There are, however, some further conceptual puzzles here. Most important, the line is sometimes thin between restrictions based on "harm" and restrictions based on viewpoint or content. Suppose, for example, that government forbids criticism of its efforts during a war. This is plainly an example of viewpoint discrimination, and it is clear that it would be invalidated. But it is not true that government cannot point to serious harms. Government might say, for example, that criticism of the war effort could undermine our recruitment efforts for military service, give aid and comfort to the enemy, and disrupt military morale. Courts might be tempted to say that these predictions are not credible—that the alleged harms would not really occur. But can they always be so sure about this? It is possible that a certain volume of public criticism of a war effort would indeed undermine that effort; actually this appears to have happened during the Vietnam War. The example shows that it makes things far too easy to say that speech cannot produce harm, and that apparently viewpoint-discriminatory regulation cannot be a plausible response to harm. Sometimes such regulation is indeed an effort to counteract serious social risks.

Would it then be reasonable to conclude that a restriction on public criticism of the war should be upheld? Surely not. Because the restriction is viewpoint-based, there is every reason to fear government's motives. Moreover, the restriction would have profound skewing effects on public deliberation. In these circumstances we should not allow the restriction unless government can make an extremely powerful demonstration that the particular speech would inevitably lead to particular harms. The government can rarely make this demonstration. I do not mean to question the speech-protective principles in current law; I say only that this approach cannot be justified simply by claiming that the restriction does not have legitimate motivations, or cannot plausibly be associated with real harms.

It might be tempting to conclude from the war example that all viewpoint restrictions should be invalidated, not because they are unconnected with harms, but on the contrary because harms are so easily invoked that their acceptance in any case would lead to intolerable censorship in many cases. If viewpoint discrimination could be defended by reference to harms, viewpoint discrimination would frequently be permitted. So perhaps we should have a per se rule against viewpoint discrimination. Laurence Tribe has said something of this kind in arguing that in the context of pornography regulation, viewpoint discrimination should not be defensible by reference to harms.[9] But there are some decisive counterexamples to Tribe's claim, in the form of cases in which viewpoint discrimination is, and should be, upheld because of the presence of sufficient harms. The point is worth discussing, because it demonstrates that there is no per se barrier to viewpoint discrimination.

Imagine, for example, that government bans advertising in favor of gambling at casinos. This restriction is clearly viewpoint-based. Such bans do not simultaneously prohibit advertising aimed *against* gambling. Nonetheless, the Supreme Court has upheld this unquestionably viewpoint-based restriction.[10] Courts have also upheld restrictions on cigarette and liquor advertising on television—even though there are no restrictions on advertising (which is plentiful) aimed against the smoking of cigarettes or the drinking of liquor. Restrictions on cigarette and liquor advertising are another example of acceptable viewpoint discrimination. Perhaps the most vivid illustration is the ban on the advertising of unlawful products or activities. I cannot sell an advertisement for cocaine or heroin, even though the government permits and even encourages advertisements designed to stop the use of drugs.

Most people agree that there is no constitutional problem with these kinds of regulation. The reason is that the restriction is based on such obvious harms that the notion that it is "viewpoint-based" does not have time even to register. Casino gambling, cigarette smoking, drinking, and use of illegal drugs all pose obvious risks to both self and others. Government controls on advertising for these activities are a means of controlling these risks.

It is even plausible to think that a liberal society should ban or regulate some or all of these activities,[11] though this is very controversial for both theoretical and practical reasons, and though our government has generally not chosen to do so. If government has the power to ban the activity, but has decided instead to permit it, perhaps it can do so only on the condition that advertising be banned. This was the Supreme Court's own reasoning in the casino gambling case. Now it would be possible to respond that this view is all wrong, because it reflects a distinctively objectionable form of paternalism, invading the autonomy of those who would listen to such speech. If we were really serious about the principle of listener autonomy, perhaps we would never allow government to stop people from hearing messages on the ground that those messages would persuade them. This is an intelligible position, but it is not relevant to my principal claim, which is purely descriptive: laws that discriminate on the basis of viewpoint are indeed upheld in certain circumstances, and we do not have a per se ban on viewpoint discrimination.

In any case the principle of listener autonomy does not seem to account for all of our considered judgments about free speech cases. Outside of the context of politics, it seems clear that in unusual cases, government can reasonably ban speech on the ground that people will be influenced by it. A prohibition on advertising for the sale of heroin is perfectly acceptable, even if the ground for the prohibition is that government does not want people to be persuaded to violate the law. The example suggests that the interest in listener autonomy is an important free speech value, but that at least if the harm is serious and the speech is low-value, the government may indeed regulate speech in violation of the interest in listener autonomy. This is an especially plausible view when we are uncertain whether listener autonomy truly justifies exposure to the relevant materials. Perhaps we fear that there is manipulation and even a degree of coercion in advertising for cigarette smoking and gambling, and perhaps this fear justifies regulation. Recall that respect for choices should not be identified with respect for autonomy; some choices reflect an absence of autonomy, as in cases of insufficient education, manipulation, or lack of options.

Or consider, as another example of viewpoint discrimination, the area of labor law, where courts have held that government may ban employers from speaking unfavorably about the effects of unionization in the period before a union election if the unfavorable statements might be interpreted as a threat against workers who support unionization.[12] Regulation of such speech is plausibly discriminatory on the basis of viewpoint, since employer speech favorable to unionization is not proscribed. As a final example, consider the securities laws, which regulate the speech that may occur in proxy statements. Restrictions on viewpoint can be found here too. Favorable views towards a company's prospects are banned, while unfavorable views are permitted and perhaps even encouraged.

We should conclude from all this that viewpoint discrimination is given a strong presumption of invalidity, but that the presumption can be overcome in certain narrow circumstances. Those circumstances occur when there is no serious risk of illegitimate government motivation, when low-value or unprotected speech is at issue, when the skewing effect on the system of free expression is minimal, and when the government is able to make a powerful showing of harm. As we will soon see, this conclusion has important implications for both hate speech and pornography.

Is Content-Neutrality Neutral?

Thus far I have largely defended current law. But if we are going to have a New Deal for speech, we will have to reassess the distinction between content-based and content-neutral restrictions on speech. In some respects, that distinction reproduces the framework of the pre-New Deal era. Is it really "neutral" to close off certain areas from expression? Is it always nonneutral to regulate on the basis of viewpoint or content? Is it really legitimate for government to take expressive capacities "as they are," which is what it does through content-neutral restrictions?

Affirmative answers to such questions tend to take the market status quo as natural and just insofar as it bears on speech. Such answers see partisanship in alteration of that status quo, and neutrality in government decisions that respect it. But this may well be wrong. There may be no neutrality in use of the market status quo when the available opportunities are heavily dependent on wealth, on the common law framework of legal entitlements, and on what sorts of outlets for speech are made available through law, and to whom. In other words, the very notions "content-neutral" and "content-based" seem to depend on the mistaken step of taking the supposedly preregulatory status quo as if it were unobjectionable.

At least two things seem to follow. The first and most important point is that many content-neutral laws should be carefully inspected to see whether they have constitutionally troublesome content-differential effects.[13] Although neutral on their face, such laws may favor some causes and disfavor others. They do so precisely because they operate against a backdrop that should not be treated as prepolitical or just. The government's refusal to allow Lafayette Park, in Washington, D.C., to be used as a place for dramatizing the plight of the homeless[14] is a prominent example. Even if government disallows all demonstrations and thus makes its restriction content-neutral, it has removed a major forum. Where can the homeless express themselves, if not in such places?

The same might be said about a refusal to allow political speech on telephone poles, or to permit protestors to place material without stamps in private mailboxes.[15] The Court has upheld these content-neutral restrictions. But such restrictions have terrible consequences for poorly financed causes. Rules that are content-neutral can, in light of an unequal status quo, have severe harmful effects on some forms of speech. Serious judicial scrutiny of content-neutral restrictions, with attention to this point, is therefore appropriate.

If we take the New Deal seriously, we will also draw into question a familiar justification for skepticism about content-based regulation of speech. That justification, referred to above, is that such regulation "skews" the marketplace of ideas. This idea has some possible infirmities. We do not have a full conception of what a well-functioning marketplace of ideas would look like. In such a system, who would be saying what? How much diversity would there be? The preconditions of an economic marketplace can be specified by the assumptions of neoclassical economics. The same is not at all true for the preconditions of a system of free expression. What, for example, would be the appropriate distribution of entitlements and authority in such a system? While it is possible to make some progress by reference to goals like political equality, attention to truth, and so forth, this question cannot be fully answered in the abstract.[16]

Moreover, the idea of "skewing" depends on taking the "marketplace" as unobjectionable in its current form. Suppose that the marketplace is already skewed; suppose that some people already

have disproportionate access to the media, and other people disproportionately little chance to be heard or even to speak at all. If
this is so, content-based regulation—even viewpoint-based regulation—may actually be a corrective. It would be exceptionally surprising, moreover, if there were no skewing in the current
process. The marketplace of ideas is of course a function of existing law, including property law, which is responsible for the allocation of entitlements that can be made into speech. The resulting
system is hardly without unjustified inequality.

Thus far, then, I have suggested that some content-neutral
restrictions should be carefully scrutinized, and that some content-based or even viewpoint-based restrictions might plausibly be
seen as a corrective to a content-based status quo. In general,
however, I do not believe that the existence of an unjust status
quo should be a reason to allow content- or viewpoint-based regulation of speech. "Affirmative action" is unlikely to be a good
principle for free speech. The basic reason is that the inquiry, for
First Amendment purposes, is probably beyond governmental
capacity. We do not want to allow government to say that some
side must be silenced because it is too powerful and because its
opponents are too weak—even though sometimes this is
undoubtedly true. There is a serious risk that judicial or legislative
decisions about the relative power of various groups, and about
who is owed redistribution, will be biased or unreliable.
Judgments about who is powerful and who is not must refer to
some highly controversial baseline. The resulting judgments are
not easily subject to governmental administration. Indeed, government will inevitably be operating with its own biases, and
those biases will affect any regulatory strategy. This risk seems
unacceptable when speech is at stake.

What is distinctive about regulation of speech is that such regulation closes off the channels of public discussion. It prevents
other views from being presented at all. Nothing like this can be
said for the social and economic New Deal. Instead of allowing
restrictions, we should encourage efforts to promote a better status quo. I have discussed some of this in connection with the
broadcasting market, campaign finance, and government funding.
Many related issues are raised by some of the most revealing
problems in First Amendment law, those raised by efforts to ban

"hate speech" and "hate crimes" on college campuses and else-where. I now turn to these problems.

Cross-Burning, the Speech/Conduct Distinction, and Racial Hatred

We might begin this discussion with a look at the many issues growing out of the important Supreme Court decision of *R.A.V. v. St. Paul.*[17] We can use this area as a case study. *R.A.V.* tests many of the principles I have discussed thus far. In that case, the Court struck down the effort of a locality to impose special restrictions on cross-burning and other forms of hate speech. I develop the analysis in detail, and some of the discussion is somewhat technical. The detail and the technicality are neces-sary, I think, in order to produce some general ideas for other applications.

Let us suppose that like St. Paul, Minnesota, a state or locality has faced a serious problem of cross-burning. Several racist groups have burned crosses on lawns of black families. The peo-ple of the locality want to regulate this form of expression as intolerable hate speech. We might be tempted to begin with the suggestion that cross-burning is action, not speech, and therefore outside of the First Amendment altogether. The state might begin by saying that it will not regulate hate "speech" at all, but only hateful "conduct" with expressive dimensions. Arguing on the state's behalf, we might suggest a proposition:

(I) Conduct is unprotected by the First Amendment. To claim con-stitutional protection, a person must be saying or writing words.

Is (I) true? I have not yet discussed the question whether gov-ernment can regulate "conduct" whenever it chooses. Some peo-ple do believe that the First Amendment's text requires this conclusion. The Constitution protects "speech," not conduct. Perhaps this simple text disposes of all cases in which people claim that by acting, they are trying to say something. Perhaps the Court's protection of expressive or symbolic conduct has gone beyond the words of the Constitution.

As a matter of basic principle, however, proposition (I) seems far too broad, for the text does not disqualify all "expressive conduct" from constitutional protection. Words are simply signs—symbols of expressive meaning. But the category of symbols of expressive meaning is not limited to words. Words are just an example of the general category of symbols.[18] Sign language, for example, does not consist of words, but it is surely entitled to constitutional protection. The same is true for the "act" of wearing an armband, or of joining a demonstration. The constitutional protection of "speech" should not be limited to words. The term "speech" is best understood to include all symbols of expressive meaning, whatever the form of those symbols. On this view, the difficulty with giving constitutional protection to expressive conduct is not that it is not "speech" in the constitutional sense—it is—but that government often has justifications for regulation that are both strong and content-neutral. The best way to handle expressive conduct is to treat it as speech, but to allow it to be regulated upon a showing of adequate justifications.

Let me sharpen the point. Suppose that we accept the Madisonian view of the First Amendment. If speech is entitled to special protection because and when it expresses a point of view about some public issue, any crisp line between "words" and "expressive conduct" becomes extremely artificial. Some forms of conduct, like flag-burning, are clearly expressive and thoroughly political in character. Their purpose and effect are to express a political message. They are part of public deliberation. In this way they seem to qualify as "speech," regulable only if the government can generate a strong, sufficiently neutral justification. A sharp line between "words" and "expressive acts" cannot, therefore, be justified in Madisonian terms. The constitutional protection is afforded to "speech," and acts that qualify as signs with expressive meaning qualify as speech within the meaning of the Constitution.

I emphasize that this is not to say that the government cannot regulate expressive conduct. Often government does have a special and sufficiently neutral justification for regulating such conduct. Protection of the President from assassination, or of the Lincoln Memorial from graffitti, can be supported by reference to powerful, legitimate reasons, such as protecting life and promoting clean public monuments. When the government regulates expressive conduct, it is usually trying to promote a purpose unrelated to the suppression of communication. But some restrictions on expressive conduct, like those on flag-burning, may well not be supportable in this way. Thus in the flag-burning cases, the Supreme Court emphasized that the government did not have a reason for regulation that was independent of the government's objection to the ideas that flag-burning embodies. The justification for regulation was illegitimate.[19]

Thus far, then, it seems that conduct carrying a political message qualifies as speech within the meaning of the First Amendment. The same conclusion seems right for other conduct, like dance, that is both expressive and communicative even if nonpolitical. When it is expressive and communicative but nonpolitical, such conduct belongs in the second tier of protection. It is regulable more easily than political speech, but it is protected in the absence of neutral justifications.

It is insufficient to respond that if people want to convey a message, they should be required to do so through words rather than action. A message cannot be so readily separated from the particular means chosen to express it; if the means are changed, the message changes too. Form and content cannot be distinguished so simply. Flag-burning conveys the relevant message more sharply and distinctively than anything else. If the speaker says instead, "My country is doing wrong," the message will be so muted as to be fundamentally transformed. The availability of purely verbal alternative forms of expression is therefore inadequate to justify failing to protect expressive conduct.

Nor—I repeat—is the constitutional text decisive against this conclusion. The question is what counts, for constitutional purposes, as "speech." Here the dictionary will not solve our problems. It is textually plausible to think that conduct that expresses a message does count as speech within the meaning of the First Amendment, and that the government needs at least a viewpoint-neutral justification to ban it. As we have seen, "the freedom of speech" is a constitutional term of art, and the speech/conduct distinction is far too crude to give it full content.

Thus far, then, cross-burning counts as speech, and it cannot simply be excluded from constitutional protection. Suppose that a criminal prosecutor, the local district attorney, invokes the law of criminal trespass to proceed against someone who has burned a cross on a private lawn. (I put to one side possible issues of selective prosecution.) Here we have a content-neutral law—the law of trespass—invoked to suppress an expressive act. Hence it might be suggested:

(II) Content-neutral restrictions on acts that qualify as speech are generally permissible.

How shall we evaluate (II)? At least in general, this use of the trespass law does seem constitutionally acceptable. Surely the law of criminal trespass could be invoked to prevent someone from drawing pictures on my house, or from using my property as a place for an antiwar demonstration. At least in general, the law of property can be invoked to protect, in a content-neutral way, private lands and dwellings from invasion, whether through expression or otherwise.

In some cases, perhaps, the law of trespass—as a content-neutral restriction on speech—might be unconstitutional if it forecloses a crucial arena for expression and if the state has no good justification for protecting property rights in this way. Consider a ban on speech at shopping centers, discussed in chapter 4. But the state has extremely strong reasons to protect ordinary homes from expressive invasion. The grant of such protection does not seriously compromise the system of free expression. It is therefore perfectly acceptable to use the trespass law to stop cross-burning. This conclusion reveals that it is misleading to ask whether cross-burning "is" or "is not" protected by the First Amendment. The answer depends on whether government has neutral justifications for regulating it. Hate crimes and hate speech, for example, can almost always be controlled through neutral regulations, such as laws prohibiting murder and rape, or trespass on private property.

Suppose, however, that a locality believes that the law of trespass is inadequate. Suppose it believes that for symbolic and deterrent reasons, it is important to enact a special statute explicitly forbidding expressive conduct of an especially harmful sort. The resulting law might be directed against racial or ethnic hate speech in particular. The law might make it a crime to "place on public or private property a symbol, including but not limited to a burning cross or a Nazi swastika, which one knows or has reason to know arouses anger or resentment in others on the basis of race, color, sex, or creed." (This is a minor variation on the law at issue in the *R.A.V.* case.) Such a law might be invoked to forbid a public or private act of cross-burning. This leads to another proposition, quite different from (II):

(III) Acts that qualify as speech can be regulated if they produce anger or resentment.

From basic principle, as well as from the flag-burning cases, we know that (III) is false. The mere fact that an expressive act produces anger or resentment cannot be a sufficient reason for regulation. An expressive act cannot, consistent with a Madisonian system of free expression, be prohibited simply because it upsets the audience.[20] If the production of anger were a sufficient reason for regulation, much speech would be regulable simply because it is out of the mainstream. This would be an impermissible prohibition on political dissent. We might go so far as to conclude that it is per se illegitimate for government to prevent the expression of ideas because people would be angered by them (see chapter 5).

To defend the law, it would therefore be necessary to show the particular properties of a burning cross (and other banned symbolic hate speech) that take it out of the realm of constitutional protection. It would be necessary to show that there is a relevant difference between the ordinary anger or resentment produced by many expressive acts and "anger or resentment on the basis of race, color, or creed." Many defenders of restrictions on hate speech have something like this in mind.[21] We therefore have to evaluate a new proposition:

(IIIa) Acts that qualify as speech can be regulated if they produce anger or resentment on the basis of race, color, or creed.

On one view, (IIIa) is really just a subcategory of (III). The anger or resentment produced by this kind of speech may be more intense than other forms; but there is at most a quantitative difference between the two. On another view, the anger or resentment produced by symbolic acts like cross-burning, and based on race, color, or creed, is qualitatively different from other forms. It is properly treated differently.

In a famous case, Justice Frankfurter, speaking for a 5–4 majority, seemed to accept a version of (IIIa). *Beauharnais v. Illinois*[22] upheld an Illinois law making it unlawful to publish or exhibit any publication which "portrays depravity, criminality, unchastity, or lack of virtue of a class of citizens, which [publication] exposes the citizens of any race, color, creed or religion to contempt, derision, or obloquy or which is productive of breach of the peace or riots." The law was applied to ban circulation of a petition urging "the need to prevent the white race from becoming mongrelized by the negro," and complaining of the "aggressions, rapes, robberies, knives, guns and marijuana of the negro."

In upholding the law, Justice Frankfurter referred to the historical exclusion of libel from free speech protection; to the risks to social cohesion created by racial hate speech; and to the need for judicial deference to legislative judgments on these complex matters. Justice Frankfurter placed less emphasis on the interest in equality—in the elimination of the caste-like features of current society—but this interest, with its roots in the Civil War Amendments to the United States Constitution, would certainly have fortified his conclusion. Many countries in Europe accept the same analysis and do not afford protection to racial and ethnic hate speech.

But most people think that after *New York Times v. Sullivan* (discussed in chapter 2), *Beauharnais* is no longer the law. In *New York Times*, the Court said that the law of libel must be evaluated in accordance with the constitutional commitment to robust and uninhibited debate on public issues. The conventional view—which the Supreme Court has not directly addressed—is that racial hate speech contains highly political ideas, and that it may not be suppressed merely because it is offensive or otherwise harmful. Importantly, *New York Times* arose in a context in which free speech interests and civil rights interests could march hand-in-hand. Perhaps the issue should be understood in a different way if these interests seem opposed.

Current constitutional law tends, however, to foreclose the claim that there is a qualitative difference between (III) and (IIIa), at least in the context of an attempt to ban otherwise protected racist speech that produces anger or resentment. Speech that contains racial hatred has not been treated differently from other speech that causes ordinary offense or anger. As noted, the Court has not had occasion to answer the precise question whether pro-hibitions on group libel might be acceptable in the wake of *New York Times v. Sullivan*. But most people think that bans on group libel or hate speech, broadly defined, are no longer permissible.

There are real complexities here, but the conventional view on the matter is probably correct, at least as applied to broad bans on hate speech that goes well beyond epithets. No one should deny that distinctive harms are produced by racist speech, especially when it is directed against members of minority groups. It is only obtuseness—a failure of perception or empathetic identification—that would enable someone to say that the word "fascist" or "pig" or even "honky" produces the same feelings as the word "nigger." In view of our history, invective directed against minority groups, and racist speech in general, create fears of physical violence, exclusion, and subordination that are not plausibly described as mere "offense." These harms are plausibly antithetical to the goal of political equality, a precondition for democracy and a goal that animates the First Amendment itself. People confronted by hate speech may experience a form of "silencing" in the sense that they are reluctant to speak and not heard when they do.

In light of all this, there is nothing obvious or clear about the view that the First Amendment should ban laws prohibiting racial hate speech. As I have noted, most European countries, including flourishing democracies committed to free speech, make excep-tions for such expression. In many countries, it is possible to think that racial and ethnic hate speech is really sui generis, and that it is properly treated differently.

On the other hand, a great deal of public debate produces anger or resentment on the basis of race. If we were to excise all such speech from political debate, we would have severely trun-cated our discussion of such important matters as civil rights, for-eign policy, crime, conscription, abortion, and social welfare policy. Even if speech produces anger or resentment on the basis of race, it might well be thought a legitimate part of the delibera-tive process. Certainly it bears directly on politics. Foreclosure of such speech would probably accomplish little good, and by stop-ping people from hearing certain ideas, it could bring about a great deal of harm. These are the most conventional Millian argu-ments for the protection of speech.[23] Claims about the inferiority of blacks, women, and homosexuals (for example) should be permitted in the public sphere and subject to open and free debate.

A possible approach would be to try to make distinctions among different categories of hate speech. We might allow racist and sexist political speech, if it is an appeal to deliberative capacities, but exempt from protection certain narrow categories of hate speech that amount to little more than mere epithets. The regulation of epithets might be supported by an analogy to the obscene telephone call. Like an obscene telephone call, a racial epithet is not plausibly taken as part of social deliberation on racial issues, and the harms that it produces go well beyond offense. Of course there will be hard intermediate cases. I take up this issue in more detail below, but as stated, proposition (IIIa) seems too broad.

Defenders of the ban on cross-burning should therefore concede that the hypothetical law is unconstitutional. We might, then, imagine that the locality proceeds greatly to narrow the reach of its ordinance, as did the state Supreme Court in the *R.A.V.* case. Suppose that the locality prohibits cross-burning that produces anger or resentment *if and only if the speech in question is otherwise regulable under existing standards as "fighting words."* Fighting words are defined as speech that is no essential part of the expression of ideas and that would cause an average addressee to fight. The Supreme Court has said that government may regulate such expression.[24] Now we have a quite different case—one in which the locality says that the prohibition will not be triggered unless the circumstances of the expressive conduct mean that the conduct fits within an already-established exception to First Amendment protection.

How does this affect the analysis? At first glance it seems to dispose of the issue.[25] By hypothesis, the law now covers only speech unprotected by the First Amendment. Surely such a law is acceptable. If so, we have a new, highly attractive proposition:

(IV) Unprotected acts of expression may be regulated by the state however it wishes.

But the first glance is misleading. We can show that (IV) is wrong. Imagine that the state attempted to regulate only those "fighting words" directed at Republicans, or at whites. Or imagine that the state made it a felony to engage in "incitement" if and only if the incitement was directed against people having a conservative political view. It is clear that such regulations would be impermissible. The reason is that laws discriminating on the basis of viewpoint are generally unacceptable. As we have seen, this principle applies even within the category of otherwise unprotected speech.

This was a major argument by the Supreme Court in the *R.A.V.* case. "Thus, the government may proscribe libel; but it may not make the further content discrimination of proscribing *only* libel critical of the government."[26] The governing principle is that the state may not regulate unprotected speech if it selects, from the class of unprotected speech, material chosen on the basis of point of view. Viewpoint discrimination is unacceptable even in the context of otherwise unprotected speech. Hence it seems clear that:

(V) Unprotected expression, or unprotected acts of expression, may not be regulated on the basis of viewpoint.

The next question becomes whether our hypothetical hate speech law violates the prohibition on viewpoint discrimination. In a critical sense, the law is different from those in the clear cases of viewpoint discrimination. The locality has not drawn a line between prohibited and permitted points of view. It has not said that one view on an issue—race relations, for example—is permitted, and another proscribed. If cross-burning were all that it banned, we might well have a case of viewpoint discrimination, since cross-burning has a particular viewpoint. But here the class of prohibited speech ("symbols that arouse anger or resentment on the basis of race, color, or creed") is far broader. Antiwhite and antiblack statements are both allowed. The locality allows speech opposed to Christians and speech opposed to Jews. It does not distinguish between the two. In this respect, the law is content-based but viewpoint-neutral.

The locality has thus built on existing public reactions to certain kinds of speech, within a subset of the category of "fighting words." It has not singled out a particular message for prohibition. It has regulated on the basis of subjects for discussion, not on the basis of viewpoint.

In *R.A.V.* the Supreme Court offers a tempting and clever response:

In its practical operation, moreover, the ordinance goes even beyond mere content discrimination to actual viewpoint discrimination. Displays containing some words—odious racial epithets, for example—would be prohibited to proponents of all views. But 'fighting words' that do not themselves invoke race, color, creed, religion, or gender—aspersions based upon a person's mother, for example—would be seemingly usable ad libitum in the placards of those arguing in favor of racial, color, etc. tolerance and equality, but could not be used by that speaker's opponents. . . . St. Paul has no such authority to license one side of a debate to fight freestyle, while requiring the other to follow Marquis of Queensbury Rules.

The short answer to this argument is that the ordinance at issue does not embody viewpoint discrimination as that term is ordinarily understood. Viewpoint discrmination occurs if the government takes one side in a debate, as in, for example, a law saying that libel of the President will be punished more severely than libel of anyone else. Viewpoint discrimination is not established by the fact that in some hypotheticals, one side has greater means of expression than another, at least—and this is the critical point—if the restriction on means is connected to legitimate, neutral justifications.

We can make this point by reference to statutes that make it a federal crime to threaten the life of the President. The Supreme Court said in *R.A.V.* that such statutes are permissible even though they make distinctions within the category of unprotected threats. In fact the presidential threat statute involves the same kind of de facto viewpoint discrimination as in the *R.A.V.* case.. Imagine the following conversation: John: "I will kill the President." Jill: "I will kill anyone who threatens to kill the President." John has committed a federal crime; Jill has not. In this sense, the presidential threat case involves the same kind of de facto viewpoint discrimination. If it is not unconstitutional for that reason[27] —and the Court indicated that it is not—the statute in *R.A.V.* should also not be found viewpoint discriminatory.

The final proposition to be evaluated is therefore this:

(VI) If government singles out unprotected acts of expression for regulation when they cause "anger or resentment on the basis of

*race, color, or creed," it does not discriminate on the basis of view-
point or otherwise on any impermissible ground.*

Is (VI) true? In the end, this was the central issue that divided
the justices in the *R.A.V.* case. It is indeed a difficult question.

The analogous cases involving "fighting words" are a helpful
start here, for they show that regulation of "fighting words" is not
by itself impermissibly viewpoint-based or otherwise objectionable. To understand this point, we need to offer a few more
remarks on the somewhat puzzling "fighting words" doctrine.
That doctrine is intended to allow government to regulate a narrow category of speech that is not an essential part of the
exchange of ideas and that would cause a fight. The doctrine is
deemed permissibly neutral because any regulation of fighting
words fails to single out for legal control a preferred point of
view.[28] The viewpoint of the speaker is relevant in the sense that
addresees will be reacting in part to the speaker's viewpoint; but
by banning fighting words in general, the government has not
endorsed a particular idea or a point of view. (It would do so if it
said, for example, that fighting words were bannable only if they
were aimed at Republicans.) This is a crucial difference.

As the *R.A.V.* Court emphasized, however, the law at issue is
not a broad or general proscription of fighting words. It reflects a
decision to single out a certain category of "fighting words,"
defined in terms of audience reactions *to speech about certain
topics.* Is this constitutionally illegitimate? The category of regulated speech—involving race, color, and creed—is based on subject matter, not viewpoint. The question is then whether a subject
matter restriction of this kind is acceptable. In *R.A.V.*, the Court,
by a 5–4 vote, concluded that it is not.

Subject matter restrictions are not all the same. We can imagine
subject matter restrictions that are questionable ("no one may discuss homosexuality on the subway") and subject matter restrictions that seem legitimate ("no high-level CIA employee may
speak publicly about classified matters relating to the clandestine
affairs of the American government"). As a class, subject matter
restricions appear to occupy a point somewhere between viewpoint-based restrictions and content-neutral ones. Sometimes subject matter restrictions are indeed upheld as a form of permissible

content regulation. As we have seen, the Court has permitted subject matter prohibitions on political advertising on buses[29] and on partisan political speech at army bases.[30] These cases show that there is no per se ban on such restrictions. When the Court upholds subject matter restrictions, it is either because the line drawn by government gives no real reason for fear about lurking viewpoint discrimination, or (what is close to the same thing) because government is able to invoke neutral, harm-based justifications for treating certain subjects differently from others.

If the subject matter restriction in the cross-burning case is acceptable, it must be because the specified catalogue of regulated speech is sufficiently neutral, and it does not alert the judge to possible concerns about viewpoint discrimination; or because (again a closely overlapping point) it is plausible to say that the harms, in the specific covered cases, are sufficiently severe and distinctive to justify special treatment. This was the issue that in the end divided the Supreme Court.

In his concurring opinion, Justice Stevens argued that the harms were indeed sufficiently distinctive. He wrote that "race based threats may cause more harm to society and to individuals than other threats. Just as the statute prohibiting threats against the President is justifiable because of the place of the President in our social and political order, so a statute prohibiting race based threats is justifiable because of the place of race in our social and political order." In his view, "[t]hreatening someone because of her race or religious beliefs may cause particularly severe trauma or touch off a riot .. ; such threats may be punished more severely than threats against someone based on, for example, his support of a particular athletic team."[31] Thus there were "legitimate, reasonable, and neutral justifications" for the special rule.

In its response, the Court said that this argument "is word-play." The reason that race-based threats are different "is nothing other than the fact that it is caused by a distinctive idea, conveyed by a distinctive method. The First Amendment cannot be evaded that easily."[32] Who is right?

At first glance, it seems that a reasonable legislature could decide that the harms produced by this narrow category of hate speech are especially severe and deserve separate treatment. Surely it is plausible to say that cross-burning, swastikas, and the like are an especially distinctive kind of "fighting word"—distinctive because of the objective and subjective harm they inflict on their victims and on society in general. An incident of cross-burning can have large and corrosive social consequences. A reasonable and sufficiently neutral government could decide that the same is not true for a hateful attack on someone's parents, or on his political convictions.

A harm-based argument of this kind suggests that the legislature is responding not to ideological message, but to real-world consequences. It is not clear that we have any special reason to suspect the government's motives. This argument draws strength from the fact that almost all industrialized nations impose special disabilities on racial and ethnic hate speech, even if they are otherwise committed to a robust principle of freedom of expression.

According to Justice Stevens, a state is indeed acting neutrally if it singles out cross-burning for special punishment, because this kind of "fighting word" has especially severe social consequences. According to the Court, on the other hand, a state cannot legitimately decide that cross-burning is worse than (for example) a vicious attack on your political convictions or your parents. A decision to this effect violates neutrality. But the Court's conception of neutrality seems implausible. There is nothing partisan or illegitimate in recognizing that distinctive harms are produced by this unusual class of fighting words.

My claim here is very narrow; I do not argue for broad bans on hate speech. Most such bans would indeed violate the First Amendment, because they would forbid a good deal of speech that is intended and received as a contribution to public deliberation. But here we are dealing with hate speech that is limited to the exceedingly narrow category of unprotected fighting words. The argument on behalf of this kind of restriction might be helped by Justice Stevens' reference to the especially severe legal penalties directed toward threats against the President. Everyone seems to agree that this restriction is permissible. Threats against the President cause distinctive harms and can therefore be punished more severely. But if the government can single out one category of threats for special punishment because of the distinctive harms that those particular threats cause, why can't it do the same for fighting words of the sort at issue here?

Justice Scalia's response is probably the best that can be offered: "[T]he reasons why threats of violence are outside the First Amendment (protecting individuals from fear of violence, from the disruption that fear engenders, and from the possibility that threatened violence will occur) have special force when applied to the President." But very much the same could be said of the hate speech ordinance under discussion—that is, the justification for exemption for fighting words has special force because of the context of racial injustice. Here, as in cases involving threats against the President, we are dealing with a subcategory of unprotected speech challenged as involving impermissible selectivity, and we have a justification for the selectivity made out in terms of the particular harms of the unprotected speech at issue. That justification seems sufficiently neutral.

An explicit set of constitutional provisions strongly supports this conclusion.[33] In the aftermath of the Civil War, the Constitution was amended by various provisions abolishing slavery, eliminating second-class citizenship, and granting the right to vote to blacks. The Thirteenth, Fourteenth, and Fifteenth Amendments fundamentally altered the Constitution by placing equality—understood as the elimination of caste, or second-class citizenship—in the forefront of constitutional concern. The Constitution itself takes a stand against second-class citizenship for any group. It is not neutral on this subject. When speech helps contribute to the creation of a caste system, the state can legitimately and neutrally attempt to respond—at least if any resulting restriction is both clear and sharply limited.

The argument to this effect depends critically on the fact that the subject matter classification occurs in the context not of a broad ban on hate speech, but of a narrowly defined category of speech that is, by hypothesis, without First Amendment protection. A subject matter restriction on unprotected speech should probably be upheld if the legislature can plausibly argue that it is counteracting harms rather than ideas.

Hate Crimes

Supplemental criminal penalties for racially motivated "hate crimes" seem to be a well-established part of current law. Most states impose such penalties. Do the penalties violate the First Amendment? In *Wisconsin v. Mitchell*,[34] a unanimous Supreme Court said that they do not, and I believe that the Court was right. But if *R.A.V.* is right, it is not so easy to answer this question. The problem comes from the fact that in imposing the additional penalty for certain crimes and not others, government may be endorsing a particular point of view, or punishing a criminal for the expressive dimension of his acts. If the government claims that hate crimes create distinctive harm, it may be referring to the symbolic or expressive nature of these crimes. This justification seems very much the same as in the cross-burning case, where it was found invalid.

We might, however, draw some distinctions between "hate crime" measures and "hate speech" laws. Perhaps we can say that hate crimes are not speech—not because we accept discredited versions of the old "speech/conduct" distinction, but because hate crimes are not intended and received as contributions to deliberation about anything. They do not communicate ideas of any kind. In this way, they are unlike cross-burning and indeed unlike all forms of hate *speech*.

This was one of the Supreme Court's major arguments in the *Mitchell* case. According to the Court, cross-burning is speech, whereas hate crimes are unprotected conduct. For many cases this answer seems right; but in some contexts it is incomplete. It may well be true that many hate crimes do not have a communicative intention or effect. But some certainly do; consider lynching of blacks or beatings of homosexuals, which are often intended to be communicative. Perhaps we can say that the hate crime statutes sweep up communicative hate crimes as an incidental part of a general category of regulated conduct, and perhaps the enhanced penalties are unobjectionable for that reason. By contrast, the hate speech statutes are directed against speech itself. Or perhaps the key justification for hate crimes statutes is the especially heinous state of mind of the criminal. The state may be punishing that state of mind, without at the same time seeking to punish any communication. Probably the state can punish the heinous state of mind without offending the First Amendment, so long as it is not trying to single out expression for special sanction. In *Mitchell*, the Supreme Court relied heavily on this point.

Arguments of this sort suggest that it is indeed possible to argue for hate crimes statutes while accepting the *R.A.V.* decision. But a lurking question remains: When there is a communicative goal to the underlying hate crime, are enhanced penalties invalid? I do not believe that there is anything illegitimate or nonneutral about the state's belief that the subjective and objective harm justifies enhancement of the criminal sentence. It is for this reason acceptable to impose enhanced penalties on hate crimes. If the hate crime cases are different from *R.A.V.*, it may be because the reason for the enhanced penalty is more neutral than the reason invoked in that case, and because punishment of expression seems less directly at stake. But in the end, some of the reasons seem very much the same.

For this reason, the line between *R.A.V.* and *Mitchell* seems quite thin. As I have emphasized, all the justices in *R.A.V.* agreed that the expressive acts at issue were unprotected by the First Amendment, because the state court said that the statute was limited to unprotected "fighting words." *R.A.V.* therefore involved constitutionally unprotected acts, just as Mitchell did. And everyone in *Mitchell* agreed that the First Amendment issue did not disappear simply because conduct was involved. The Court said that "a physical assault is not by any stretch of the imagination expressive conduct protected by the First Amendment"; but it rightly added that a genuine First Amendment issue is raised when a state "enhances the maximum penalty for conduct motivated by a discriminatory point of view."

Understood in these terms *R.A.V.* and *Mitchell* are very close, and the Court did not adequately explain the difference between them. Perhaps the major distinction between the two cases is that the Minnesota law in *R.A.V.* covered speech as well as expressive conduct, and cross-burning is characteristically expressive— whereas the enhancement statute was directed only at conduct, and many hate crimes are not intended and received as a communication on anything at all. For this reason, the enhancement penalty can perhaps be seen as a content-neutral restriction on conduct that is not ordinarily expressive, while the Minnesota law was a content-based restriction on speech, including expressive conduct. This is a reasonable distinction. But it is not clear that the distinction really rescues *R.A.V.* The question remains whether the state had a legitimate justification for doing what it did. The *Mitchell* Court emphasized that the state treated "bias-inspired conduct" more severely because that conduct inflicts "greater individual and societal harm." This was Justice Stevens' argument in *R.A.V.*, and it seems to have equal weight in both cases.

To make the point especially vivid, consider a federal ban on lynching, limited to lynching of blacks by whites. Is this unconstitutional? Is it unacceptably partisan? I do not believe so. It would seem reasonable to think that an anti-lynching law, even if limited to racial lynchings or those committed by blacks against whites, is a plausible response to a distinctive harm. In view of history, and the subjective and objective injury of lynching of blacks by whites, the nation could neutrally decide that this form of murder is especially heinous and warrants special punishment.

One final analogy seems to draw *R.A.V.* into doubt. The civil rights laws say that you may not fire someone because of his race, even though you may fire him for many other reasons. If *R.A.V.* is right, the civil rights laws might even be said to be unconstitutional, since they penalize someone because of his political convictions. It is certainly possible to imagine a white employer firing a black employee as a way of expressing his view that blacks do not belong in the workforce. Perhaps the civil rights laws are just like a content-based prohibition on flag-burning or cross-burning. They single out conduct for special penalty simply because of the message communicated by that conduct. To be sure, many discriminatory discharges are not intended to communicate a message; but some such discharges do have a communicative intention.

This argument is not unintelligible. But it would be odd, to say the least, to claim that the civil rights laws cannot be lawfully applied to discriminatory acts that are politically motivated. And if the civil rights laws are permissible, the hate crimes statutes are permissible as well, as the Court said explicitly in *Mitchell*. For this reason, the analysis in *R.A.V.* seems doubtful.

Here too some responses are possible. Perhaps most discriminatory discharges lack an expressive purpose. Perhaps most people who fire blacks or women are not intending to communicate a message. Alternatively, we might think that the prohibition on discriminatory discharge has a sufficiently neutral basis, and that any restriction on speech is neutrally justified—like a ban on criminal trespass applied to cross-burning on a private lawn. These are certainly plausible distinctions, but they seem a bit thin. Fairly applied, *R.A.V.* does seem to cast doubt on a legislative judgment to forbid certain forms of discharge (produced through speech) and not others. I think that this doubt is unwarranted (as the *Mitchell* Court confirmed), because a state could neutrally decide that discriminatory discharges are subjectively and objectively worse than other discharges. And if the state could make this judgment, we have reason to question *R.A.V.* itself, where a similar decision was ruled impermissibly selective.

I conclude that as the *Mitchell* Court held, the First Amendment is not violated by laws enhancing the punishment of hate crimes. I also conclude that no serious First Amendment problem is raised by the civil rights laws, even though those laws sometimes punish speech. And contrary to the outcome in *R.A.V.*, a restriction on cross-burning and other symbolic speech is a permissible subject matter classification, so long as the restriction is narrowed in the way described.

Hate Speech on Campus

We can use this discussion as a basis for exploring the complex problems resulting from recent efforts to regulate hate speech on campus. Some regulations have been associated with alleged efforts to impose an ideological orthodoxy on students and faculty, under the rubric of "political correctness." Perhaps left-wing campuses, under pressure from well-organized groups, are silencing people who disagree. Are the campus speech codes constitutional?

To the extent that we are dealing with private universities, the Constitution is not implicated at all, and hence all such restrictions are permissible. Private universities can do whatever they like. They can ban all speech by Republicans, by Democrats, or by anyone they want to silence. But many private universities like to follow the Constitution even if they are not required to do so. In any case, public universities are subject to the Constitution, and so it is important to try to establish what the First Amendment means for them.

On the analysis I have provided, we can offer an important

provisional conclusion: If campus speech restrictions at public universities cover not merely epithets, but speech that is part of social deliberation, they might well be seen as overbroad and unconstitutional for that very reason.[35] At least as a presumption, speech that is intended and received as a contribution to social deliberation is constitutionally protected even if it amounts to hate speech—even if it is racist and sexist.

Consider, for example, the University of Michigan's judicially invalidated ban on "[a]ny behavior, verbal or physical, that stigmatizes or victimizes an individual on the basis of race, ethnicity, religion, sex, sexual orientation, creed, national origin, ancestry, age, marital status, handicap, or Vietnam-era veteran status, and that . . . creates an intimidating, hostile, or demeaning environment for educational pursuits." This broad ban forbids a wide range of statements that are part of the exchange of ideas. It also fails to give people sufficient notice of what statements are allowed. For both reasons, it seems invalid.

The argument to the contrary would stress that distinctive harms are produced by certain forms of hate speech, and that the university (and perhaps the state) should have a degree of flexibility in counteracting those harms. The *Beauharnais* case, discussed above, has not been overruled, even if its authority is doubtful. That case suggests that it is constitutional to prevent libel of certain social groups. Perhaps courts should permit a hate speech restriction limited to a few "status" categories—at least if the restriction is narrow and designed to carry forward the post–Civil War commitment to eliminate social castes. But the Michigan ban was far too broad. On the other hand, it should be permissible for government to build on the basic case of the epithet in order to regulate certain categories of hate speech. Standing by themselves, or accompanied by little else, epithets are not intended and received as contributions to social deliberation about anything. The injury to dignity and self-respect is a sufficient harm to allow regulation. (See my discussion of the Stanford regulation below.)

The provisional conclusion is that a public university should be allowed to regulate hate speech in the form of epithets, but that it should be prohibited from reaching very far beyond epithets to forbid the expression of views on public issues, whatever those views may be. Under current law, moreover, even narrow restrictions might be invalidated as viewpoint-based. A university might well, post-*R.A.V.*, be forbidden from singling out for punishment speech that many universities want to control, such as (1) a narrowly defined category of insults toward such specifically enumerated groups as blacks, women, and homosexuals, or (2) a narrowly defined category of insults directed at individuals involving race, sex, and sexual orientation. How would restrictions of this kind be treated?

Under current law, a restriction that involves (1) is viewpoint-based, and to that extent even worse than the restriction in *R.A.V.* itself. On the analysis of the *R.A.V.* Court, restriction (1) tries to silence one side in a debate. A restriction that involves (2) is a subject matter restriction, not based on viewpoint. But it too is impermissibly selective in the same sense as the restriction invalidated in the *R.A.V.* case. For reasons offered above, I believe that the conclusions in *R.A.V.* are incorrect in principle, because there are sufficiently neutral grounds for restrictions (1) and (2). A university could neutrally decide that epithets directed against blacks, women, and homosexuals cause distinctive harms. But this conclusion is hard to reconcile with the *R.A.V.* decision.

Colleges and universities do, however, have some arguments that were unavailable to St. Paul, and in order to make the conclusions thus far more than provisional, we have to address those arguments. If *R.A.V.* does not apply to the campus, it might be because public universities can claim a degree of insulation from judicial supervision. The largest point here is that colleges and universities are often in the business of controlling speech, and their controls are hardly ever thought to raise free speech problems.[36] Indeed, controlling speech is, in one sense, a defining characteristic of the university. There are at least four different ways in which such controls occur.

First, universities impose major limits on the topics that can be discussed in the classroom. Subject matter restrictions are part of education. Irrelevant discussion is banned. Students cannot discuss the presidential election, or Marx and Mill, if the subject is math. Schools are allowed to impose subject matter restrictions that would be plainly unacceptable if enacted by states or localities.

Second, a teacher can require students to treat each other with at least a minimum of basic respect. It would certainly be legiti-

mate to suspend a student for using consistently abusive or profane language in the classroom. This is so even if that language
would receive firm constitutional protection on the street corner.
The educational process requires at least a measure of civility.
Perhaps it would be unacceptable for universities to ban expressions of anger or intense feeling; the notion of civility should not
be a disguise for forbidding irreverance or disagreement. But so
long as requirements of civility are both reasonable and neutral
with respect to viewpoint, a university may limit abusive or profane comments within the classroom.

The problem goes deeper, for—and this is the third kind of
academic control on speech—judgments about quality are pervasive. Such judgments affect admissions, evaluation of students in
class and on paper, and evaluation of prospective and actual faculty as well. Academic decisions about quality are based on a
conception of appropriate standards of argument and justification. These standards involve judgments about merit or excel-
lence that would of course be unacceptable in the setting of
criminal punishment or civil fine, but that are a perfectly and
nearly inescapable part of the educational function. At least this
is so if there is no discrimination on the basis of viewpoint—that
is, if the person involved in making the assessment offers judgments on the basis of standards of quality that are applied neutrally to everyone (an ambitious aspiration, and one that is
conceptually complex).

But there is a fourth and more troublesome way in which universities control speech, and this involves the fact that some academic judgments are viewpoint-based, certainly in practice. In
many places, a student who defends fascism or communism is
unlikely to receive a good grade. In many economics departments, sharp deviation from the views of Adam Smith may well
be punished. History and literature departments have their own
conceptions of what sorts of arguments are retrograde, or beyond
the pale. Viewpoint discrimination is undoubtedly present in
practice and, even if we object to it in principle, it is impossible
and perhaps undesirable for outsiders to attempt to police it.

Thus far I have been discussing students, but much the same is
true for faculty members. Universities can impose on their faculty
restrictive rules of decorum and civic participation. A teacher

who refuses to teach the subject, fails to allow counterarguments, treats students contemptuously, or vilifies them in class can be penalized without offense to the Constitution. The job performance of teachers consists mostly of speech. When that performance is found wanting, it is almost always because of content, including judgments about subject matter and quality, and sometimes because of viewpoint.

It is worthwhile pausing over this point. Initial hirings, tenure, and promotion all involve subject matter restrictions and sometimes viewpoint discrimination in practice. All this suggests that universities are engaged in regulating speech through content discrimination and at least implicit viewpoint discrimination. The evaluation of students and colleagues cannot occur without resort to content, and it would be most surprising if viewpoint discrimination did not affect many evaluations.

These examples do not by any means compel the conclusion that any and all censorship is acceptable in an academic setting. A university can have a good deal of power over what happens in the classroom, in order to promote the educational enterprise, without also being allowed to decree a political orthodoxy by discriminating on the basis of viewpoint. If a public university were to ban students from defending, let us say, conservative or liberal causes in political science classes, a serious free speech issue would be raised. Therefore there are real limits to permissible viewpoint discrimination within the classroom, even if it is hard to police the relevant boundaries. Certainly the university's permissible limits over the classroom do not extend to the campus in general. We could not allow major restrictions on what students and faculty may say when they are not in class. A university could not say that, outside of class, students can talk only about subjects of the university's choice.

From these various propositions, we might adopt a principle: *The university can impose subject matter or other restrictions on speech only to the extent that the restrictions are closely related to its educational mission.* This proposition contains both an authorization to the university and sharp limitations on what it may do. There is a close parallel here with decisions about what to include or exclude from libraries and about how to fund the arts;[37] in all these contexts, certain forms of content discrimination are inescapable (see chapter 7). But in cases in which the educational mission is not reasonably at stake, restrictions on speech should be invalidated. Certainly this would be true in most cases in which a university attempts to impose a political orthodoxy, whether inside or outside the classroom. We might react to the existence of implicit viewpoint discrimination by saying that it is hard for courts to police, but nonetheless a real offense to both academic aspirations and free speech principles.

How does this proposition bear on the hate speech issue? Perhaps a university could use its frequently exercised power over speech in order to argue for certain kinds of hate speech codes. Perhaps it could say that when it legitimately controls speech, it does so in order to promote its educational mission, which inevitably entails limits on who may say what. Perhaps a university could be allowed to conclude that its educational mission requires unusually firm controls on hate speech, so as not to compromise the values of education itself.

In this regard the university might emphasize that it has a special obligation to protect all of its students as equal members of the community. This obligation calls for restrictions on what faculty members may say. The university might believe that certain narrowly defined forms of hate speech are highly destructive to the students' chance to learn. It might think that black students and women can be effectively excluded by certain forms of hate speech. Probably a university should be given more leeway to restrict hate speech than a state or locality, precisely because it ought to receive the benefit of the doubt when it invokes concerns of this kind. Surely the educational mission ought to grant the university somewhat greater room to maneuver, especially in light of the complexity and delicacy of the relevant policy questions. Courts might also hesitate before finding viewpoint discrimination or impermissible selectivity. Perhaps there should be a presumption in favor of a university's judgment that narrowly defined hate speech directed at blacks or women produces harm that is especially threatening to the educational enterprise.

This conclusion is buttressed by two additional factors. First, there are numerous colleges and universities. Many students can choose among a range of alternatives, and a restriction in one, two, or more imposes an extremely small incursion into the system of free expression. Colleges that restrict a large amount of speech may find themselves with few students, and in any case other institutions will be available. Second, the Constitution is itself committed to the elimination of second-class citizenship, and this commitment makes it hard to say that an educational judgment opposed to certain forms of hate speech is impermissibly partisan.

I think that an analysis of this kind would justify two different sorts of approaches to the general issue of hate speech on campus. First, a university might regulate hate speech, narrowly defined, as simply a part of its general class of restrictions on speech that is incompatible with the educational mission. On this approach, there would be no restriction specifically directed against hate speech—no campus "speech code"—but a general, suitably defined requirement of decency and civility, and this requirement would regulate hate speech as well as other forms of abuse. Just as a university might ban the use of profanity in class, or personally abusive behavior on campus, so it might stop racial epithets and similar expressions of hatred or contempt. This is not to say that students and teachers who violate this ban must be expelled or suspended. Generally informal sanctions, involving conversations rather than punishment, are much to be preferred. But the Constitution should not stand as a barrier to approaches of this sort, so long as the university is neutral in this way.

Second, courts should allow narrowly defined hate speech restrictions even if those restrictions are not part of general proscriptions on indecent or uncivil behavior. For example, Stanford now forbids speech that amounts to "harassment by personal vilification." (Stanford is a private university, free from constitutional restraint, but it has chosen to comply with its understanding of what the First Amendment means as applied to public universities.) Under the Stanford rule, speech qualifies as regulable "harassment" if it (1) is intended to insult or stigmatize an individual or a small number of individuals on the basis of their sex, race, color, handicap, religion, sexual orientation, or national and ethnic origin, (2) is addressed directly to the individual or individuals whom it insults or stigmatizes, and (3) makes use of insulting or "fighting" words or nonverbal symbols. To qualify under (3), the speech must by its "very utterance inflict injury or tend to incite to an immediate breach of the peace," and must be "commonly understood to convey direct and visceral hatred and contempt for human beings on the basis of" one of the grounds enumerated in (2).[38]

The Stanford regulation should not be faulted for excessive breadth. It is quite narrowly defined. If a public university adopted it, the major constitutional problem, fueled by the outcome in *R.A.V.*, would not be breadth but unacceptable selectivity. Why has the university not controlled other forms of "fighting words," like the word "fascist," or "commie," or "bastard"? Does its selectivity show an impermissible motivation? Shouldn't we find its selectivity to be impermissibly partisan? I do not think that we should. A university could reasonably and neutrally decide that the harms caused by the regulated fighting words are, at least in the university setting, more severe than the harms caused by other kinds of fighting words. I conclude that public universities may regulate speech of the sort controlled by the Stanford regulation and probably go somewhat further, and that such restrictions should not be invalidated as impermissibly selective.

We can also use this discussion as a basis for exploring the question of the university's power over employees, recently arising out of the highly publicized decision of the City University of New York to remove Dr. Leonard Jeffries as chair of the black studies department at City College. Jeffries had reportedly made a range of apparently anti-Semitic remarks, blaming rich Jews for the black slave trade, complaining that Russian Jews and "their financial partners, the Mafia, put together a financial system of destruction of black people," and claiming that Jews and Italians had "planned, plotted, and programmed out of Hollywood" to denigrate blacks in films. Could the City University take these alleged remarks as a reason to remove Jeffries from his position as department chair? (We should agree that removal could be justified if, as some say, it was a response to an inadequate record of publication, to poor research, or to low-quality work.)

The answer depends on whether the removal was based on an effort neutrally to promote educational goals, or whether it was instead an effort to punish the expression of a controversial point of view. In the abstract this question is hard to answer, but it can be clarified through examples. Under the First Amendment, a public university could not fire a mathematics professor because he is a Republican, extremely conservative, or a sharp critic of the Supreme Court; such a discharge could not plausibly be connected with legitimate concerns about job performance. Even if the mathematics professor was a department chair, these political convictions are unrelated to job performance.

On the other hand, a university could surely fire the head of an admissions committee who persisted in making invidiously derogatory comments about blacks, women, and Jews. It would be reasonable for the university to say that someone who makes such comments cannot perform his job, which includes attracting good students, male and female, and of various races and religions. The discharge of the admissions head would not really be based on viewpoint; it would be part of a viewpoint-neutral effort to ensure that the head can do what he is supposed to do. Much the same could be said of a university president or many other high-visibility public employees. Consider the fact that the President, or a Governor, is freely permitted to fire high-level officials who make statements that compromise job performance, even if those statements are political in nature; if the Secretary of State says publicly that the President is a fool, or even that the President's policy toward Russia is senseless, the President can tell the Secretary to seek employment elsewhere.

It seems to follow that a university could remove a department chair if his comments make him unable successfully to undertake his ordinary duties as chair. The governing principle seems to be this: *A university can penalize speech if and only if it can show that the relevant speech makes it very difficult or impossible for the employee adequately to perform his job.* Whenever a university seeks to punish speech, it should face a large burden to show that it is behaving neutrally, and not trying to punish a disfavored point of view. On this approach, teachers and researchers will almost always be protected. Controversial political statements will not be a sufficient basis for punishment or discharge. A political science professor may criticize (or endorse) the President without becoming less able to perform the job, and most teachers will be able to say whatever they like without subjecting themselves to the possibility of discipline. It follows that the City College could not punish (as it tried to do) a philosophy professor for publishing the view that blacks are, on average, intellectually inferior to whites. It also follows that the City College could not remove Jeffries from his tenured position merely because he made actually or apparently anti-Semitic statements.

But we can imagine a range of statements that might make job performance quite difficult, at least for someone in a high-level administrative position—statements, for example, expressing general contempt for students and colleagues, a refusal to participate in the academic enterprise, or hatred directed against people who are part of the university community. Perhaps such statements would not be sufficient to allow discharge from a faculty position, but they could make it hard for the relevant speakers to perform as deans, as admissions officers, or as chairs of departments. In the Jeffries case, the best argument in favor of the City University of New York would be that it is difficult for someone to succeed as chair of a prominent black studies department if he has made sharply derogatory statements about members of other groups defined in racial, religious, or ethnic terms. This argument would not allow Jeffries to be discharged from his position as professor, but it should allow him to be removed from the position of department chair, which involves a range of distinctive public tasks. It follows that, on the facts I have assumed, the City College did not violate Jeffries' First Amendment rights. Of course, the case would be different if Jeffries could prove that the City College was reacting not to impaired job performance but to its own disapproval of Jeffries' point of view.

An opposing principle would take the following form. *A university should not be permitted to burden or to deny benefits to an employee on the basis of the employee's point of view, even if the point of view does damage job performance.* On this view, people who disapprove of the point of view—students, other faculty, potential contributors—should not be permitted to enshrine their own views by affecting the university's decisions about employees. We might argue for this principle on the ground that there should be no "heckler's veto" against unpopular opinions. We should not have a system in which people who dislike a certain point of view can stop dissenters from assuming prominent positions in the university.

This argument is not without force, but I do not think that it should be adopted. Everyone seems to agree that the President and the Governor may make hiring decisions on the basis of viewpoint; it would not make sense to disable the President from ensuring that high-level employees do not try, through speech, to undermine the President's program. Any resulting interference with the system of free expression seems minimal, and the President has a strong need for a loyal staff. Similarly, universities have powerful and legitimate reasons to expect their employees to perform their jobs, especially if those employees are engaged in highly public administrative tasks, and especially if professors who are not performing such tasks are not threatened. At least under ordinary circumstances, there will be no substantial interference with the system of free expression if universities are given the narrow authority for which I have argued. I conclude that outside of legitimate judgments about quality and subject matter, universities may punish employees for their speech only in a narrow set of circumstances—almost always involving highly public, administrative positions—in which the relevant speech makes it difficult or impossible for employees to perform their jobs.

It follows from all this that the national government should abandon its efforts to subject private universities to the constraints of the First Amendment. This is an area in which national authorities should proceed with caution. Of course, we could imagine experiments that we might deplore, but there is no reason for the federal government to require uniformity on this complex matter.

It is often said that government may not regulate speech on the basis of viewpoint. The claim contains a good deal of sense. It explains much of free speech law. It helps us make sensible distinctions between different restrictions on speech.

But the ban on viewpoint discrimination is hardly self-applying. Whether we have a case of viewpoint discrimination is itself a function of viewpoint, or more accurately of a complex set of judgments about the harms produced by speech. In the context of cross-burning and other forms of hate speech, I have argued that we ought not to see impermissible partisanship in a social judgment on behalf of narrow restrictions on speech. The government

may neutrally attempt to counter the threat of race-related violence and the subjective and objective harms produced by certain,
narrowly defined hate speech. The point suggests that there is no
constitutional problem with enhanced penalties for hate crimes. I
conclude that the prohibition on viewpoint discrimination does
lie at the core of the First Amendment, but that there is no impermissible discrimination in these restrictions. This claim is important, for similar issues arise in other areas, including that of
pornography, where we will soon find a number of surprises.

Chapter 7

More Hard Cases

Pornography, Government Arts Funding, and Corporate Speech

ALL OVER THE COUNTRY, states and localities—not to mention the federal government—are considering new proposals to regulate pornography. At the national level, government has started to reassess its current policies for funding art. May government money be denied to feminists or homosexuals? In the next decade, it is likely that government will try to regulate speech by corporations. Here the constitutional standards are especially ill-developed. May a state say that a corporation cannot speak on behalf of a political candidate?

In this chapter I attempt to answer these questions. I conclude that government should not regulate sexually explicit speech because it is "offensive," but that it may enact narrowly drawn restrictions on materials that combine sex with violence or coercion; that government has broad discretion to fund or not to fund art, but that it must avoid conspicuous or explicit viewpoint discrimination; and that government may not impose special controls on corporate speech. These are simple statements, but they conceal some real complexities. The complexities go to the heart of the constitutional prohibition on impermissible selectivity in the regulation of speech.

209

Pornography

The area of pornography has fueled some of the most intense debates in all of constitutional law—not just in the last few years, but in many of the major periods of free speech doctrine. Restrictions on sexually explicit materials raise problems of discrimination and selectivity in an especially difficult and illuminating place. It is therefore worthwhile to devote a fair amount of space to the issue.

With respect to regulation of sexually explicit speech, two positions have captured the current constitutional landscape. They also seem to dominate popular debate. According to the first view, often coming from religious groups, some categories of expression are simply excluded from the category of protected "speech." They consist of words and pictures, to be sure, but they are not "speech" within the meaning of the First Amendment. They are degrading, disgusting, subversive to traditional morality, and offensive, and they do not promote the purposes for which speech is given constitutional protection. In the well-known formulation from the Supreme Court's *Miller* case, "obscenity" is defined to include materials that appeal to the prurient interest, are patently offensive by contemporary community standards, include sexual conduct specifically described by state law, and lack serious social value when the materials are taken as a whole.[1] Under current law, obscenity appears not to count as speech within the meaning of the First Amendment.

There are many puzzles in the *Miller* test. For one thing, the test seems to require an odd psychological state from the judge and jury. In order to be regulable, the materials must be simultaneously sexually arousing (the "prurient interest" part of the test) and "patently offensive." This is not an unrecognizable psychological state, but it entails a certain dissonance, and a certain attitude about sexuality, that are likely to be unusual or at least to be rarely confessed. For this reason, among others, the *Miller* test is highly speech-protective. It is extremely difficult to win an obscenity prosecution except in the case of materials that consist solely of masturbatory aids. Most art and literature, even if it is sexually explicit, will have serious value as a matter of law, and this part of the test will immunize it from regulation. There are some frivolous and highly publicized prosecutions—like those based on the work of the gay artist Robert Mapplethorpe and the rap group 2 Live Crew—but realistically speaking, most people involved in the production of sexually explicit work have little to fear from the *Miller* test.

The "serious value" part of the test has proved particularly helpful to defendants in obscenity cases. Some people think that courts should not be entitled to ask whether speech has "serious value" or not. But under any two-tier system, this question will be relevant, and as it is administered, the "value" test has not allowed courts to engage in ad hoc inquiries into whether they approve of the material at issue. Instead, it has helped distinguish between materials that are basically masturbatory aids and other sorts of speech, and done so in a way that makes it extremely hard for the state to succeed in a prosecution.

Despite the protectiveness of the *Miller* standard, it is unclear whether the justifications for regulating obscenity are consistent with a proper interpretation of the First Amendment. "Patent offensiveness" is the central defining harm of obscene speech, with offensiveness understood as including both revulsion at certain sexually explicit material and a social concern about the changed and debased tone of a society that is pervaded by obscenity. These justifications are typical moral reasons for regulation. Although controversial, they should not always be disparaged. The problem is that under the First Amendment, government is not supposed to regulate speech because people are offended at the ideas that it contains. Is the regulation of obscenity an effort to censor speech containing ideas that people dislike? This is not a simple question. Perhaps the obscenity approach is directed not at ideas, but only at a particular means of expression. Perhaps it is more akin to a ban on loud noises than to a ban on speech containing officially disapproved views. But these lines are thin, and it is certainly plausible to say that the justification for regulating obscenity is much like a ban on objectionable ideas.

Does the *Miller* test discriminate on the basis of viewpoint? It seems clear that a decision to regulate obscenity is far from entirely neutral, since it makes regulation turn on the content of the speech and even on existing social attitudes. Critics of *Miller* make this point in support of their view that all sexually explicit materials should be protected by the First Amendment. But the Court appears to think that so long as something as general and legitimate as "contemporary community standards" is the basis for regulation, controls on obscenity are at least neutral with respect to point of view. Such controls are nonpartisan in the crucial sense that the government does not single out certain views for disapproval, or make those views the trigger for the imposition of legal restrictions. At least so it is ordinarily thought; I will return to the point.

The opposing view, coming from civil libertarians, is that all speech stands on the same ground and that government has absolutely no business censoring speech merely because some people, or some officials, are puritanical or offended by it.[2] On this view, obscenity is speech, not sex—just as a movie filled with violence is a representation rather than the thing itself. And on this view, a decision to single out obscenity for special treatment, and to censor it, is a conspicuous violation of the neutrality requirement of the First Amendment. The use of contemporary community standards just aggravates this problem of partisanship because those standards are themselves biased or affected by viewpoint.

More recently, an entirely new position, originally developed by Andrea Dworkin and Catharine MacKinnon, has emerged on the question of legal control of pornography.[3] This position is frequently confused with the "contemporary community standards" approach, but it is actually quite different. As I understand it here, the third position is that sexually explicit speech should be regulated not because it is offensive and sexually explicit (the problem of "obscenity") but instead because and when it produces harm through merging sex with violence or coercion (the problem of "pornography"). The violence and coercion may occur either in the production of the material or in its use.

I will therefore be dealing principally with violent pornography and with the claim that pornography should be regulated because and when it causes harm, especially against women. Not all of those who focus on this problem understand it in this way. Some people treat pornography as a problem of sex discrimination not only because it is associated with violence, but because it is associated with subordination and dehumanization more generally.[4] It is certainly reasonable to think that nonviolent material might nonetheless portray women in a subordinate way, or involve subordination in its production, or treat women as objects for the use and control of others, and that here too there is a reason for legal concern. If we moved beyond violence, we might ask more broadly about the role of pornography in creating inequality, in part through its place in the sexual subordination or objectification of women. I restrict the discussion here, however, to pornography as an object of regulation only to the extent that it is associated with violence or coercion either in its production or in its use. It need not be emphasized that subjection to violence and coercion is an especially important ingredient in sexual inequality. I focus on violent material because the broader understanding of the harms that pornography produces raises some trickier First Amendment difficulties, and it is helpful to begin with a relatively narrow understanding.

On this third view, the problem of pornography does not stem from offense, from public access to sexual explicit materials, from an unregulated erotic life, or from violation of traditional values or community standards. Instead the problem consists of tangible real-world harms, produced by the portrayal of women and children as objects for the control and use of others, most prominently through sexual violence. On this view, the goal of regulation is not to stop "offense" or to protect current social values, but to recognize and counteract sexual practices that are a vehicle for sex discrimination. Materials that eroticize rape and other forms of violence should be treated as a part of sex discrimination.

Because of its focus on harms, this third approach creates not a criminal ban, but a civil remedy for those who can prove harm as a result of pornography. This remedy would work most simply for women who have been abused in the production of pornography. It would also offer a remedy for women who can prove, under the normal legal standards, that they have been harmed by the use of pornography in sex crimes. In both cases, the usual remedy would be an award of monetary damages for actual harm. Under some proposals, an injunction would be available to prevent continued distribution or use of harmful material. For example, a woman forced to participate in a pornographic movie might be permitted to enjoin further sale of the movie. Of course no one would be required to bring suit; this decision would be made by individual victims.

It is notable that under this third approach, the category of regulable speech might be relatively broad or extremely narrow. We might, for example, adopt the basic approach, but use it to allow regulation or private remedies against some subset of speech that is already regulable as obscenity under *Miller*. We might decide to protect all material with serious social value, or refuse to regulate speech unless it not only combines sex with violence, but also has little real cognitive content and amounts to "hard-core" pornography. In any case, it is fully possible that the category of regulable speech would be smaller than the category that is now subject to regulation under the antiobscenity approach. This important point is often missed. The real difference between the third approach and the first lies not in greater breadth of coverage or in more censorship, but in the emphasis on discrimination and harm to women rather than offense or contemporary community standards.

How is the First Amendment issue affected if women injured by pornography are given a civil action and if criminal prosecutors have no enforcement authority? In some ways, the civil action helps alleviate the First Amendment concerns. There is a special problem whenever the government decides to proceed against speech that it deems harmful, and a private suit does not pose this problem. There seems to be no serious free speech issue if a woman injured in the production of pornography brings suit to recover damages for the harms done to her, at least if the speech is not political. On the other hand, the state is unquestionably involved when it awards damages for harms done by speech, and we know from *New York Times v. Sullivan* (discussed in chapter 2) that the First Amendment imposes barriers to government efforts to use civil actions to force speakers to pay for the real costs of their speech. The parallel to *New York Times* is very close if the government said that anyone who produces art or literature must pay for injuries that result from his work.

The question is not limited to material with sexual violence. Dostoevsky's *Crime and Punishment* is said to have been followed by a series of copycat murders in Russia. One problem with a civil action is that any judge or jury decision about causation might be unreliable, suspect, or affected by bias of various sorts. And if we are talking about speech that is genuinely protected by the First Amendment, or at the free speech core, *New York Times* seems to say that government may not require speakers to "internalize" the costs of what they say. It is possible to question this view, but it seems to be the law, and so long as it is, a civil action for harms that result from speech is not fundamentally different from criminal prosecution.

It is often suggested that the antipornography position raises especially serious free speech questions and that the antiobscenity and "no regulation" positions are far preferable. In fact, however, there is a quite straightforward argument for regulating at least some narrowly defined class of pornographic materials. The first point, made by traditional obscenity law as well, is that much pornographic material lies far from the center of the First Amendment concern. Under current doctrine, and under any sensible system of free expression, speech that lies at the periphery of constitutional concern may be regulated on the basis of a lesser showing of harm than speech that lies at the core. As we have seen, the definition of the core and the periphery is not simple. Under the Madisonian view or nearly any alternative standard, however, at least some pornographic materials should be placed in the periphery. Such materials fall in the same category as commercial speech, libel of private persons, conspiracies, unlicensed medical or legal advice, attempted bribes, perjury, threats, and so forth. The reason is that these forms of speech do not amount to part of social deliberation about public matters, or about matters at all—even if this category is construed quite broadly, as it should be, and even if we insist, as we should, that emotive and cognitive capacities are frequently intertwined in deliberative processes, and that any sharp split between "emotion" and "cognition" would be untrue to political and social discussion.

An important qualification is necessary here. Those who write or read sexually explicit material often can claim important expressive and deliberative interests. Sexually explicit works can be highly relevant to the development of individual capacities. For many, it is an important vehicle for self-discovery and self-definition.[5]

Even if such speech is not political in the constitutionally relevant sense, it is entitled to a degree of constitutional protection
because of its close connection with other free speech values. In
light of the complexity of sexuality, perhaps the same can be said
of some of the most graphic forms of sexually explicit material,
even if it features violence. But even if all this is true, at least
some sexually explicit material seems far from the center of constitutional concern. It can be regulated on the basis of a lesser
showing of harm.

The second point is that pornographic material causes sufficient harms to justify regulation under the more lenient standards
applied to speech that does not fit within the free speech core. Of
course it is possible to question the extent of the relevant harms.
The empirical debates are complex, and I will only summarize
some of the evidence here. But the harms do create a far stronger
case for regulation than underlies the antiobscenity position,
which relies on less tangible aesthetic goals and on the vaguer and
constitutionally troublesome idea of adherence to conventional
moral standards. Notably, the relevant harms consist generally of
acts committed against women by men. I suggest that the category
of regulable speech might well exclude homosexual pornography,
for which the same showing of harm cannot be made (so far as I
am aware).

The harms fall in three categories. First, the existence of the
pornography market produces a number of harms to models and
actresses.[6] Many women, usually very young, are coerced into
pornography. Others are abused and mistreated, often in
grotesque ways, once they enter the pornography "market." To be
sure, some women who participate are not abused or coerced in
the way made relevant by the criminal law (though many of these
begin when they are very young and are treated as, or are, prosti-
tutes). It is therefore tempting to respond that government should
adopt a less restrictive alternative. Rather than regulating speech,
government should ban the coercion or mistreatment, as indeed
current state law does. Usually this is the better strategy: If someone has unlawfully gotten access to confidential materials relating
to the government, he should be punished for the illegal behavior,
but not for the publication unless the ordinary "clear and present
danger" standard can be met. But in this peculiar setting, with

low-value speech and special enforcement problems, such an alternative would probably be a recipe for disaster, since it would simply allow existing practices to continue. The explanation is straightforward.

It is hard enough to bring an action for rape and sexual assault. The difficulty becomes all the greater when the victims are young women coerced into and abused during the production of pornography. Often the victims will be reluctant to put themselves through the experience, and possible humiliation and expense, of initiating a proceeding. Often they will have extremely little credibility even if they are willing to do so. In this light, the only realistically effective way to eliminate the practice is to eliminate or reduce the financial benefits.[7]

As noted, some or even much participation in pornography may well be voluntary in the legally relevant sense, and a regulatory approach would therefore ban far more material than should be controlled if the argument is based solely on coercion in the production. But it appears that if we really want to stop the abuse and coercion, we must accept regulation that is overly broad in just this way.

To make a final assessment of this matter, it would probably be necessary to have a full understanding of the actual degree of coercion in the production of pornographic materials. If the degree is relatively low, the level of overbreadth would be unacceptable. On the other hand, no serious problem seems to be created by a damages remedy for those who can prove **actual harm** in the production of the material.

Second, there is a causal connection between pornography and violence against women.[8] The extent of the effect and the precise relationship between exposure to pornography and sexual violence are sharply disputed. No one thinks that sexual violence would disappear if pornography were eliminated, or that most consumers of pornography act out what they see or read. But a review of the literature suggests that pornography does increase the incidence of sexual violence against women. The evidence includes laboratory experiments, longitudinal studies of the effects of increased availability of pornography, and victim and police testimony.[9] In laboratory experiments, male interest in rape increases after exposure to certain kinds of pornography. In some longitudinal studies, there appears to be a connection between sexual violence and free availability of pornography. There is a good deal of victim and police testimony tending to show a causal relation or at least a correlation between use of pornography and some violent acts. All three sources indicate a plausible connection between exposure to sexually violent material and sexually violent acts.

There are of course severe methodological problems with any evidence of this kind. Laboratory experiments may inadequately connect to the real world. Victim and police testimony is anecdotal. Longitudinal studies cannot easily control for other variables. Even if there were a close causal connection between violent pornography and real-world violence, social science would have a hard time in proving it. But the current evidence suggests quite a bit. It indicates that the real question is not the existence of a causal connection but its degree. In light of current information, it is at least reasonable to think that there would be significant benefits from regulation of violent pornography.

It would probably be best to respond to this evidence by creating a private cause of action for those who can prove that they have been harmed through the production or use of pornography. This approach would be preferable to a new criminal action brought by prosecutors. The incentives of the prosecutor may not always be aligned with the interests of injured parties. As noted in earlier discussion, it would be an advantage of a private cause of action that the plaintiff would be required to plead and prove actual harm.

The first two points I have mentioned—involving harm to participants and a causal connection with violent acts—may well suggest that antipornography legislation should be addressed only to movies and pictures, and exempt the written word. Of course, it is only in movies and pictures that abuse of performers will occur. (One might similarly support a law against child pornography in movies and pictures while allowing written essays that amount to child pornography.) Moreover, the evidence on pornography as a stimulus to violence deals mostly with movies and pictures, and the immediacy and vividness of these media suggest a possible distinction from written texts. I do not discuss the appropriate breadth of an antipornography statute here. But the possibility of exempting written texts, no matter what they contain, suggests the weakness of the objection from neutrality. A statute that is directed at violent or coercive pornography, but that exempts written texts, is very plausibly treated as harm-based rather than viewpoint-based.

The third point is that pornography promotes behavior toward women that is degrading and dehumanizing and that includes illegal conduct, including sexual harassment. The pornography industry operates as a conditioning factor for some men and women, a factor that has some consequences for the existence of equality between men and women. Of course it is more symptom than cause; but it is cause as well. One need not believe that the elimination of violent pornography would bring about sexual equality, eliminate sexual violence, or change social attitudes in any fundamental way, in order to agree that a regulatory effort would have an effect in reducing violence and in diminishing views that contribute to existing inequalities.

It is revealing to consider in this connection the general public reaction to the recent feminist attack on pornography. The *New Republic*—a journal priding itself on its belief in racial and sexual equality—gave the title "Big Boobs" to its response to a Justice Department Report that was sympathetic to feminist claims.[10] It thus sought to ridicule the authors of the report by depicting them as parts of the female anatomy. On the cover, the *New Republic* carried a drawing of Attorney General Edwin Meese as an attractive woman, with the description, "Fast, Loose, and Stacked." The cover caricatured the Commission by describing the Attorney General as a woman and, more particularly, as a pornographic model. There are of course limits to how much we can learn from journalistic attempts at humor. But I suggest that the New Republic's dismissive coverage of the report quite inadvertently and unself-consciously confirmed some of the anti-pornography movement's argument about the relationships among sexuality, pornography, and inequality.

The point suggests that it is indeed plausible to think that pornography sometimes plays a part in "silencing women." It does this not by criminalizing their speech, but by helping to discredit it in a way that has consequences for the attitudes of men and women alike. The notion that "no means yes" has grotesque consequences in the context of women's complaints about pornography. In general, it seems fair to say that women's speech is not given the same respect as men's speech, and this phenomenon will naturally lead women to speak less than men. All this is partly a result of the sexual objectification of women. No one should claim that pornography is the ultimate cause of sexual objectification, or that sexual violence and inequality are attributable above all to pornography. But pornography can be a contributing factor.

Hard questions, however. are raised by the claim that the argument from "silencing" properly plays a significant role in the First Amendment inquiry. This form of silencing is produced by social attitudes resulting from speech itself, and probably one cannot find that to be a reason for regulation without making excessive inroads on a system of free expression. Many forms of speech do indeed have silencing effects, and it is not clear that this is a sufficient reason to regulate them.[11] There are two problems here. The first is that it is uncertain whether the form of silencing that results from speech itself should be, in principle, a basis for regulating speech. The second problem is that even if we resolve the question of principle in favor of the "silencing" argument, our institutions are peculiarly unlikely to be able to make reliable judgments on the issue. It is plausible to think that would-be speakers are often silenced by especially vigorous challenges, and government regulation of those challenges, based on "silencing," might well be rooted in objectionable motivations and untrustworthy conclusions. Much remains to be done on this difficult subject. But in this area, it is best to try to avoid the most controversial and adventurous claims, and so I do not rely on the silencing argument here.

Taken as a whole, these various considerations suggest a quite conventional argument for regulation of certain forms of pornography, one that fits well with the rest of free speech law. We have seen, for example, that misleading commercial speech is regulable because it is not entitled to the highest form of protection and because the harms produced by such speech are sufficient to allow for regulation. The same is true of libel of private persons, criminal solicitation, unlicensed legal or medical advice, and conspiracy. In these and other areas, it is inadequate to offer the usual response, coming from Justice Brandeis, that "more speech" rather than "forced silence" is the appropriate remedy for harmful speech. When speech falls in the second tier and produces significant predictable harm, more speech is not always the constitutionally required remedy; consider false or misleading commercial speech. It is also possible to think that more speech is an insufficiently effective remedy for the harms produced by pornography, in part because of the odd method by which pornography communicates its "message." I suggest that certain forms of pornography, especially violent material, should be approached similarly. Indeed, the argument for regulation—in view of the nature of the material and the evidence of harm—is far more powerful than the corresponding argument for many forms of speech now subject to government control.

The antipornography approach also has significant advantages over the two more prominent approaches to the subject. As compared with the view that all sexually explicit speech is protected, the antipornography approach recognizes that it is extremely difficult to run a system of free expression without distinguishing among different categories of expression in terms of their centrality to the First Amendment guarantee. It also recognizes, as that position does not, that violent pornography is a serious problem, at least as serious as many of the problems that have been found sufficient to call for governmental controls on speech. As compared with the "moral consensus" position, the antipornography approach has the advantage of concentrating on real-world harms rather than the less tangible, more aesthetic problems captured in the use of contemporary community standards.

Strikingly, however, the antipornography position is by far the least well-represented of the three, not only in popular debate but also in current constitutional law. I believe that part of what has made the antipornography approach so controversial is that it is rooted in beliefs that the sexual and reproductive status quo, as between men and women, is sometimes a place for inequality, that women are treated unequally to men, that sexual violence by men against women is a greater social problem than sexual violence by women against men, and that social inequality can be both expressed and perpetuated through sexuality. The rejection of this insistence on the need for a movement in the direction of sex equality—a refusal to recognize existing inequality, turned into a claim of partiality—has become critical to constitutional law. The objection here is that the antipornography position is selective (especially compared with the antiobscenity approach), and that in its selectivity lies in its partisanship, which is what makes it fatally inferior to its competitors. Here we can find many of the same issues I have discussed in connection with the cross-burning issue.

In the leading decision on the subject, the United States Court of Appeals for the Seventh Circuit, in a case affirmed summarily by the Supreme Court,[12] invalidated an antipornography ordinance. The court reasoned that an argument that would allow regulation of pornographic materials by reference to the harms referred to above is worse, not better, than the obscenity approach. Indeed, it would be worse than the obscenity approach even if the category of suppressed speech turned out to be far narrower than the category that can be suppressed under existing law. According to the court, any statute that imposed penalties on a subcategory of obscene speech, defined by reference to these harms, would be unconstitutional. It would discriminate on the basis of viewpoint and thus violate a core First Amendment constraint.

For the court, the key point is that such an approach would constitute impermissible "thought control," since it would "establish[] an 'approved' view of women, of how they may react to sexual encounters, [and] of how the sexes may relate to each other." Under the antipornography approach, depictions of sexuality that involve rape and violence against women may be subject to regulation. But depictions that do not are uncontrolled. Sexually explicit materials that portray men and women on a place of equality are not subject to restriction. It is the nonneutrality of antipornography legislation—its focus on the subordination of women—that is its central defect. People with the approved view can speak; people with the disapproved view cannot. That, in the court's view, is what the First Amendment centrally prohibits.

The general point is both correct and important: Viewpoint

discrimination usually offends the First Amendment. Indeed, the pornography restriction might seem even worse than the restriction in *R.A.V.*: the latter restriction was based on subject matter and not viewpoint-discriminatory on its face. But especially in this setting, the category of viewpoint-neutrality turns out to be far more difficult to understand than appears at first glance. As we saw in chapter 6, First Amendment law contains several categories of speech that are subject to ban or regulation even though they are nonneutral, or viewpoint-discriminatory, in very much the same sense as antipornography legislation. Consider the bans on advertising for casino gambling, cigarette smoking, and alcohol; the SEC's regulation of proxy statements; the controls on what employers may say during a union election; the prohibition of advertising for illegal products. In these cases, the partisanship of the regulation is not apparent because there is so firm a consensus on the presence of real-world harms that the objection from neutrality does not even register. The spectre of partisanship does not arise because a decision to control the speech in question has obvious legitimate justifications. An extension of the prohibition to other areas appears not compelled by neutrality but instead an unnecessary form of gratuitous censorship.

More fundamentally, the current law of obscenity might readily be regarded as nonneutral. In one sense, it is not a bit less partisan than antipornography legislation. The line drawn by existing law makes it critical whether the speech in question departs from contemporary community standards. Those standards are the trigger for regulation as prurient and "patently offensive." But if contemporary community standards are, with respect to offensiveness and prurience, themselves partisan and reflective of a particular viewpoint (and it would be most surprising if they were not), then a decision to make contemporary standards the basis for regulation might well be thought unacceptably partisan. Imagine if the government said that contemporary community standards would be the basis for regulating depictions of race relations. Surely this would be invalid. On what theory, then, can antiobscenity law be treated as neutral and antipornography law as partisan?

The answer lies in the fact that antiobscenity law takes existing social consensus as the foundation for decision, whereas antipornography law is directed against that consensus. Existing practice is the target of the antipornography approach, or what that approach seeks to change. Existing practice is the very basis of the antiobscenity approach, or what that approach seeks to preserve. Obscenity law, insofar as it is tied to community standards, is deemed neutral, but only because the class of prohibited speech is defined by reference to existing social values. Antipornography legislation is deemed impermissibly partisan because the prohibited class of speech is defined by less widely accepted ideas about equality between men and women—more precisely, by reference to a belief that equality does not always exist even in the private realm, that sexual violence by men against women is a greater problem than sexual violence by women against men, and that the sexual status quo is an ingredient in sexual inequality.

Along the axis of neutrality, however, the distinction between antiobscenity and antipornography law cannot be sustained. That distinction would be plausible only if existing norms and practices themselves embodied equality. Since they do not, the distinction fails. Indeed, one could imagine a society in which the harms produced by pornography were so widely acknowledged and so generally condemned that an antipornography ordinance would not be regarded as viewpoint-based at all.

Perhaps it could be responded that the state acts with sufficient neutrality if it makes existing social standards—whatever their content—the basis for regulation. Perhaps the state does not act neutrally if and only if it selects a specific set of standards as the basis for regulation. But this argument would not be easy to sustain. Everyone knows the content of existing social standards, at least in general terms. In adopting an obscenity law, the state may have refused to make particular choices among those standards, but its endorsement of prevailing attitudes can hardly be deemed neutral. In principle, there is no real difference between a state's decision to use existing attitudes toward race relations as the basis for regulation, and a state's decision to single out a particular attitude toward race relations as the basis of choice. The same is true for sexually explicit material.

I conclude that the regulation of pornography is no more partisan than regulation of obscenity, and indeed that the argument for regulation of materials that combine sex with violence or coercion is more powerful than the corresponding argument for regulating obscenity. From this we might be tempted to conclude that both obscenity law and antipornography law are invalid—that they both violate the neutrality requirement. I suggest a different conclusion. Since perfectly conventional measures regulating speech are similarly partisan, and have properly been upheld, the objection from nonneutrality should be unpersuasive here as well. The standards for accepting laws that contain viewpoint discrimination seem to be met here. There are sufficient justifications made out in terms of tangible harms to women and children. There is a sufficient connection between the end—preventing those harms—and the means of allowing a remedy for demonstrable injury. Moreover, it is not impermissibly selective to aim at material that contains and promotes violence against women. This is so especially in light of the Constitution's commitment to the elimination of caste or second-class citizenship, a commitment that is violated by disproportionate violence against any social group defined in terms of a morally irrelevant characteristic. It should be recalled that the equal protection clause was originally an effort to counteract the disproportionate subjection of black people to private and public violence. An effort to counteract the disproportionate subjection of women to such violence is very much in keeping with the aspirations of the equal protection clause. Such an effort should not be deemed inconsistent with neutrality.

I do not say that it will be simple to design a regulation with sufficient clarity and narrowness. The Constitution protects most forms of sexually explicit speech. Experimentation with various clear and narrow alternatives should be encouraged in the future. A regulation of pornography might, for example, make an exception for material having serious social value—although even for such material, women should be allowed to recover damages for actual harms done to them in its production. In any case, we should be addressing issues of clarity and narrowness, not the question of neutrality. So long as any antipornography law has the requisite clarity and narrow scope, the appropriate forum for deliberation on this contested subject is the democratic process, not the judiciary. There should be no constitutional barrier to a narrowly defined prohibition on material that combines sex with coercion or violence against women.

It seems clear, for example, that a state should be allowed to impose special restrictions on a subset of speech that is already bannable under *Miller*, where the subset is defined by reference to materials containing sexual violence. A state should probably be allowed to extend its restrictions modestly further than *Miller*. In any case, much more enforcement effort should be directed to preventing the abuse of women and children in the production of pornography.

A final note. Nothing I have said here argues in favor of regulation of sexually explicit writing in general, or of the work of (say) Robert Mapplethorpe, an artist depicting (among other things) homosexual relations and recently subject to criminal prosecution. The antipornography argument is quite specific in its aims. It is not directed against sexually explicit materials as a whole. Indeed, we might find it an exceedingly strange artifact of current legal and popular thinking that an attack on material featuring sex and violence against women should be believed simultaneously to endanger art relating to homosexuality. The antipornography argument, rightly understood, calls for fierce protection of speech that complains explicitly or implicitly about discrimination against homosexuals, because that speech is "high-value" in the relevant sense and because it contains precisely none of the harms that call for regulation of pornography.

Funding the Arts

I now turn to the issue of government funding of the arts. This is an area of great interest in its own right. It is also an especially helpful place to explore problems of discrimination and selectivity in the distinctive context of funding (on current law and the *Rust* case, see chapter 4).

Some people think that government should remove itself from arts funding and allow all such decisions to be made through private markets. The argument seems extreme, because such markets contain strong biases of their own. They may well provide insufficient support for controversial or experimental work, or for art that questions the conventional wisdom. The removal of government funding would hardly return financial contributions to the arts to a neutral or just system. Just as political speech should be encouraged, so as to promote democratic deliberation, so too it is proper to fund art by public dollars, so as to improve cultural life and available opportunities for the citizenry.[13]

If government is to be involved in the process, however, there will be some hard free speech questions. Let me begin by illustrating some permissible funding decisions. The central point here is that government has limited resources with which to fund the arts, and its allocation is necessarily selective. Full funding is simply inconceivable. There are at least three conclusions that seem to follow.

First, government may refuse to fund speech that it can ban through the criminal law. A refusal to fund obscenity, or libelous speech, or incitement to crime, is therefore unobjectionable. The only qualification is that there must be procedural safeguards to ensure that the relevant speech is actually unprotected by the First Amendment.

Second, funding decisions that are based on qualitative or aesthetic judgments should be entirely legitimate, at least in most cases and at least as a presumption. The government should be permitted to fund projects that it considers to be of high caliber. Indeed, such judgments are inescapable for people who must allocate limited resources. Unless we are to use a lottery system, which would create obvious arbitrariness, selection among applicants would be impossible without aesthetic or qualitative judgments.

Third, decisions to fund projects on the basis of their subject matter should generally be uncontroversial. If the government wants to fund projects related to American history, Chaucer, World War II, the civil rights movement, Egypt, or the film industry, there is no basis for complaint. Surely it is legitimate for government to select some topics or areas for financial assistance. If we say that government may be in the business of funding the arts, we have almost concluded that government may select subjects or topics that it considers worthy of approval. (I discuss limits on this principle below.) Here too limited funds make any alternative approach unrealistic.

Taken together, these conclusions will authorize most of current practice for funding the arts. In all of these cases, government has legitimate reasons for selectivity. If government may make decisions by reference to subject matter, and if decisions about quality are allowed, current policies will generally be upheld.

Under what circumstances might serious First Amendment objections arise? The most obvious occur when government discriminates against people because of their point of view. Suppose that government decides to fund projects by Democrats but not Republicans, or only by people who have voted in favor of the current President. The case is an easy one; this is invalid. We have seen that the prohibition on discrimination based on point of view lies at the heart of the First Amendment. In this case, both the purpose and the effects of governmental action are objectionable. Moreover, government cannot provide a justification that shows why the context of funding calls up neutral justifications to allow it to act in this way.

The only possible reason for allowing this form of discrimination would rest on the taxpayers' unwillingness to subsidize art that they find abhorrent. This argument has played a major role in public debate, as people ask the supposedly rhetorical question: Shouldn't taxpayers be allowed to ensure that their money is allocated as they choose? But the question is anything but rhetorical. The taxpayers could not fund white artists and not black artists, or only artists who agreed to criticize affirmative action. If we allowed taxpayers to fund as they wished, we would permit funding decisions to skew artistic creations in accordance with prevailing political convictions, especially those of the government or of current majorities. This would allow government to give money only to people whose point of view it shared. At least in a world in which the government engages in a wide range of funding, this skewing effect on expression could not possibly be tolerated. It would run afoul of the core of the free speech guarantee.

Only slightly harder are cases in which government decides to fund only those projects that contain a particular, approved viewpoint. Imagine, for example, a law to the effect that the National Endowment for the Arts (NEA) will fund only those projects that deal favorably with the current performance of the American government, or only projects involving the Civil War that portray President Lincoln and General Grant in a certain light. The government cannot justify this kind of selectivity in constitutionally acceptable terms; it is plainly discriminating on the basis of viewpoint. An across-the-board ban on the funding of projects critical of government or embodying governmentally disapproved views would, at least usually, be impermissible.[14]

I say that viewpoint discrimination is "at least usually" impermissible, because there will be some possible counterexamples. Suppose, for example, that the government decides to fund programs for the celebration and possible export of democracy. Or suppose that it says that governmentally-funded portrayals of the Civil War cannot advocate slavery. Or suppose that it funds projects to discourage cigarette smoking or drug addiction. For reasons to be explored shortly, viewpoint discrimination of this kind may be acceptable in some circumstances.

From these claims, and with this qualification, it is possible to develop some tentative conclusions. The clearest constitutional violation consists of discrimination on the basis of point of view. Most other funding decisions will be permissible, for they will generally involve judgments covering subject matter or aesthetics. It follows that some of the hardest cases will arise when the relevant discrimination seems to involve subject matter or aesthetics but is in fact an effort to control a particular point of view.

We could do much worse than to build free speech principles on these conclusions. The only problem is that the line between the key categories is an elusive one. This is so, first, in the relatively uninteresting sense that there will be hard intermediate cases—cases that are at the borderline and for that reason difficult to decide. But it is also true in the far more troubling sense that the distinction is difficult to draw even as a conceptual matter. I have said that viewpoint discrimination is generally prohibited and that aesthetic or qualitative judgments are generally permitted. But judgments about aesthetics or quality often depend, at root, on ideas having a political or ideological component.

This is most obvious for people who think that art celebrating nazism or communism at least ordinarily cannot qualify as good art. Perhaps such people are right. Perhaps artistic creations must have a greater degree of nuance and humanity than is characteristic of artistic celebrations of pernicious ideologies. But the relationship between aesthetic judgments and political commitments is very general. The idea that yellow marks on a page, or a sentimental drawing of a kitten, or American flags marked with swastikas, should or should not qualify for funding might well be rooted in views, at least broadly speaking political in nature, about the appropriate character and aims of the arts. This claim seems to find confirmation in the numerous recent debates about the role played by point of view in evaluating artistic creations.[15] To say the least, judges and lawyers are not well-suited to assess these debates.

In these circumstances, the available options for law are few, and none of them is especially appealing. Realistically there are only three possibilities. The first is a constitutional principle that would forbid even aesthetic or subject matter judgments on the ground that these too are rooted in politics and in a sense point of view. But this principle would be intolerable. It would forbid selective funding of any sort, which is to say that it would forbid government funding entirely (short of an arbitrary lottery system). Such a solution would hardly be desirable in a world in which public funding is an important individual and collective good.

The second possible route would be to permit even the most conspicuously partisan funding decisions on the ground that sensible lines cannot be drawn between supposedly banned politically motivated decisions and supposedly permissible aesthetically motivated decisions. But this approach would also be intolerable. It would authorize the most egregious government interferences with artistic expression for the state's own partisan purposes. The result would be conspicuous violations of the free speech principle. We could not reasonably say that the state can award funds only to those artists who support the administration and its current programs.

The third and probably the only sensible solution is to apply the constitutional prohibition solely in the most straightforward cases of viewpoint discrimination, and to permit aesthetic or qualitative judgments so long as they are not conspicuously or explicitly based on partisan aims. Of course anyone who accepts this approach must recognize that it rests on some conceptually shaky ground.

There are two final hard cases here. The first involves a restriction that does not clearly discriminate on the basis of viewpoint but that nonetheless amounts to an attempt to impose conventional morality on artists. The second involves cases in which viewpoint discrimination might be permitted—including "hate literature" or art that offends a significant portion of the community because it degrades them.

With respect to the first problem, suppose that government says that it will refuse to fund projects containing profanity or sexually explicit scenes, even if those projects are not technically obscene. The constitutional concern is that in such cases, government will be distorting artistic processes by imposing financial pressures that incline people toward officially sanctioned views about what is morally fitting in art. In a system containing some public funding, this problem cannot be altogether avoided. But it can be minimized rather than increased. I suggest that the appropriate constitutional strategy here is to refuse to permit any general or across-the-board measures that deny funding to art that offends conventional morality. For this reason, courts should strike down any nationwide statutory ban on funding projects with profanity or sexually explicit scenes.

A different result, however, might make sense if the regulation is limited in time or in space. A decision by the NEA to forbid the funding of all art with nudity would be far more objectionable than a decision not to allow nudity in just one or two governmentally funded projects. The latter measure would have some of the characteristics of time, place, and manner restrictions. It would have a far better claim to constitutionality. If there is no conspicuous discrimination on the basis of point of view, restrictions of this kind might well be acceptable in the funding context so long as they are only occasional.

The point suggests a broader one. Government may be permitted to discriminate on the basis of point of view if (1) it is doing so in the context of sharply limited, discrete initiatives and (2) the viewpoint discrimination does not involve taking sides in a currently contested political debate. For example, it seems clear that a fund for democracy may permissibly promote democratic causes. Perhaps this is so because democracy has come to be understood[16] as a sufficiently shared, sufficiently nonpartisan goal as to escape the prohibition on viewpoint discrimination. Similarly, a anticigarette campaign may legitimately fund people who will campaign against cigarette smoking; the government need not also fund people who approve of smoking. But these are unusual cases. Most across-the-board laws containing viewpoint discrimination would be impossible to justify.

The next category is at least equally troublesome. What if the government decides not to fund Nazi art, pro-slavery art, art of the Klu Klux Klan, or art glorifying rape and sexual violence, on the ground that the relevant causes are filled with hatred, are abhorrent, or are perceived as abhorrent by a large segment of the community? The basic problem here, noted above, is that conventional morality cannot be permitted to be the arbiter of governmental funding of expression. A system in which conventional morality played that role would be inconsistent with the First Amendment guarantee, which is designed precisely to protect views that do not accord with conventional morality. What would be required, in the cases at hand, is a principle of sufficient generality to pick up any legitimate concerns with the use of taxpayer money in these areas, without at the same time amounting to impermissible dictation of point of view.

It would be good if we could find such a principle; but it is far from simple to do so. Surely government should not be permitted to decline to fund any project simply because a significant number of taxpayers have a conscientious objection. Taxpayers have such objections to many possible projects. If this were a basis for restrictions on funding, we would be enshrining conventional morality as the basis for funding decisions. Perhaps we can find in the Civil War Amendments a constitutional principle that allows government not to fund projects that promote the social subordination of groups facing caste-like disabilities. This is the most likely principle; but it would obviously be susceptible to abuse.

However the hardest cases may be resolved, it follows from all this that government has considerable power to grant funds to artistic projects, even if it does so on a selective basis. The only clear prohibition operates against straightforwardly partisan motives, as in the case of discrimination against a particular point of view; and even here there are some exceptions. A similar prohibition might be triggered when a subject matter restriction embodies a form of illegitimate discrimination, as in the exclusion of art containing profanity. For these cases, much will depend on the particular context. A constant question is whether any form of viewpoint or content discrimination is limited in time and place. Under these general standards, difficult cases will remain. But the approach I have outlined would resolve the vast majority of cases, and help orient treatment of the rest.

One final note. There are lurking questions here about the government's own speech. It seems clear that government has unlimited authority over what it will say.[17] Some people think that it follows from this that government should have similarly broad authority over people it pays. The government, after all, consists only of human beings who are its agents. When government is paying out its own money, perhaps all recipients of taxpayer funds have become government agents or government employees. Perhaps it follows that no one has a legitimate basis for constitutional complaint. On this view, the government's power to say what it wishes necessarily entails the conclusion that there are no limits on government's power to give funds to causes that it favors. Government can fund speech however it chooses, simply because it can speak however it likes.

This is a tempting and crisp argument, and there is, perhaps, no similarly crisp response. But I think that the argument should be rejected. It would be unacceptable to say that because government officials may speak freely, government funding decisions are unconstrained. Part of the difference between government speech and government funding lies in the fact that when government is speaking, the public knows who the speaker really is. This knowledge has a healthy effect on political deliberation. It allows the people to take what is said with full knowledge and perhaps a dose of skepticism. The same cannot be said when the government is paying a private person to say what it wants. Here people do not know that the private speaker may not really believe that he is saying, and that government has influenced his expression. From this point we should conclude that government's power to speak freely does not at all justify the view that government may allocate funds to favored causes.

There is a further point. When government pays people to speak as it wishes, there is a significant risk of government co-optation of the private sphere. Indeed, this risk conspicuously arises whenever government imposes conditions on private people who are receiving government money. Fear of this risk retains its full authority even in a post–New Deal era. Indeed, the fear of co-optation is all the more urgent in an era in which it is a constant threat.

All this suggests that there are grave dangers in the claim that if government speech is unconstrained, the same is true for funding decisions. Indeed, it is possible to draw the opposite inference. If government wants a certain point of view to be heard, it should require real government officials to advocate that point of view. It should not bribe ordinary citizens to do its work for it.

Corporate Speech

This discussion bears on our final hard case: government controls on spending by corporations. The issue is extremely important to democratic processes. Imagine, for example, that a state bans corporations from making expenditures to influence referenda on public issues. Does the ban violate the First Amendment?

This issue arose in *First National Bank of Boston v. Bellotti*,[18] in which the Supreme Court held that such a prohibition was indeed unconstitutional. In that case, Massachusetts attempted to limit corporate expenditures on a proposed "bottle bill," requiring recycling of all bottles. The state feared that corporations having a financial stake in the issue would drown out other positions, and thus distort political debate. The vast amount of funds in the corporate treasury could certainly dwarf other expenditures on the bottle bill. Indeed, the state was able to show that the political committee opposing the amendment had raised $120,000, whereas its opponent raised merely $7,000.

In invalidating the restriction, the Supreme Court stressed that corporations frequently offer political speech that is "indispensable to decisionmaking in a democracy" and "at the heart of the First Amendment's protection." Emphasizing the democratic interest of listeners in hearing speech about public matters, the Court concluded that the restriction was an unacceptable interference with the system of free expression. Recalling Justice Brandeis in *Whitney*, the Court said that more speech was the appropriate response to corporate expression, not mandatory silence. In these ways the Court insisted that a Madisonian understanding of the First Amendment entailed protection of corporate speech.

The dissenting opinion by Justice White invoked democratic considerations too, but for the opposite conclusion. Justice White argued that corporations have acquired "vast amounts of money which may, if not regulated, dominate not only the economy but also the very heart of our democracy, the electoral process." According to Justice White, it is important to ensure that corporations do not use their wealth to pervert electoral processes. The limitation on corporate speech is therefore acceptable. In an especially striking separate dissenting opinion, Justice Rehnquist emphasized a different point: the fact that the corporation owes its existence only to law. Since law gives corporations their various properties—their powers and duties—law may similarly condition the grant of these benefits through a constraint on speech, or so Justice Rehnquist argued.

Let us begin with Justice White's claim that restrictions on corporate speech are a reasonable effort to promote political equality. If this is the rationale for such restrictions, I believe that Justice White is wrong, and that such restrictions should be invalidated as impermissibly selective. Many corporations are relatively poor. Many individuals are relatively rich. A limit on corporate speech is insufficiently connected to the general interest in ensuring equality in political campaigns. It is far too indirect, even discriminatory. To the extent that Justice White is concerned with the distorting effects of wealth, he is really arguing not for restrictions on corporate expenditures, but for restrictions on electoral expenditures in general. A claim for political equality is powerful if it is general (see chapter 4, defending campaign finance restrictions); but it is inadequate to support a restriction on corporate speech alone.

At first glance, the Court's conclusion in *Bellotti* seems to fit well with the view I have offered in this book. The corporate speech in that case appears to fall in the center of Madisonian concerns. There is a large social interest in hearing what corporations have to say about public issues. If corporations are sharply opposed to (for example) environmental regulation, it is important for people to know this and to hear the reasons for their opposition. Consider the issue of governmentally mandated recyclable bottles. This policy may or may not be good, but it is certainly important for people to know the costs, and corporate speech is admirably well-suited to identifying them. Of course no one is forced to believe what the corporations claim.

Thus far, then, it seems that the *Bellotti* Court was right, and that restrictions on corporate speech are impermissible. But there is an intriguing argument for the opposite view. Justice Rehnquist offers the best place to start. He thinks that the case is like a restriction on government funding of the arts. In his view, limits on corporate speech are simply an instance of a permissible condition on the grant of a government benefit—in this case, the grant of the valuable government benefit of corporate status. In Justice Rehnquist's view, *Bellotti* turns out to be just like the abortion funding "gag rule" case, *Rust v. Sullivan*, which he (not incidentally) wrote.

More specifically: Just as the government can condition the grant of Medicaid funds on an agreement to maintain silence with respect to abortion, so too can government condition the grant of corporate status on an agreement to maintain silence with respect to politics. This is a view that Justice Rehnquist has often defended; but I think that it is much too simple (see chapter 4). Some conditions are unconstitutional; they are impermissible in their purposes and in their effects. The government could not, for example, condition corporate status on an agreement to speak only in favor of the President. We always need to ask about the particular condition at issue. We answer such questions by seeing whether the government has legitimate reasons for the imposition of the relevant condition, and whether that condition is sufficiently related to those legitimate reasons.

The strongest argument for allowing restrictions on corporate speech would make several points. First, imagine a hypothetical case: The President offers a range of special benefits to people who engage in certain entrepreneurial activity—these benefits include huge tax relief, federal assistance, special rules in litigation, and so forth. Suppose the President is concerned that people who take advantage of this program will use their accumulated assets to influence politics. Suppose he says that as a condition for participating in the program, people must agree to restrict their profits to economic rather than political activity. Would this be unconstitutional? In Justice Rehnquist's view, surely not; and it is hard to see why he might be wrong.

The hypothetical is far from exotic. By granting use of the corporate form, government offers corporate officials a good deal of assistance in the accumulation of assets. This assistance includes the limited liability of shareholders, who are generally made immune to claims from creditors; potentially perpetual life; generous provisions for the accumulation and distribution of assets; and favorable tax treatment. Government denies this assistance to everyone else. It might be argued that a limitation on political speech is a permissible condition on the receipt of these various benefits insofar as it prevents wealth accumulated for special, limited economic purposes from being used for political purposes. This is especially so to the extent that corporate political speech reflects the economically motivated decisions of investors and customers rather than popular support for political ideas. In short: If the political power of the corporation reflects economic power made possible only by the government's general provision of the corporate form, perhaps the restriction on corporate speech can be justified as an effort to protect against the distortion of electoral processes by institutions that have been especially benefited by the state.

An argument of this kind lay at the center of the Supreme Court's reasoning in the *Austin* case. There the Court upheld a prohibition on the use of corporate treasury funds for independent expenditures on campaigns for state offices.[19] Under the program in *Austin*, any corporate expenditures must be obtained through a specially segregated fund, in which participants would know they were making political contributions. In upholding this program, the Court emphasized the special benefits extended by the state to corporations and the potential abuse of shareholder funds for political activity. *Austin* is in obvious tension with *Bellotti*. In the latter case, the Court emphasized the public interest in hearing corporate speech; in the former, the Court stressed the need to ensure against the abuse of the corporate form through the expenditure of corporate assets on politics.

The two cases are not the same. *Austin* involved expenditures in campaigns, whereas *Bellotti* dealt with referenda. Perhaps more important, *Austin* involved a mere segregation requirement, whereas *Bellotti* dealt with a flat ban. But it is unclear that these are decisive differences, and in any case Justice Rehnquist's dissenting view in *Bellotti* appears to have enjoyed a surprising rebirth in *Austin*.

The outcome in *Austin*, based on the concerns I have just outlined, is rooted in a strong argument; but in the end I am not sure that it is persuasive. Many associations and individuals—including labor unions and partnerships of various kinds—are also given assistance by government, and their speech is not regulated or regulable. The tax system is filled with special benefits and incentives for various groups. It is probably wrong to think that corporations are uniquely benefited, or that the assistance offered to them by the state is qualitatively different from the assistance offered by the state to others. All wealth is "artificial" in the sense that it is made possible by legal arrangements. Property itself depends on law. The hypothetical case I have offered is a bit different from the ordinary corporate speech case. It may be legitimate to condition new corporate benefits on new agreements to refrain from speech. But in the long history of the corporate form, we have reason to fear that the new restrictions on that old form are not an effort to prevent abuse of the form, but amount instead to highly selective effort to stop businesses from speaking to the public about matters that concern them.

Moreover, corporate shareholders can and do exercise a degree of control over corporate actitivies. The expenditure of corporate funds for speech is at least plausibly a reflection of the shareholders' will. In these circumstances, protection of shareholders does not seem to be an especially strong argument for government restrictions on corporate speech. It may be true that corporate expenditures do not reflect popular support; but the same is true of individual expenditures by, for example, rich people. For this reason, it seems illegitimate to invoke this argument to single out corporations for special treatment.

The appeal of the *Austin* ruling ultimately stems, I think, from a general concern about political equality. It does not result from the specific concern about the use of the state-created corporate framework with which to accumulate assets. I have argued that political equality is indeed a legitimate goal and that the state can take steps to promote that goal (see chapter 4). But the state should not be permitted to be selective about this—to enact limitations on corporate speech without limiting the speech of others, and without generally seeking to prevent the distortion of deliberative processes through wealth.

It would be tempting to respond that this is a form of pre–New Deal thinking. Perhaps corporations have disproportionate political influence, and in these circumstances controls on their speech might be a corrective to a viewpoint-based status quo, in which businesses can dominate speech processes. It is surely plausible to claim that corporations have disproportionate influence, though the claim raises some complex issues of fact and value. But it is doubtful whether restrictions on speech should often be justifiable on this ground, at least in light of the extreme difficulties posed by governmental efforts to claim that some speakers should be silenced because they have disproportionate power. The difficulties arise not because some speakers do not have such power, but because no government institution is well-suited to embark on this sort of inquiry. Precisely because of their breadth, limits on expenditures that are general in character pose far less problem on this score.

The restriction on corporate speech might therefore be seen as a form of speaker-based discrimination that properly creates suspicion. It follows that a limitation on corporate speech should be treated as an unconstitutional condition. Despite its apparent neutrality, it may well reflect a form of implicit viewpoint discrimination. It is impermissibly selective. If government is to reduce corporate expenditures, it should do so as part of a general effort to reduce the effects of wealth, not as an independent program designed to stop business from speaking.

In general, it is sensible to distinguish among content-based, content-neutral, and viewpoint-based restrictions. These distinctions help explain when government regulations on speech are most likely to be harmful and least likely to be based on legitimate reasons. Usually courts can administer these distinctions without great difficulty, and the distinctions can therefore claim to combine the virtues of substantive reasonableness and ease of application.

But three general qualifications are necessary. First, some content-neutral restrictions are especially troublesome because of their destructive effects on expressive opportunity and because of their content-differential effects. Second, some unusual viewpoint-based restrictions are and should be upheld; the category should not operate as a substitute for close examination of particular contexts. Third, it is difficult to apply these distinctions to the context of government funding, though I have argued that courts should generally invalidate viewpoint discrimination in the allocation of taxpayer money. In any case, I have tried to suggest the enduring truth of the proposition that discrimination on the basis of point of view is the core violation of the free speech guarantee.

Chapter 8

Deliberative Democracy

THUS FAR I HAVE NOT said much about the political functions of the free speech guarantee or about the conception of democracy that it should be taken to embody. Some general remarks are in order.

The American constitutional system is emphatically not designed solely to protect private interests and private rights. Private interests and private rights are of course protected; but this is not the entire point of the system. Even more emphatically, its purpose is not to furnish the basis for struggle among self-interested private groups. Although the framers recognized the existence and indeed the inevitability of self-interest in government, the notion of politics as interest-group deals is anathema to American constitutionalism.[1] Interest-group deals reflect existing preferences and existing distributions of wealth and authority. In the American conception, the function of law is far more ambitious.

Instead, a large point of the system is to ensure discussion and debate among people who are genuinely different in their perspectives and position, in the interest of creating a process through which reflection will encourage the emergence of general truths. A distinctive feature of American republicanism is extraordinary hospitality toward disagreement and heterogeneity, rather than fear of it. The framers believed that a diversity of opinion would be a creative and productive force. The prominent antifederalist Brutus, an eloquent opponent of the proposed Constitution, insisted: "In a republic, the manners, sentiments, and interests of the people should be similar. If this be not the case, there will be a constant clashing of opinions; and the representatives of one part will be continually striving against those of the other."[2] Speaking for the Federalists, Alexander Hamilton responded that in a heterogeneous republic, discussion will be improved. Indeed, "the jarring of parties . . . will promote deliberation."[3] The American Federalists did not believe that heterogeneity would be an obstacle to political discussion and debate. On the contrary, they thought that it was indispensable to it. If people already agree, what will they talk about? Why would they want to talk at all?

A good deal of light is cast on the resulting system of free expression by a decision in the first Congress. Through that decision, the representatives rejected a proposal to give citizens, as part of the Bill of Rights, a "right to instruct" their representatives. For the founding generation, a right to instruct was thought to be inconsistent with the point of meeting, which was deliberation. Sherman's statement was especially clear: "[T]he words are calculated to mislead the people, by conveying an idea that they have a right to control the debates of the Legislature. This cannot be admitted to be just, because it would destroy the object of their meeting. I think, *when the people have chosen a representative, it is his duty to meet others from the different parts of the Union, and consult, and agree with them to such acts as are for the general benefit of the whole community. If they were to be guided by instructions, there would be no use in deliberation.*"[4]

We can find in these words many of the foundational commitments of the system of free expression. On this view, even desires, or current beliefs about what courses of action are best, should not be frozen. The political system was one of deliberation rather than aggregation. The framers insisted that existing views might be a product of partial perspectives, of limited experience, or of incomplete information. People engaged in democratic discussion should "meet others from the different parts of the Union, and consult." People should be "open to the force of argument." They should be prepared to give up their initial views when shown "the general benefit of the whole community." There is a good deal of empirical evidence that deliberation can have a transformative function on beliefs.[5] And through this process of discussion, public deliberation should produce better public decisions.

In coming to terms with these ideas, we can begin with some modest claims. Public deliberation may reveal the truth or falsity of factual claims about the state of the world or about the likely effects of policy proposals.[6] Through confrontation among people who disagree, errors of fact may be revealed as such. A candidate for electoral office claims that a tax on gasoline will have good effects on the environment, by reducing automobile pollution; another candidate disagrees. At least if reasoned analysis can be made to play a large role in public debate, better outcomes should result from public deliberation simply through this process of correction.

Only somewhat more ambitiously, we might think that the presence of diverse perspectives will cast light not only on the correctness of factual claims but also on how much weight they should be given. Let us take some controversial current issues. It is highly relevant if affirmative action programs turn out to be unpopular among the people they are intended to help. Exposure to this perspective may cast a new light on the problem. Or consider the issue of sexual harassment. It is important for a public concerned with this issue to get a full sense of the number, nature, and perceptions of actual or potential victims of sexual harassment. How often are people harassed? Are the victims only or nearly only women? What forms does harassment take?

The judgments of victims (or of any other particular group) cannot by themselves be decisive. But they are highly relevant. In a system of free expression, exposure to multiple perspectives will offer a fuller picture of the consequences of social acts. This should help make for better law.

There is also what Jon Elster describes as *the civilizing force of hypocrisy*.[7] Without making heroic assumptions about the human capacity for virtue and the transcendence of self-interest, we might observe that a system of public discussion requires people to speak in public-regarding terms. Policies must always be justified on the basis of reasons, or on the ground that they promote the public good. In a deliberative politics, even the most venal or self-interested participants in politics must invoke public justifications in their support. If "hypocrisy is the tribute that vice pays to virtue,"[8] at least we can say that in a system of public deliberation, everyone must speak as if he were virtuous even if he is not in fact.

The requirement of justification in public-regarding terms—the civilizing force of hypocrisy—might well contribute to public-regarding outcomes. It may "launder" preferences by foreclosing certain arguments in the public domain, including, for example, those involving racial or sexual prejudice.[9] It might even bring about a transformation in preferences and values, simply by making venal or self-regarding justifications seem off-limits.

A system of free expression should also increase the likelihood that political outcomes will be responsive to the will of the public. This is an important aspect of political freedom, as the framers insisted.[10] To be sure, there are notorious difficulties in the claim that political outcomes can actually reflect the "public will." It is doubtful that private desires or even aspirations can be well-aggregated through the process of majority rule.[11] Even if a process of aggregation were possible, it would not be entirely desirable in light of the broader goals of deliberation in producing reasoned agreement rather than simple aggregation. But for the moment, these complexities may be put to one side. It seems clear that a well-functioning deliberative process will increase the likelihood that political outcomes will respond to people's desires and aspirations at the same time that it will help shape them for the better. In these ways as well, it should improve political outcomes.

Most ambitiously, we might hope that a well-functioning system of free expression will ultimately encourage a degree of public virtue and produce high levels of participation and genuine deliberation.[12] The achievement of these goals would reinforce the connection between deliberative democracy and better political outcomes. But it would also connect with Brandeis' civic conception and with Madison's notion of sovereignty. Recall that Brandeis thought that in our constitutional system, freedom of speech is valued "both as an end and as a means"; that liberty is "the secret of happiness and courage . . . the secret of liberty"; that "the greatest menace to freedom is an inert people." A well-functioning system of free expression does not simply promote better outcomes; it also has salutary effects on individual character. Such a system tends to diminish feelings of social and political powerlessness, to increase political involvement, and to create a "courageous, self-reliant" people. Note also the words of James Madison, often labeled a great skeptic about human nature, during the Virginia Ratifying Convention: "Is there no virtue among us? If there be not, we are in a wretched situation. No theoretical checks, no form of government, can render us secure."[13] The free speech principle should be understood as benefiting from and helping to inculcate certain personal characteristics that amount to both collective and individual goods.

In the American tradition, a norm of political equality is central to democratic deliberation. What counts is "the force of the argument." Politics is emphatically not a process in which desires and interests remain frozen, before or during politics. The protection accorded to free speech is designed to allow the polity's judgments to emerge through general discussion and debate. And for this process to occur, it is necessary for people to be exposed to reasoned debate from a broad range of perspectives. This view does not depend on a sharp distinction between public interest and private interest, or on an unrealistic insistence that private interest is not and should not be a motivation for political action. Private interests often motivate political behavior; this is inevitable and often even desirable. But there are many advantages to a deliberative politics in producing good outcomes, and these advantages help sharpen the contrast between "consumer sovereignty" and the Madisonian conception. Because that contrast has played a central role in this book—especially in the claims on behalf of a free speech New Deal—it is worthwhile to explore the contrast in some detail. Several points are important here.

First, the collective character of politics might overcome the problem of preferences and beliefs that have adapted, or to some extent adapted, to an unjust status quo or to limits in available opportunities. Without the possibility of collective action, the status quo may seem intractable, and private behavior and even beliefs will adapt accordingly. But if people can act in concert, preferences might take on a quite different form. There are many examples; consider social movements involving the environment, labor, and race and sex discrimination. Political deliberation is central to this process of overcoming preferences and beliefs that are produced by limited opportunities or social injustice.

Second, social and cultural norms might lead people to express aspirational or altruistic goals more often in political behavior than in markets. Reasons must generally be offered on behalf of political outcomes. The same is not true of consumption decisions. Norms of this kind may press people, in their capacity as citizens, in the direction of a concern for others, for justice, or for the public interest.

Third, the collective character of politics is critical here. People may not want to implement their considered judgments, or to be altruistic, unless there is assurance that others will do so as well. The satisfaction of aspirations or altruistic goals will sometimes have the characteristics of the provision of public goods.[14]

Indeed, one can think of both altruism and aspirations as having the features of a public good, that is, something that cannot be proved to one person without simultaneously being provided to many or all people. Aspirations are not conventional public goods, because the market does not fail according to ordinary understandings of "market failure." But if the most preferred option is to reflect and carry out aspirational or altruistic goals, political action may be the best alternative. Social deliberation is indispensable to this task.

Fourth, consumption decisions, for information as for other things, are a product of the criterion of private willingness to pay. Willingness to pay is a function of ability to pay, and it is an extremely crude proxy for utility or welfare. Poor people may be unwilling to pay much for something that they very much want. Rich people may be willing to pay a good deal for things toward which they feel relatively indifferent. Political behavior removes this distortion (which is not to say that it does not introduce distortions of its own).

Finally, and most fundamentally, the deliberative aspects of politics, bringing new information and perspectives to bear, may affect preferences as expressed through governmental processes. A principal function of a democratic system is to ensure that through representative processes, new or submerged voices, or novel depictions of where interests lie and what they in fact are, can be heard and understood. It should hardly be surprising if preferences, values, and perceptions of both individual and collective welfare are changed as a result of that process.

None of these points suggests that politics always works well. A deliberative process will not result in unanimity or even consensus. Nor should we deny the inevitable role in politics of greed, ignorance, hatred, myopia, self-interest, confusion, compromise, and logrolling. Sometimes people really disagree, and the deliberative process will not bring them together. Sometimes debates will produce intense differences, leading at best to compromises among competing positions. Sometimes altruists disagree more sharply than anyone else. It would be foolish to think that a good system of political deliberation will or should eliminate the place of self-interest in politics. But these are hardly arguments against the process I have described. If people disagree, it should always be for reasons, and these should be publicly stated. Compromises ought to be permitted only after everyone has had a chance to speak and to be heard. It is only under these conditions that compromises can be found necessary, and that people can be sufficiently informed to choose one compromise rather than another.

Nor does the commitment to a deliberative politics entail disrespect for private rights and the private sphere, or an unwillingness to ensure that government's functions are sharply limited.[15] On the contrary, respect for private rights, the private sphere, and limited government should themselves be justified by publicly articulable reasons, and thus they too will be either the preconditions for or the appropriate outcomes of a well-functioning deliberative process. Much of the American Constitution can be understood as an effort to set out the preconditions for political deliberation; the First Amendment is only the most conspicuous example. And in a system of free expression, the belief in limited government—in free markets, private rights, and civil society—is neither dogma nor theology. In the United States, any particular conception of the private sphere must be defended by a substantive argument.

The Madisonian conception, understood in this light, can draw strength from a wide variety of philosophical traditions. The most attractive forms of utilitarianism place a high premium on political deliberation and certainly do not take existing preferences and distributions as the basis for social choice.[16] So understood, utilitarianism is fully compatible with the account I have suggested here. John Dewey, the leading American pragmatist, emphasized the need to develop a conception of liberty dedicated to establishing the social preconditions for political deliberation.[17] This form of pragmatism has close links to the Madisonian conception of free speech; it has a similar understanding of political truth. The contemporary revival of Aristotelianism[18] places a high premium on political deliberation, freedom of choice, and expressive liberty. The Madisonian conception sees political deliberation in a broadly similar way, and Madisonianism, as I have understood it here, also fits well with the neo-Aristotelian view in its emphasis on the importance of the range of human goods associated with speech falling within the second tier.

Above all, perhaps, the forms of liberalism associated with such figures as Kant, Mill, and Rawls lead naturally to an approach of the general sort that I have offered. One of the most important liberal innovations was the commitment to "government by discussion,"[19] and this idea, especially influential in early America, helps account for many of the recommendations that I have offered here. Liberal rights are pervasively democratic. One of their prime functions is to furnish the preconditions for democratic deliberation.[20] Hence the classical liberals believed that **correct results would be** far more likely to be achieved through broad discussion, under conditions of equality, among people who were differently situated. The liberals thought that if one of the purposes of a political system was to reach good outcomes, general discussion was indispensable. The liberal account of truth and deliberation is part and parcel of the Madisonian system along all of its central dimensions: its skepticism about external or transcendental foundations; its fear of institutional bias and partiality; its self-consciously experimental character; its insistence on the principle of political equality; its modest perfectionism, captured in its belief that a system of free expression has **salutary effects** on the development of character;[21] and perhaps above all in its association of truth in politics with what emerges from a well-functioning political process.[22]

Because the Madisonian conception can emerge from otherwise diverse foundations, it is possible for people who disagree on many issues to converge on that conception of free speech. The possibility of convergence surely strengthens the appeal of the general approach.

From all this it should be clear that understandings of politics as an aggregation of interests, or as a kind of "marketplace," inadequately capture the American system of free expression. Justice Holmes' metaphor of a "marketplace of ideas"[23] has produced considerable good, but it is also misleading. Aggregative or marketplace notions disregard the extent to which political outcomes are supposed to depend on discussion and debate, on a commitment to political equality, and on the reasons offered for or against the alternatives. The First Amendment is the central constitutional reflection of the commitment to deliberative democracy. It is part of the constitutional commitment to citizenship. And this commitment should be understood in light of the American conception of sovereignty, placing governing authority in the people themselves.

The proposals I have set out here flow directly from this conception of the First Amendment. The belief that politics lies at the core of the amendment is of course a conspicuous outgrowth of the structural commitment to deliberative democracy. The concern for ensuring the preconditions for open discussion among the citizenry is closely associated with this commitment. It is in this respect that the proposals suggested here fit with the constitutional aspirations of which the First Amendment is the most tangible expression.

We have come far from many of the ideas that characterize current thinking about free speech. The aversion to line-drawing with respect to speech leads to insoluble conundrums. It is better to be candid and to insist that as far as the First Amendment is concerned, all speech is not the same. Threats to free speech do indeed come from government, but the general understanding of what this means is far off the mark. Such threats take the form not only of conventional, highly visible censorship, but also of what is in some respects the same thing, that is, the allocation by government of rights of property, ownership, and exclusion that determine who can speak and who cannot, and that involve the use of civil and criminal law to carry out the rights of exclusion. Government neutrality is the right aspiration, but properly understood, neutrality does not mean respect for free markets in speech, or for rights of speech as these can be vindicated in light of existing distributions of rights and entitlements. It is thus necessary to rethink some of the commitments that have, with respect to speech, come to represent the general consensus about the meaning of the Constitution's first guarantee.

Over the last forty years, the American law of freedom of speech experienced nothing short of a revolution. The revolution accomplished enormous good. It would be hard to argue that a return to the pre-1950 law of free speech would provide a better understanding of the free speech principle. As the twentieth century draws to a close—in a period when an appreciation for freedom of speech seems to be exploding throughout the world—it is fully appropriate to celebrate our tradition of liberty, and to recognize that ours is an extraordinary and precious achievement.

At the same time, a crucial part of that achievement is a dynamic and self-revising free speech tradition. Our liberty of expression owes much of its content to the capacity of each generation to rethink the understandings that were left to it. To the economists' plea that "the perfect is the enemy of the good," we should oppose John Dewey's suggestion that "the better is the enemy of the still better."[24] The particular conception of free speech in any decade of American history is often quite different from the conception twenty years before or after.

It is increasingly clear that our current understandings are inadequate to resolve current controversies, and that they threaten to protect both more and less speech than they should. They are inadequate for current controversies, because they are poorly adapted to the problems raised by campaign finance regulation, scientific speech, regulation of broadcasting, content-neutral restrictions on speech, hate speech, commercial advertising, and pornography. They protect more than they should, because they include, within the category of protected expression, speech that promotes few or none of the goals for which speech is protected, and that causes serious social harms. They protect less than they should, because current doctrine does not sufficiently serve the central goal of producing a deliberative democracy among free and equal citizens.

Ironically, the existing system owes many of its failures to the supposed mandates of contemporary conceptions of the First Amendment. In some areas, the First Amendment is imposing an unfortunate "chilling effect" on our thinking about how to improve public deliberation.[25] The current problems often stem from conceptions of neutrality and action that predated the New Deal. They apply pre-New Deal understandings about the naturalness and justice of existing distributions to contemporary problems of free expression. They do not see "regulation" when it actually exists. They disfavor as "regulation" entirely legitimate governmental efforts to improve the system of free expression. They show the sharp split between Justice Brandeis' civic conception of free speech on the one hand and Justice Holmes' marketplace metaphor on the other. In the current period, Holmes' view is clearly ascendant. This is most unfortunate.

I have suggested two fundamental changes in existing understandings. Both of them derive from the American contribution to the theory of sovereignty, a theory to which Brandeis' view is a conspicuous heir. Both of them are designed to help equip constitutional law for the extraordinary challenges and opportunities provided by new technology, which will make it necessary to adapt free speech practices to cover a bewildering range of expressive outlets. We can be sure that before long, the technology of expression will be very different from what it is now. It is important to approach the changing system with a clear view of the goals of a well-functioning system of free expression.

First, our existing "markets" in speech are in many ways a Madisonian failure. We do not have enough substantive discussion of public issues, and we are not exposed to sufficient diversity of view. Democratic deliberation about remedies should not be foreclosed by the First Amendment. Some forms of apparent government intervention into free speech processes can actually improve those processes. They should not be understood as an objectionable intrusion into an otherwise law-free social sphere. Intervention should not always be seen as an impermissible "abridgment" of the free speech right.

Efforts of this sort ought not to be taken to argue for a "positive" understanding of free speech in lieu of the heretofore dominant belief in "negative" liberty. Instead these efforts would entail a democratic recognition of the dangers to free speech posed by content-neutral restrictions that limit access to arenas in which expression should occur, and might make a difference. Thus I have suggested a range of reforms for the broadcasting industry and a series of changes in current approaches to government funding, public forums, campaign finance, and perhaps newspapers as well.

Second, the free speech principle should be understood to be centered above all on political thought. In this way the free speech principle should be seen through the lens of democracy. To be sure, free speech values are plural. It is important to understand that diverse human interests—including autonomy and development of the faculties—underlie the First Amendment guarantee. But many forms of speech may be regulated on the basis of a lesser showing of harm than is required for political speech.

Taken together, these principles would bring about significant changes in the legal treatment currently given to many free speech issues. They would alter our approach to electoral campaigns, electronic broadcasting, public forums, speech-related "conditions" on the use of government funds, pornography, and the assertion of ownership rights in order to exclude political speech from the media. Even in their most modest form, the principles would provide a major step toward resolving current free speech controversies, and toward fortifying democratic processes, without fundamentally restructuring existing law. Rightly understood, these principles might well counteract the novel, sometimes invisible, and often serious obstacles that now lie in the path of free speech in America, and that threaten to do so in an increasingly severe way in the twenty-first century. Taken seriously, the resulting reforms would create a system of free expression that is both old and new—old in its emphatic reaffirmation of Madisonian aspirations; new in its willingness to adapt our practices to sustain those aspirations under changing social conditions.

Notes

Introduction

1. See Leonard W. Levy, *Emergence of a Free Press* 272-74 (Oxford, 1985).
2. William Blackstone, 4 Commentaries 150-53 (1769) (emphasis in original).
3. Joseph Story, *A Familiar Exposition of the Constitution of the United States* §§445-47 at 316-18 (Regnery Gateway, 1986).
4. The Act can be found as Act of July 14, 1798, 1 Stat. 596. For the contemporaneous reaction, see Philip Kurland and Ralph Lerner, eds., 5 *The Founders' Constitution* (Chicago, 1987).
5. This interpretive strategy is defended in many places. See, e.g., Ronald Dworkin, *Taking Rights Seriously* (Cambridge, 1977).
6. The equal protection and due process clauses might be very different on this score. We might think that use of the original understanding is important because here the dangers of judicial discretion are very high, and the threats to democratic processes are substantial. By contrast, a robust free speech principle seems a precondition for well-functioning democratic processes, and a system of interpretation that takes the First Amendment as a general concept rather than a particular conception appears to fortify the democratic system rather

than to override it. But these interpretive issues raise many complexities that I cannot address here.

7. On constitutional interpretation in general, see, e.g., Ronald Dworkin, *Law's Empire* (Cambridge, Mass., 1988); Ronald Dworkin, *A Matter of Principle* (1985); Robert Bork, *The Tempting of America* (New York, 1990). For my own views, see Cass R. Sunstein, *The Partial Constitution* chs. 4 and 5 (Cambridge, Mass., 1993).

8. J. Madison, Report on the Virginia Resolution, Jan. 1800, in 6 *Papers of James Madison* 385-401 (Charlottesville, 1991). See the discussion of the shifting understanding of sovereignty in Samuel H. Beer, *To Create A Nation* (Cambridge, Mass., 1993).

9. James Madison, "Report of 1800," January 7, 1800, in 17 *Papers of James Madison* (David Mattern et al. eds., Charlottesville, 1991), at 346, 344, 341.

10. For Madison, the governing ideal was best described as republican, not as democratic. A republican system involved decision by representatives, as distinguished from a democracy, "by which I mean, a Society, consisting of a small number of citizens, who assemble and administer the Government in person" The Federalist No. 10. For present purposes, however, we may understand Madison's conception of republicanism as a version of democracy, not as an alternative to it.

11. See also 14 James Madison, *The Papers of James Madison* 197-98 (Charlottesville, 1983) (describing political equality as first cure for spirit of faction); 3 Max Farrand, *The Records of the Federal Convention of 1787* 479 (New Haven, 1911) (discussing closing of constitutional convention as a means of promoting deliberation).

12. For a helpful discussion, see Mark Graber, *Transforming Free Speech* (Berkeley, 1990).

Chapter 1: The Contemporary First Amendment

1. See Barbara Gamarekian, "Ads Aimed at Children Restricted," The New York Times, Oct. 18, 1990, section D, p. 1, column 3.

2. On the development of this practice, see Tom Engelhardt, "The Shortcake Strategy," in *Watching Television* 68 (Todd Gitlin ed., New York, 1986).

3. Statement on the Children's Television Act of 1990, Government Printing Office, Weekly Compilation of Presidential Documents, vol. 26, no. 2, p. 1611 (Oct. 22, 1990).

4. Dennis v. United States, 341 U.S. 494 (1951).
5. FCC, Editorializing by broadcast licensees, document no. 856, 1 June 1949.
6. David Rabban, "The First Amendment in Its Forgotten Years," 90 Yale L.J. 514 (1981). For an example of the bad tendency idea, see Shaffer v. United States, 255 F. 886 (9th Cir. 1919).
7. The developments here are traced, and the key opinions reprinted, in Geoffrey Stone et al., *Constitutional Law* ch. 7 (Boston, 1989).
8. New York Times Co. v. U.S., 403 U.S. 713, 714 (1971) (Black, J., joined by Douglas, J., concurring); New York Times v. Sullivan, 376 U.S. 254, 293 (1964) (Black, J., joined by Douglas, J., concurring); Miller v. California, 413 U.S. 15, 37 (1973) (Douglas, J., dissenting).
9. Much of this is stated in Robert H. Bork, "Neutral Principles and Some First Amendment Problems," 47 Ind. L. J. 1 (1971). See also Dennis v. United States, 341 U.S. 494 (1951). For Justice Frankfurter's views, see id. at 517 (Frankfurter, J., concurring); Bridges v. California, 314 U.S. 252, 279 (1951) (Frankfurter, J., dissenting); Beauharnais v. Illinois, 343 U.S. 250 (1952).
10. See, e.g., Brandenburg v. Ohio, 395 U.S. 444, 449 (Black, J., concurring).
11. Virginia State Bd. of Pharmacy v. Virginia Citizens Consumer Council, 425 U.S. 748 (1976) (commercial speech); New York Times v. Sullivan, 376 U.S. 254 (1964) (libel); Cox Broadcasting Corp. v. Cohn, 420 U.S. 469 (1975) (names of rape victims); Brandenburg v. Ohio, 395 U.S. 444 (1969) (advocacy of illegality); Buckley v. Valeo, 424 U.S. 1 (1976) (campaign expenditures); First National Bank of Boston v. Bellotti, 434 U.S. 765 (1978) (corporate speech).
12. Brandenburg v. Ohio, 395 U.S. 444 (1969).
13. This emerges from Virginia State Bd. of Pharmacy v. Virginia Citizens Consumer Council, 425 U.S. 748 (1976). Note also that some truthful, nondeceptive advertising can be regulated. See Posadas de Puerto Rico v. Tourism Co. of Puerto Rico, 478 U.S. 328 (1986), suggesting that the government can regulate advertisements for casino gambling because it could instead have forbidden gambling altogether, even though such advertisements are truthful and not misleading.
14. Hustler Magazine v. Falwell, 485 U.S. 46 (1988). Technically, this case involved not libel but intentional infliction of emotional distress; but the Supreme Court applied the basic principles developed in the libel cases.

15. See New York Times v. Sullivan, 376 U.S. 254 (1964); Gertz v. Welsh, 418 U.S. 323 (1974).
16. Miller v. California, 413 U.S. 15, 24 (1973): "The basic guidelines for the trier of fact must be: (a) whether the average person, applying contemporary community standards would find that the work, taken as a whole, appeals to the prurient interest; (b) whether the work depicts or describes, in a patently offensive way, sexual conduct specifically defined by the applicable state law; and (c) whether the work, taken as a whole, lacks serious literary, artistic, political, or scientific value."
17. New York Times v. Sullivan, 376 U.S. 254 (1964) (invoking democratic goals); Chaplinsky v. New Hampshire, 315 U.S. 568 (1942) (invoking exchange of ideas).
18. The best discussions are Geoffrey R. Stone, "Content Discrimination and the First Amendment," 25 Wm. & Mary L. Rev. 189 (1983); Geoffrey R. Stone, "Content-Neutral Restrictions," 54 U. Chi. L. Rev. 46 (1987).
19. I am assuming here that the libelous speech meets the standards for regulation and therefore does not qualify as "high value."
20. Lehman v. Shaker Heights, 418 U.S. 298 (1974); Greer v. Spock, 424 U.S. 828 (1976).
21. See, e.g., Rodney Smolla, *Free Speech in a Democratic Society* (Oxford, 1992); E. deGrazia, *Girls Lean Back Everywhere* (New York, 1992); Nat Hentoff, *Free Speech for Me but Not For Thee* (New York, 1992).
22. See Valentine v. Chrestensen, 316 U.S. 52 (1942). Justice Douglas eventually concluded that he had been wrong. See Pittsburgh Press Co. v. Pittsburgh Human Relations Commission, 413 U.S. 376, 397–98 (1973).

Chapter 2: A New Deal for Speech

1. Policies of the Federal Communications Commission require some qualifications, but in the wake of deregulation, the qualifications are relatively minor. For a useful outline, see *Mass Media Law*, part 4, especially pp. 761–89 (Marc Franklin and David Anderson eds., New York, 1990).
2. On deliberative democracy, see Joseph Bessette, "Deliberative Democracy: The Majority Principle in Republican Government," in *How Democratic Is the Constitution?* 102, 112–16 (Robert Goldwin and William Schambra eds., Washington,

D.C., 1980). For more elaboration, see chapter 8; see also Cass R. Sunstein, *The Partial Constitution* chs. 5 and 6 (Cambridge, Mass., 1993).

3. Conceptions of appropriate conditions are set out in John Rawls, *A Theory of Justice* (Cambridge, Mass., 1971) and Jurgen Habermas, *The Philosophical Discourse of Modernity* 336–67 (Cambridge, Mass., 1987). See also Hilary Putnam, *Renewing Philosophy* (Cambridge, Mass., 1992).

4. I do not discuss here the problems shown by Arrow's Impossibility Theorem for this understanding. See Kenneth Arrow, *Social Choice and Individual Values* (2d ed., New Haven, 1963). An overview is Elizabeth Anderson and Richard Pildes, "Slinging Arrows at Democracy," 89 Colum. L. Rev. 2121 (1989).

5. See Samuel H. Beer, *To Make a Nation* (Cambridge, Mass., 1993); Stephen Holmes, *Passions and Constraint* (forthcoming 1994). See also the discussion of the need to ensure the "fair value" of equal political liberties in John Rawls, *Political Liberalism* 324–31 (Cambridge, Mass., 1993). The promotion of "fair value" is at least part of the reason for distinguishing between deregulated markets and a well-functioning system of free expression.

6. See Jon Elster, *Sour Grapes* (Cambridge, 1983); John Rawls, "Fairness to Goodness," 84 Phil. Rev. 537 (1975); John Rawls, "Kantian Constructivism in Ethical Theory," 77 J. Phil. 515 (1980); Amartya Sen, *Commodities and Capabilities* (North-Holland, 1985); Amartya Sen, *Inequality Reexamined* (Cambridge, Mass., 1992).

7. See Jon Elster, *Sour Grapes* 35–42 (Cambridge, 1983).

8. Something of this general sort is suggested in Onora O'Neill, "Practices of Toleration," in *Democracy and the Mass Media* 155 (J. Lichtenberg ed., Cambridge, 1990); Thomas Scanlon, "Content Regulation Reconsidered," in id. at 331; Owen M. Fiss, "Free Speech and Social Structure," 71 Iowa L. Rev. 1405 (1986); Owen M. Fiss, "Why the State?" 100 Harv. L. Rev. 781 (1987); J. M. Balkin, "Some Realism about Pluralism," 1990 Duke L. J. 375. See also the important discussion in Lee Bollinger, *Images of a Free Press* (Chicago, 1991), which examines two different conceptions of the First Amendment, one involving a deregulated marketplace, the other involving attention to public affairs. Bollinger's treatment overlaps a good deal with what I say here, and I have learned much from his discussion.

Many of the concerns expressed here were set out long ago in Commission on Freedom of the Press, *A Free and Responsible Press* (Chicago, 1947). That Commission, headed by Robert Hutchins and Zechariah Chafee, included among its members John Dickinson, Harold Lasswell, Archibald MacLeish, Charles Merriam, Reinhold Niebuhr, and Arthur Schlesinger. It did not recommend legal remedies for the current situation, but it suggested the need for private measures to control novel problems. "The press has been transformed into an enormous and complicated piece of machinery. As a necessary accompaniment, it has become big business. . . . The right of free public expression has therefore lost its earlier reality. Protection against government is now not enough to guarantee that a man who has something to say shall have a chance to say it. The owners and managers of the press determine which persons, which facts, which versions of the facts, and which ideas shall reach the public." Id. at 15–16.

9. See, e.g., Abrams v. United States, 250 U.S. 616, 624 (1919) (Holmes, J., dissenting); Gitlow v. New York, 268 U.S. 652, 672 (1925) (Holmes, J., dissenting); Whitney v. California, 274 U.S. 357 (1927) (Brandeis, J., dissenting).
10. 250 U.S. 616 (1919) (Holmes, J., dissenting).
11. On Holmes' theory of politics, see Yosal Rogat, "Mr. Justice Holmes: Some Modern Views—The Judge as Spectator," 31 U. Chi. L. Rev. 213 (1964).
12. See David Strauss, "Persuasion, Autonomy and Freedom of Expression," 91 Colum. L. Rev. 334 (1991). See also William James, *Pragmatism and The Meaning of Truth* (Cambridge, Mass., 1978).
13. Charles Peirce, "How To Make Our Ideas Clear," *Collected Papers of Charles Sanders Peirce*, 248, 268n (Charles Hartshorne and Paul Weiss eds., New York, 1934).
14. Gitlow v. New York, 268 U.S. 652, 672 (1925) (Holmes, J., dissenting).
15. 274 U.S. 357, 372 (1927) (Brandeis, J., concurring).
16. A superb discussion is Vincent Blasi, "The First Amendment and the Ideal of Civic Courage: The Brandeis Opinion in Whitney v. California," 29 Wm. & Mary L. Rev. 653 (1988). See also the illuminating discussion of the Brandeis opinion in John Rawls, *Political Liberalism* 351–56 (Cambridge, Mass., 1993).

17. Bruce Ackerman goes so far as to treat the New Deal as a constitutional amendment. See Bruce A. Ackerman, *We the People, vol. 1: Foundations* (Cambridge, Mass., 1991). One need not see things in this way in order to recognize the relevance of the New Deal to the American constitutional tradition. Some of the details of the New Deal are outlined in Cass R. Sunstein, *After the Rights Revolution* (Cambridge, Mass., 1990).

18. Two qualifications are necessary. First, redistribution through taxation—most notably by way of the poor laws and other welfare measures—was permissible. Second, some forms of regulation were permissible even if they had redistributive features. The "police power" extended, for example, to protection of workers' health, although the Court was sometimes skeptical that a health justification was plausible. See Lochner v. New York, 198 U.S. 45 (1905).

19. See Adkins v. Children's Hospital, 261 U.S. 525 (1923); Lochner v. New York, 198 U.S. 45 (1905). Of course minimum wage and maximum hour legislation has complex redistributive consequences; it does not simply transfer resources from employers to employees. The New Deal period is discussed in some detail, from this angle, in Cass Sunstein, *The Partial Constitution* ch. 2 (Cambridge, Mass., 1993).

20. Franklin D. Roosevelt, "Message to Congress," June 8, 1934, reprinted in *Statutory History of the United States: Income Security* 61 (Robert B. Stevens ed., New York, 1970);

21. 1 *Public Papers of Franklin D. Roosevelt* 657 (Washington, D.C., 1938).

22. Amartya Sen, *Poverty and Famines* (Oxford, 1981), is a striking contemporary illustration of similar ideas, demonstrating that famines are a result not solely of a decrease in the supply of food, but also of social choices, prominent among them legal ones, deciding who is entitled to what. See especially id. at 165–66: "Finally, the focus on entitlement has the effect of emphasizing legal rights. Other relevant factors, for example market forces, can be seen as operating *through* a system of legal relations (ownership rights, contractual obligations, legal exchanges, etc.). The law stands between food availability and food entitlement. Starvation deaths can reflect legality with a vengeance." Sen's claim can be seen as a special case of the New Deal understanding of "laissez-faire."

23. The classic statement is J. S. Mill, "Nature", in 10 *The Collected Works of John Stuart Mill* 373 (J. M. Robson ed.,

Toronto, 1967): "If the artificial is not better than the natural, to what end are all the arts of life? To dig, to plough, to build, to wear clothes, are direct infringements on the injunction to follow nature. . . . All praise of Civilization, or Art, or Contrivance, is so much dispraise of Nature; an admission of imperfection, which it is man's business, and merit, to be always endeavoring to correct or mitigate. . . . In sober truth, nearly all the things which men are hanged or imprisoned for doing to one another, are nature's every day performances. . . . [I]t remains true that nearly every respectable attribute of humanity is the result not of instinct, but of a victory of instinct; and that there is hardly anything valuable in the natural man except capacities—a whole world of possibilities, all of them dependent upon eminently artificial discipline for being realized. . . . [T]he duty of man is the same in respect to his own nature as in respect to the nature of all other things, namely not to follow but to amend it. . . . Conformity to nature, has no connection whatever with right and wrong. . . . That a thing is unnatural, in any precise meaning which can be attached to the word, is no argument for its being blamable."

24. Robert Hale, unpublished manuscript, quoted in B. Fried, *Robert Hale and Progressive Law and Economics*, ch. 3 at 26 (1992 draft, forthcoming).

25. Morris Cohen, "Property and Sovereignty," 13 Cornell L. Q. 8, 14 (1927).

26. 376 U.S. 254 (1964). Anthony Lewis, *Make No Law* (New York, 1991), is an especially illuminating discussion of the case.

27. See A. Meiklejohn, *Free Speech and Its Relation to Self-Government* (New York, 1948). The link is made explicitly in Brennan, "The Supreme Court and the Meiklejohn Interpretation of the First Amendment," 79 Harv. L. Rev. 1 (1965). See also Kalven, "The New York Times Case: A Note on 'the Central Meaning of the First Amendment," 1960 Supreme Court Review 1.

28. NYT v. Sullivan, 273 Ala, 656, 144 So. 2d 25 (1962). It is notable here that in *Sullivan*, the government was not a party—something that distinguishes the case from most others in which First Amendment objections had been raised. But this does not mean that there is no state action; to think that it does is simply another version of the problem discussed in the text.

29. See Onora O'Neill, "Practices of Toleration," in *Democracy and the Mass Media* supra note 8, 177–78: "[N]o society can institutionalize zero-regulation of public discourse. The choice can only be between differing patterns of regulation. . . . No society can guarantee that all communications will be able to express every possible content in every possible context. Supposed attempts to do this by laissez-faire communications policies merely assign the regulation of communication to nonstate powers. They secure a particular configuration of freedom of expression, which may leave some unable to find their voices and does not guarantee the expression of diverse views. A better and less abstract aim for a democratic society is a set of practices that enables a wide range of communication, especially of public communication, for all."

30. CBS, Inc. v. Democratic National Committee, 412 U.S. 94 (1973). In this case the justices were split, and the underlying theory did not emerge with clarity.

31. See Metromedia, Inc. v. San Diego, 435 U.S. 490 (1981).

32. Lloyd Co. v. Tanner, 407 U.S. 551 (1972); Hudgens v. NLRB, 424 U.S. 507 (1976).

33. It is sometimes so argued. See David Strauss, "Persuasion, Autonomy, and Freedom of Expression," 91 Colum. L. Rev. 334 (1991).

34. Lloyd Co. v. Tanner, 407 U.S. 551 (1972); Hudgens v. NLRB, 424 U.S. 507 (1976).

35. CBS v. Democratic National Committee, 412 U.S. 94 (1973). In that case only three justices said that there was no state action. But those three justices may now represent the majority view. See Flagg Bros. v. Brooks, 436 U.S. 149 (1978).

36. See Jeremy Waldron, "Homelessness and the Problem of Freedom," 39 UCLA L. Rev. 295 (1991). The same point is made about hunger in Amartya Sen, "Ingredients of Famine Analysis: Availability and Entitlements," in Amartya Sen, *Resources, Values and Development* 452, 458 (1984).

37. To say this is not to say that the distinction itself is untenable. We can understand a positive right as one that requires for its existence some act by government, and a negative right as one that amounts merely to an objection to some such act. There is nothing incoherent about this distinction. (Note, however, that on this view a right becomes positive if it is created by government, and thus the class of genuinely negative rights becomes very small.) The argument in text is directed against

the view that an objection to rights of exclusive ownership is a call for a positive right; in fact that objection is mounted against something that government is actually doing.

38. It also fails to explain constitutional law in general. The eminent domain clause creates a positive right, that is, a right to affirmative governmental protection of property. The contracts clause creates a right to governmental protection of contractual agreements. In both cases, the Constitution is violated by a governmental withdrawal from the scene.

39. See, e.g., Kunz v. NY, 340 U.S. 290 (1951); Edwards v. South Carolina, 372 U.S. 229 (1963); Cox v. Louisiana, 379 U.S. 536 (1965); Gregory v. Chicago, 394 U.S. 111 (1969). See also Thomas M. Scanlon, "Content Regulation Reconsidered," in *Democracy and the Mass Media*, supra note 8, at 338–39, and Fiss, "Free Speech and Social Structure," supra note 8, both discussing this point. The Court has not said, however, that there is a positive right in the sense that police officers are obliged to protect the speaker from a hostile crowd. The Court has only said that the police officers must not silence the speaker if it can protect him. It therefore remains possible that the police could constitutionally stand by while a hostile crowd descends on the speaker.

40. See Richard A. Epstein, "Was *New York Times v. Sullivan* Wrong?" 53 U. Chi. L. Rev. 703 (1984), for a criticism of the case from this foundation. A qualification is necessary here. To decide whether there is a subsidy, one needs a baseline, in the form of a description of the initial set of endowments. To see reputation as part of that initial set is to proceed in the common law fashion. Some forms of social contract thinking — the state must protect certain rights in return for the decision of citizens to leave the state of nature—support the same view. But it would of course be possible to say that on the right theory, people do not have such an antecedent right to reputation, and that therefore no subsidy is involved in the libel cases. See also the Court's decision invalidating "user fees" for expression, Forsyth County v. Nationalist Movement, 112 S.Ct. 2395 (1992).

41. Red Lion Broadcasting Co. v. FCC, 395 U.S. 367 (1969).

42. See Robert M. Entman, *Democracy without Citizens* (Oxford, 1986).

43. 395 U.S. at 389. See also Commission on Freedom of the Press, supra note, at 18: "To protect the press is no longer

automatically to protect the citizen or the community. The freedom of the press can remain a right of those who publish only if it incorporates into itself the right of the citizen and the public interest."

44. 395 U.S. at 390 (citations omitted, including a reference to the Brennan article referred to earlier).

45. Mark Fowler, former Chairman of the Federal Communications Commission, quoted in Bernard D. Nossiter, "The FCC's Big Giveaway Show," The Nation 402 (October 26, 1985).

Chapter 3: Broadcasting, Politics, Liberty

1. The key decision is Syracuse Peace Council, 2 FCCR 5043, 5055 (1987).

2. See, e.g., L. Scot Powe, *American Broadcasting and the First Amendment* (Berkeley, 1988).

3. See Thomas M. Scanlon, "Content Regulation Reconsidered," in *Democracy and the Mass Media* 350 (Judith Lichtenberg ed., Cambridge, 1989): "The case for or against such powers must be made out on the basis of their consequences. Statutes requiring that opponents of newspaper or television editorials be given the opportunity to reply are not, on the face of it, inconsistent with the right of freedom of expression. Everything depends on what the consequences of such statutes would be as compared with the likely alternatives." See also Commission on Freedom of the Press, *A Free and Responsible Press* (New York, 1947), at 23–24 ("the great agencies of mass communication should regard themselves as common carriers of public discussion. . . . All the important viewpoints and interests in the society should be represented in its agencies of mass communication").

4. The point raises the complex question of "affirmative action" as a regulatory policy in the speech area. In principle, the idea makes some sense; some views are genuinely unrepresented, and special efforts to equalize the process could improve the system of free expression, certainly in theory. But there are probably insuperable problems in deciding on the right degree of representation, especially in light of (1) the inevitably value-laden character of the judgment about what a good speech market looks like and (2) the absence of trustworthy institutions to make these decisions even if we had a good

theory from which to work. In these circumstances, the best route is probably to ban viewpoint discrimination in regulation even if it plausibly has a market-correcting rationale.

5. Steven Shiffrin, *Democracy, Free Speech, and Romance* (Cambridge, Mass., 1990), emphasizes the role of the First Amendment in protecting dissent. Although the Madisonian view does not place special stress on the dissenter, its concerns overlap a good deal with Shiffrin's insofar as both are intended to promote diversity of view and to allow critical scrutiny of current conventions.

6. See Phyllis Kaniss, *Making Local News* 102 (Chicago, 1991), on which I draw for the information in this and the following paragraphs.

7. See id.; Robert M. Entman, *Democracy Without Citizens* (Oxford, 1986). See the prescient discussion in John Dewey, *The Public and Its Problems* 179–81 (Chicago, 1954), lamenting "the triviality and 'sensational' quality of so much of what passes as news."

8. Kaniss at 110.

9. Id. at 129–30. Similar concerns were expressed in the 1940s; see Commission on Freedom of the Press, supra note 3, at 68: "The news is twisted by the emphasis on firstness, on the novel and sensational; by the personal interests of owners; and by pressure groups. Too much of the regular output of the press consists of a miscellaneous succession of stories and images which have no relation to the typical lives of real people anywhere. Too often the result is meaninglessness, flatness, distortion, and the perpetuation of misunderstanding among widely scattered groups whose only contract is through these media."

10. Shanto Iyengar and Donald Kinder, *News That Matters* 122 (Chicago, 1987)

11. See generally Kathleen Hall Jamieson, *Dirty Politics* (Oxford, 1992).

12. Id. at 105.

13. See Aaron Tversky and Daniel Kahneman, "Availability: A Heuristic for Judging Frequency and Probability," 5 Cognitive Psychology 207 (1973).

14. See Stephen Breyer, *Breaking the Vicious Circle* (Cambridge, Mass., 1993).

15. See W. Kip Viscusi, *Fatal Tradeoffs* (Oxford, 1992).

16. See Jamieson, supra note 11, ch. 7, on which I draw for some of the suggestions in this paragraph.

17. See James Fishkin, *Democracy and Deliberation* 63 (New Haven, 1991).
18. Robert Entman, "Super Tuesday and the Future of Local News," in *The Future of News* 53, 55 (Philip Cook, Douglas Gomery, and Lawrence Lichty eds., New York, 1992).
19. Bruce Buchanan, *Electing a President: The Markle Commission Research on Campaign '88* 39 (Austin, 1991)
20. S. Robert Lichter, Daniel Amundson, Richard Noyes, *The Video Campaign* 14–15, 12 (New York, 1988).
21. Kiku Adatto, "Sound Bite Democracy: Network Evening News Presidential Campaign Coverage, 1968 and 1988" (Research Paper R–1) (Cambridge, Mass.: John F. Kennedy School of Government, Harvard University, 1990), at 4.
22. See Jamieson, supra note 11, at 206.
23. Some shows about the media could of course be about public affairs; but most are not.
24. J. Max Robins, "Nets' Newscasts Increase Coverage of Entertainment," Variety 3 and 63 (July 18, 1990).
25. Id.
26. Id.
27. See Lawrence Lichty and Douglas Gomery, "More Is Less," Cook, Gomery, and Lichty, supra note 18, at 3, 26–27.
28. Harvey Levin, *Fact and Fancy in Television Regulation* 269 (New York, 1983).
29. See Iyengar and Kinder, supra note 10; Shanto Iyengar, *Is Anyone Responsible?* (Chicago, 1991).
30. *News That Matters*, at 133.
31. See Ronald Collins, *Dictating Content: How Advertising Pressure Can Corrupt a Free Press* (Washington, D.C., 1991).
32. See C. Edwin Baker, "Advertising and a Democratic Press," 140 U. Pa. L. Rev 2097 (1992).
33. Id. at 2111.
34. Steven Waldman, "Consumer News Blues," 117 Newsweek 48 (May 20, 1991).
35. Collins, supra note 31, at 20–25.
36. Baker, supra note 32, at 2149.
37. Id. at 2151.
38. "Advertisers Drop Program about the Timber Industry," The New York Times, Sept. 23, 1989. p. 32.
39. See Baker, at 2141–42, drawing on Les Brown, *Television: The Business Behind the Box* 196–203 (New York, 1971).
40. Verne Gay, "NBC v. Sponsors v. Wildman RE: Telepic 'Roe v. Wade'," 335 Variety 71 (May 10, 1989).

41. Baker, at 2143.
42. Quoted in Baker, at 2155–56.
43. B. Shanks, *The Cool Fire: How to Make It in Television* 98 (New York, 1976).
44. Baker at 2153–56.
45. Statements of Bruce Christensen, President of the National Association of Public Television Stations before the Hearing on Children and Television, 98th Cong, 1st Sess 36–37 (March 16, 1983).
46. Tom Enselbadt, The Shortcake Strategy, in Todd Gitlin, ed., *Watching Television* (New York, 1986), at 70.
47. See Aletha Huston et al., *Big World, Small Screen* 54 (Lincoln, 1992).
48. Fred M. Hechinger, *Fateful Choices* (New York, 1992).
49. See Huston et al. at 54–56; National Institute of Mental Health, *Television and Behavior* (D. Pearl, L. Bouthilet, and J. Lazar eds., Washington, D.C., 1982); Jerome Singer, Dorothy Singer, and Wanda Rapaczynski, "Family Patterns and Television Viewing as Predictors of Children's Beliefs and Aggression, "34 J. of Communication 73 (1984); L. D. Eron, "Relationship of TV Viewing Habits and Aggressive Behavior in Children," 67 J. Abnormal. & Soc. Psych. 253 (1963); W. Wood, F. Y. Wong, and J. G. Chachere, "Effects of Media Violence on Viewers' Aggression in Unconstrained Social Interaction," 109 Psych. Bulletin 371 (1984); L. D. Eron and L. R. Huesmann, "Television as a Source of Maltreatment of Children," 16 School Psych. R. 200 (1987); L. R. Huesman and L. S. Miller, "Long-Term Effects of Repeated Exposure to Media Violence in Childhood," in *Public Communication and Behavior* 3 (G. Comstock ed., New York, 1992).
50. See George Gerbner and Nancy Signorielli, "Violence Profile 1967 through 1988–89: Enduring Patterns," 117 Broadcasting 97 (Dec. 4, 1989).
51. G. Rakow and P. Kranich, "'Women' as Signs in Television News," 42 J. of Communication 8 (1991); see also Huston et al., supra note 47, at 26–31. Concerns about social stereotyping in the mass media were set out long ago in Commission on Freedom of the Press, supra note 3, at 26–27.
52. Kathy Pollitt, "The Smurfette Principle," The New York Times, April 7, 1991, section 6, p. 22, column 3.
53. Id.
54. John J. Corry, "Children's TV Found Dominated by White

Men," The New York Times, July 15, 1982, section C, p. 14, column 4.

55. See Daniel A. Farber, "Free Speech without Romance: Public Choice and the First Amendment," 105 Harv. L. Rev. 554 (1991). Information is not a pure public good, for it is often feasible to provide it only to those who pay for it, and copyright and patent laws can guarantee appropriate incentives for its production. But it does have much in common with pure public goods.

56. For a lucid discussion, see Jon Elster, *The Cement of Society* (Cambridge, 1989).

57. Some of the underlying issues are well discussed in Elizabeth Anderson, *Value in Ethics and Economics* (Cambridge, Mass., 1993). Of course some democratic decisions would violate the First Amendment even if those decisions could be classed as aspirations; consider the foreclosure of a particular, broadly despised point of view. But this form of viewpoint discrimination should not be confused with what I am discussing here.

58. See Jon Elster, *Ulysses and the Sirens* (Cambridge, 1979); Howard Margolis, *Selfishness, Altruism, and Rationality* (Chicago, 1982).

59. See Jon Elster, *Sour Grapes* (Cambridge, 1984); see also the discussion of autonomy in Joseph Raz, *The Morality of Freedom* (Oxford, 1986).

60. See George Will, *Restoration* (New York, 1992).

61. See Huston et al., supra note 47, at 115.

62. 12 BVerfGE 205, 259–60, 262–63 (1961) (emphasis added). A good discussion is David Currie, "Freedom of Expression in the Federal Republic of Germany" (unpublished manuscript 1992).

63. 57 BVerfGE 295 (1981). The case can be found in Donald Kommers, *The Constitutional Jurisprudence of the Federal Republic of Germany* 409–13 (New York, 1989).

64. 73 BVerfGE 118, 155–56 (1986).

65. Id. at 158–60.

66. 83 BVerfGE 238, 310–12 (1991).

67. Decision 225/1974 [1974] Giurisprudenza costituzionale 1775.

68. See the discussion in Eric Barendt, "The Influence of the German and Italian Constitutional Courts on their National Broadcasting Systems," Public Law 93 (Spring 1991).

69. See Huston et al., supra note 47, ch. 7, from which I draw for much of the information in this paragraph.
70. This is the message of Jamieson, supra note 11.
71. See id. at 261.
72. For general discussion, quite outside the area of free speech, see David Osborne and Ted Gaebler, *Reinventing Government* (Washington, D.C., 1991); Cass R. Sunstein, "Democratizing America through Law," 25 Suffolk L. Rev. 949 (1991); Cass R. Sunstein, *After the Rights Revolution* (Cambridge, Mass., 1990).
73. 47 U.S.C. 303 (c).
74. See Huston et al., supra note 47, ch. 7; Amy Gutmann, *Democratic Education* 238–55 (Princeton, 1987).
75. See especially the excellent discussion in Baker, supra note 32, at 2178–2219, on which I draw here. Baker does not deal specifically with the broadcasting context, but many of his ideas apply there as well.
76. Under the Noerr-Pennington Doctrine, there is an exemption from the antitrust laws for joint efforts to influence government. Moreover, the Newspaper Preservation Act, 15 U.S.C. 1801 et seq., allows joint operating arrangements.
77. Royal Commission on the Press, 1961–1962 Report 93–95 (1962).
78. Baker, supra note 32, at 2193–95.
79. See the parallel suggestions, set out for self-policing, in Commission on Freedom of the Press, supra note 3, at 92–96 (suggesting the "responsibility of the industry for diversity and quality" and arguing that "Radio cannot become a responsible agency of communication as long as its programming is controlled by the advertisers").
80. See Sushil Bikhchandani, David Hirshleifer, and Ivo Welch, "A Theory of Fads, Fashion, Custom, and Cultural Change as Informational Cascades," 100 J. Polit. Econ. 992 (Oxford, 1992).
81. See Raz, supra note 59.
82. See the discussion in A. Meiklejohn, *Free Speech and Its Relation to Self-Government* 103–5 (New York, 1948) of the failure "of the commercial radio": "The radio as it now operates among us is not free. Nor is it entitled to the protection of the First Amendment. It is not engaged in the task of enlarging and enriching human communication. It is engaged in making money. And the First Amendment does not intend

to guarantee men freedom to say what some private interest pays them to say for its own advantage. . . . The radio, as we now have it, is not cultivating those qualities of taste, or reasoned judgment, of integrity, of loyalty, of mutual understanding upon which the enterprise of self-government depends. On the contrary, it is a mighty force for breaking them down. It corrupts both our morals and our intelligence. And that catastrophe is significant for our inquiry, because it reveals how hollow may be the victories of the freedom of speech when our acceptance of the principle is merely formalistic. Misguided by that formalism we Americans have given to the doctrine merely its negative meaning. We have used it for the protection of private, possessive interests with which it has no concern. It is misinterpretations such as this which, in our use of the radio, the motion picture, the newspaper and other forms of publication, are giving the name 'freedoms' to the most flagrant enslavements of our minds and wills."

83. Consider Meiklejohn at 16–17: "Congress is not debarred from all action upon freedom of speech. Legislation which abridges that freedom is forbidden, but not legislation to enlarge and enrich it. The freedom of mind which befits the members of a self-governing society is not a given and fixed part of human nature. It can be increased and established by learning, by teaching, by the unhindered flow of accurate information, by giving men health and vigor and security, by bringing them together in activities of communication and mutual understanding. And the federal legislature is not forbidden to engage in that positive enterprise of cultivating the general intelligence upon which the success of self-government so obviously depends. On the contrary, in that positive field the Congress of the United States has a heavy and basic responsibility to promote the freedom of speech."

84. On the general point, see Laurence Sager, "Fair Measure: The Legal Status of Underenforced Constitutional Norms," 91 Harv. L. Rev. 1212 (1978).

Chapter 4: Does the First Amendment Undermine Democracy?

1. 424 U.S. 1, 48–49 (1976).
2. See, e.g., Austin v. Michigan Chamber of Commerce, 110 S.Ct. 1391 (1990); FEC v. Massachusetts Citizens for Life, 479 U.S. 238 (1986).

3. See Dan Clawson, Alan Neustadtl, and Denise Scott, *Money Talks* (New York, 1992).
4. FEC v. NCPAC, 470 U.S. 480 (1985).
5. California Medical Assn. v. FEC, 453 US 182 (198).
6. 198 U.S. 45 (1905).
7. "Basic Liberties and Their Priority," in 3 *The Tanner Lectures on Human Values* 76 (S. McMurrin ed. 1982). See also Thomas M. Scanlon, "Content Regulation Reconsidered," in *Democracy and the Mass Media* 349–50 (Judith Lichtenberg ed., Cambridge, 1989): "It seems clearly mistaken to say that freedom of expression never licenses government to restrict the speech of some in order to allow others a better chance to be heard." See also the criticism of *Buckley v. Valeo* and the identification of the case with *Lochner v. New York* in John Rawls, *Political Liberalism* 362–63 (Cambridge, Mass., 1993). Rawls' discussion of the fair value of equal political liberties bears importantly on issues of campaign finance and broadcast regulation.
8. See, e.g., Michael Malbin, ed., *Parties, Interest Groups, and Campaign Finance Laws* (Washington, D.C., 1981).
9. See Clawson, Neustadtl, and Scott, supra note 3. See also David Magleby and Candice Nelson, *The Money Chase* (Washington, D.C., 1990); Larry Sabato, *Paying for Elections* (Washington, D.C., 1989).
10. See Bruce A. Ackerman, "Crediting the Voters," 13 *The American Prospect* 71 (1993).
11. See, e.g., United States v. Grace, 461 U.S. 171 (1983); Clark v. Community for Creative Non-Violence, 468 U.S. 288 (1983); Boos v. Berry, 485 U.S. 312 (1988); Frisby v. Shultz, 487 U.S. 474 (1988); Ward v. Rock against Racism, 491 U.S. 781 (1989); Heffron v. International Society for Krishna Consciousness, 452 U.S. 640 (1981).
12. See Davis v. Massachusetts, 418 U.S. 241 (1974), where this idea is explicit.
13. This approach was suggested in Grayned v. Rockford, 408 U.S. 104 (1972), but it no longer represents the law.
14. International Society for Krishna Consciousness, Inc. v. Lee, 112 S.Ct. 2701 (1992).
15. Food Employees Local 590 v. Logan Valley Plaza, 391 U.S. 308 (1968); Lloyd Corp. v. Tanner, 407 U.S. 551 (1972); Hudgens v. NLRB, 424 U.S. 507 (1976).
16. See Schneider v. State, 308 U.S. 147 (1939); Martin v. City of Struthers, 319 U.S. 141 (1943).

17. See, e.g., Pell v. Procunier, 417 U.S. 817 (1974).
18. See id.
19. Alexander Bickel, *The Morality of Consent* 82 (New Haven, 1975).
20. This claim casts doubt on the outcome or at least the rationale in Miami Herald Publishing Co. v. Tornillo, 418 U.S. 241 (1974), in which the Court struck down a "right of reply" law. The special problem with that law was that it was limited to candidates for office who had been attacked in the press. There was thus reason for the Court to suspect that the law was an effort by political candidates to insulate themselves from attack.
21. FCC v. Pacifica Foundation, 438 U.S. 726 (1978); Red Lion Broadcasting Co. v. FCC, 395 U.S. 367 (1969); National Broadcasting Co. v. U.S., 319 U.S. 190 (1943).
22. See Bruce Owen and Steven Wildman, *Video Economics* (Cambridge, Mass., 1992).
23. The scarcity rationale is sharply attacked in Ronald Coase, "The Federal Communications Commission," 2 J. L. & E. 1 (1959).
24. See Lee Bollinger, *Images of a Free Press* (Chicago, 1991).
25. See C. Edwin Baker, "Advertising and a Democratic Press," 140 U. Pa. L. Rev. 2097 (1992).
26. FCC v. Pacifica Foundation, 438 U.S. 726 (1978).
27. See the discussion in Kathleen Hall Jamieson, *Dirty Politics* (Oxford, 1992).
28. Rust v. Sullivan, 111 S.Ct. 1759 (1991); Harris v. McRae, 448 U.S. 297 (1980); FCC v. League of Women Voters, 468 U.S. 364 (1984); Regan v. Taxation with Representation, 461 U.S. 540 (1983).
29. Snepp v. United States, 444 U.S. 507 (1980).
30. 111 S.Ct. at 1759.
31. Id. at. 1772. In response to the claim that the regulations conditioned the receipt of a benefit on the relinquishment of a right, the Court said that "here the government is not denying a benefit to anyone, but is instead simply insisting that public funds be spent for the purposes for which they were authorized." The Court added: "To hold that the Government unconstitutionally discriminates on the basis of viewpoint when it chooses to fund a program dedicated to advancing certain permissible goals, because the program in advancing those goals necessarily discourages alternate goals, would render numerous government programs constitutionally suspect.

When Congress establishes a National Endowment for Democracy to encourage other countries, it is not required to fund a program to encourage competing lines of political philosophy such as Communism and Fascism."

32. Technically, the gag rule did apply to advocacy, but the case did not involve an advocate, and the Court approached the case as if it involved limits on services.

33. I do not argue what some have, that government may silence "the powerful" to protect "the powerless." Such a position would create a legitimate risk that judicial or legislative decisions about the relative power of various groups, and about who should receive redistribution, will be biased or unreliable. Judgments about who is powerful and who is not must refer to some baseline. That baseline will of course be politically contested. When the powerful are free to redistribute speech, it is likely they will distribute it in ways that advantage them. The resulting judgments are not easily subject to governmental administration. This risk seems unacceptable when speech is at stake.

Moreover, we should regard a decision to silence the views of the powerful as an objectionable interference with freedom, even if it might promote the goal of equality. Well-off people might not have any strong claim of right to distributions of wealth and property that the common law grants them; but surely they have a right to complain if they are silenced. It is obvious that what they have to say may turn out to be correct, may spur better approaches to current problems, or may add a great deal to the debate simply by virtue of the reasons offered by those who respond. These are the most conventional Millian arguments for the distinctiveness of speech. See J. S. Mill, *On Liberty* (New York, 1926), at 20–21. They do not apply to the recommendations set out here. These recommendations turn not on "power" or on "silencing the powerful," but on the application of First Amendment scrutiny to all legal rules, including those that create markets.

Chapter 5: Political Speech and the Two-Tier Amendment

1. A. Meiklejohn, *Free Speech and Its Relation to Self-Government* (New York, 1948): "The guarantee given by the First Amendment is not . . . assured to all speaking. It is assured only to speech which bears, directly or indirectly, upon which voters have to deal—only, therefore, to the con-

siderations of matters of public interest. Private speech, or private interest in speech, on the other hand, has no claim whatever to the protection of the First Amendment." Id. at 94.

2. Here I depart from Meiklejohn, who believed that nonpolitical speech was not covered by the First Amendment at all. (Note, however, that in his later writing Meiklejohn came to see much speech as political. See Alexander Meiklejohn, "The First Amendment is an Absolute," 1961 Supreme Court Review 245.) Much of the analysis in this chapter is devoted to an exploration of why and how to protect nonpolitical speech in a two-tier First Amendment.

3. Central Hudson Gas v. Public Serv. Comm. of NY, 447 U.S. 557 (1980); Posadas de Puerto Rico Associates v. Tourism Co., 478 U.S. 32 (1986); Miller v. California, 413 U.S. 15 (1973); compare New York Times v. Sullivan, 376 U.S. 254 (1964), with Gertz v. Welsh, 418 U.S. 323 (1974).

4. This would be an effort to build on Austin's notion of "speech acts" for First Amendment purposes. See Kent Greenwalt, *Speech, Crime, and the Uses of Language* (Oxford, 1989).

5. See Thomas Scanlon, "Freedom of Expression and Categories of Expression," 40 U. Pitt. L. Rev. 519 (1979).

6. It would be possible to respond that misleading commercial speech is more harmful than misleading political speech; but this is not clearly true.

7. As is expressly urged in Ronald Dworkin, "The Coming Battles over Free Speech," New York Review of Books 55 (June 11, 1992), in the context of an argument for raising the protection of libel of private persons to that now given to libel of public figures.

8. This is explicitly urged in Edward DeGrazia, *Girls Lean Back Everywhere* (New York, 1992).

9. On the plurality of values, see Elizabeth Anderson, *Value in Ethics and Economics* (Cambridge, Mass., 1993).

10. For different views on this subject, see, e.g., Ronald Dworkin, *A Matter of Principle* (Cambridge, Mass., 1985); Robert Bork, *The Tempting of America* (New York, 1989).

11. The point emerges from L. Levy, *The Emergence of a Free Press* (Oxford, 1985), and also from a reading of the materials collected in Philip Kurland and Ralph Lerner, eds., 5 *The Founders' Constitution* (Chicago, 1987).

12. New York Times Co. v. US, 403 U.S. 713 (1971); New York Times v. Sullivan, 376 U.S. 254 (1964); Bridges v. California,

314 U.S. 252 (1941); Brandenburg v. Ohio, 395 US 444 (1969).

13. This is an application of the notion of reflective equilibrium as famously discussed in John Rawls, *A Theory of Justice* (Cambridge, Mass., 1971). Notably, a distinction is made between political and nonpolitical speech in John Rawls, *Political Liberalism* 363–65 (Cambridge, Mass., 1993). See also Cass R. Sunstein, "On Analogical Reasoning," 106 Harv. L. Rev. 741 (1993).

14. See Frederick Schauer, *Free Speech: A Philosophical Inquiry* (Cambridge, 1982); see also Joshua Cohen, "Freedom of Expression" 22 Phil. & Pub. Aff. (forthcoming 1993) (discussing "the Fact of Power").

15. See George Stigler ed., *Chicago Studies in Political Economy* (Chicago, 1988).

16. See the discussion of the supposed liberal taboo on "external preferences," in Ronald Dworkin, "Liberalism," in *A Matter of Principle*, supra note 10. I do not believe that there is any such general taboo, see Cass R. Sunstein, *The Partial Constitution* ch. 6 (Cambridge, Mass., 1993), but religious domination of public processes does call up a characteristic and legitimate liberal fear.

17. It might be thought that the First Amendment itself is a response here—that the First Amendment calls for special skepticism about any regulation of speech. But I think this begs the question, which is the appropriate interpretation of the First Amendment. Where there is special reason to suspect government, there is special reason to police government carefully; where there is no such reason for suspicion, there is no such reason to police.

18. See John Hart Ely, *Democracy and Distrust* (Cambridge, Mass., 1981), for a general statement to this effect.

19. See id.

20. T. M. Scanlon, "A Theory of Free Expression," 1 Phil. & Pub. Aff. 204 (1972); David Strauss, "Persuasion, Autonomy, and Freedom of Expression," 91 Colum. L. Rev. 334 (1991); Martin Redish, "The Value of Free Speech," 130 U. Pa. L. Rev. 591 (1982). A popular treatment is Ronald Dworkin, "The Coming Battles over Free Speech," supra note 7, at 55. In an important essay, Scanlon revised his position on grounds analogous to those invoked here: see Scanlon, "Freedom of Speech and Categories of Expression," supra note 5; see also Thomas Scanlon, "Content Regulation Reconsidered," in

Democracy and the Media 346 (Judith Lichtenberg ed., Cambridge, 1989).

21. An understanding of this sort emerges from Richard Epstein, *Forbidden Grounds* (Cambridge, Mass., 1991), with the usual qualifications for force and fraud.
22. See Jon Elster, *Sour Grapes* (Cambridge, 1985); Amartya Sen, *Inequality Reexamined* (Cambridge, Mass., 1991).
23. See Ronald Dworkin, "Liberalism," in *A Matter of Principle*, supra note 16.
24. See Joseph Raz, *The Morality of Freedom* (Oxford, 1986).
25. Scanlon, "A Theory of Free Expression," supra note 20; Strauss, supra note 20.
26. Some such distinctions are offered in C. Edwin Baker, *Human Liberty and Freedom of Speech* (Oxford, 1990).
27. See Strauss, supra note 20. On the other hand, perhaps government should allow the citizenry to sort out truth from falsehood.
28. As is explicitly urged in Dworkin, "The Coming Battles over Free Speech" supra note 7.
29. This would be an Aristotelian approach, for which there is no clear defense in current legal writing. Cf. Baker, supra note 26; Martha Nussbaum, *Love's Knowledge* (Oxford, 1991).
30. Cohen, supra note 14.
31. Quoted in Gerald Gunther, "Learned Hand and the Origins of Modern First Amendment Doctrine: Some Fragments of History," 27 Stan. L. Rev. 719, 749 (1975).
32. See American Booksellers Ass'n v. Hudnut, 771 F.2d 323 (7th Cir. 1985), aff'd, 475 US 1001 (1986).
33. See Dennis v. United States, 341 U.S. 494 (1951).
34. See R.A.V. v. City of St. Paul, 112 S.Ct. 2538 (1992) (Stevens, J., dissenting). A good criticism of balancing can be found in J. H. Ely, *Democracy and Distrust* (Cambridge, Mass., 1980).
35. See Vince Blasi, "The Pathological Perspective and the First Amendment," 85 Colum. L. Rev. 449 (1985).
36. See Cass R. Sunstein, "On Legal Theory and Legal Practice," in *NOMOS: Theory and Practice* (forthcoming 1994).
37. See Gerald Rosenberg, *The Hollow Hope* (Chicago, 1991).
38. See Blasi, supra note 35.
39. Of course persuasive speech can be regulated on grounds of its persuasiveness in some exceptionally narrow circumstances, as when it creates a "clear and present danger."
40. 403 U.S. 15 (1971).
41. See Young v. American Mini-Theatres, 427 U.S. 50 (1976); City of Renton v. Playtime Theatres, 475 U.S. 41 (1986).

42. 438 U.S. 726 (1978).
43. See Geoffrey Stone, "Content Regulation and the First Amendment," 25 Wm. & Mary L. Rev. 185 (1983).
44. See Central Hudson Gas & Elec. v. Public Serv. Comm'n, 447 U.S. 557 (1980). But see Posadas v. Louis Co. of Puerto Rico, 478 U.S. 328 (1986), in which the Court upheld a truthful, nondeceptive ban on advertising for casino gambling.
45. Gertz v. Welch, 418 U.S. 323 (1974).
46. A possible response would be that many famous people in fact have governmental associations of some sort, and that the notion of "public figures" is designed to overcome the difficulties of case-by-case inquiries into such questions. Note also that many people not involved in government are involved in activities in which the public is legitimately concerned on democratic grounds; consider attempted bribery of public officials by corporate executives. Probably the best approach, suggested by Justice Marshall and urged in the text, would involve an inquiry into whether the issue is one of public importance. See Rosenbloom v. Metromedia, 403 U.S. 29, 78 (1971) (Marshall, J., concurring).

   Ronald Dworkin contends that the First Amendment should be interpreted to protect against any libel unless actual malice can be shown. See Ronald Dworkin, "The Coming Battles over Free Speech," supra note 7. Dworkin would therefore prevent private people, as well as celebrities, from recovering for most libel. His justification is the interest in "autonomy," which, he says, applies in all libel cases. Though the point is unclear, he appears to mean listener autonomy. But the argument seems unconvincing. Certainly it is not clear that listener autonomy argues in favor of protection of falsehoods; indeed, if we are interested in protecting the moral autonomy of listeners, we might be especially concerned to forbid falsehoods; see Strauss, supra note 20. Perhaps we must protect falsehoods to protect truth; but this is a complex empirical claim. In fact much of the Court's work in the libel area has depended on empirical judgments that have not been identified or defended. Large advances in our thinking about libel could be produced by careful attention to the actual incentives of the press and the effects of different libel rules on press behavior.

   Speaker autonomy cannot be the operative principle behind Dworkin's recommendation, for if we require protection of libelous falsehoods, we would also probably require renovation of many other areas as well, calling for, among other things, the constitutional protection of false commercial speech.

47. A possible counterexample would be a case in which names are mentioned in order to focus public attention on the real nature and frequency of rape—as in cases in which names of AIDS victims are mentioned as part of social deliberation about AIDS. Here the point of disclosure might be to counter misconceptions about the nature of the victimized class and to bring concreteness to public discussion. In a case of this kind, disclosure of names might be constitutionally protected.

48. See Barnes v. Glen Theatre, Inc., 111 S.Ct. 2456, 2468 (1991) (Souter, J., concurring in the judgment).

Chapter 6: Discrimination and Selectivity: Hard Cases, Especially Cross-Burning and Hate Speech

1. International Society for Krishna Consciousness v. Lee, 112 S. Ct. 2701 (1992).

2. See, e.g., Martin Redish, "The Content Distinction in First Amendment Analysis," 24 Stan. L. Rev. 113 (1981).

3. See Geoffrey R. Stone, "Content Regulation and the First Amendment," 25 Wm. & Mary L. Rev. 189 (1983); Geoffrey R. Stone, "Content-Neutral Restrictions," 54 U. Chi. L. Rev. 46 (1987).

4. Related discussion can be found in Bernard Williams, "Utilitarianism," in *Utilitarianism: For and Against* (Cambridge, 1972) and Elizabeth Anderson, *Value in Ethics and Economics* (Cambridge, Mass., 1993), both attacking consequentialism of a certain sort.

5. As the Court held in R.A.V. v. St. Paul, 112 S. Ct. 2356 (1992), discussed infra; see also American Booksellers Assn. v. Hudnut, 771 F.2d 323 (7th Cir. 1985), aff'd mem., 475 U.S. 1001 (1986). I believe that both of these cases misapply the general principle; but it is important that they identify the right principle.

6. Greer v. Spock, 418 U.S. 298 (1974).

7. Lehman v. Shaker Heights, 418 U.S. 298 (1974).

8. See chapter 3 above.

9. See Laurence H. Tribe, *American Constitutional Law* (2d ed., New York, 1988).

10. See Posadas v. Louis Co. of Puerto Rico, 478 U.S. 328 (1986). It would be possible to argue that the restriction is not really viewpoint-based, because there is no real category called "advertisements against gambling." Speech of that kind is really public-interest announcements. True viewpoint discrimination would consist of a ban on "pro-gambling" messages, which are not banned. The prohibition on advertisements for casino gambling does not prevent people from advertising their view that gambling is a good idea. On this view, the ban on casino gambling—and the other examples offered in the text—are not real examples of viewpoint discrimination.

I do not think that this argument is persuasive. It seems to amount to a reshuffling of the categories, not an effort to come to terms with the real discrimination in the examples. It remains true that people cannot buy advertising time or space to stimulate demand for certain activities, whereas people can do precisely this in order to dampen demand for those activities.

11. See Robert Goodin, *No Smoking* (Chicago, 1987).
12. See NLRB v. Gissel Packing Co., 395 U.S. 575, 618–19 (1969).
13. See Stone, "Content-Neutral Restrictions," supra note 3.
14. Clark v. Community for Creative Non-Violence, 468 U.S. 288 (1984).
15. Widmar v. Vincent, 454 U.S. 263 (1981); U.S. Postal Service v. Council of Greenborough, 453 U.S. 114 (1981); Heffron v. Intl Society, 452 U.S. 640 (1981).
16. See David Strauss, "Persuasion, Autonomy, and Freedom of Expression," 91 Colum. L. Rev. 334 (1991).
17. 112 S.Ct. 2538 (1992).
18. For a good discussion, see Akhil R. Amar, "The Case of the Missing Thirteenth: R.A.V. v. City of St. Paul," 106 Harv. L. Rev. 124 (1992).
19. See Texas v. Johnson, 109 S.Ct. 2533 (1989).
20. See Terminiello v. Chicago, 337 U.S. 1 (1949).
21. See Charles R. Lawrence, "If He Hollers Let Him Go," 1990 Duke L. J. 431; Mari Matsuda, "Public Response to Racist Speech," 87 Mich. L. Rev. 2320 (1989); Richard Delgado, "Words That Wound," 17 Harv. C.R.-C.L. L. Rev. 133 (1982).
22. 343 U.S. 250 (1952).
23. See J. S. Mill, *On Liberty* (New York, 1926).

24. Chaplinsky v. New Hampshire, 315 U.S. 568 (1942).
25. I am putting issues of overbreadth to one side, by assuming that with the narrowing construction, the law applies only to speech unprotected by the First Amendment. In the *R.A.V.* case itself, four justices concluded that there had been no sufficient narrowing construction.
26. Id. at 2543. The dissenters in *R.A.V.* argue that this is an equal protection principle, not a First Amendment principle. But it is surely sensible to think that the First Amendment of its own force prohibits government from acting on the basis of the motive of self-insulation.
27. See the discussion of pornography in chapter 7. If my argument on that point is unpersuasive, the Court may well be right in finding viewpoint discrimination.
28. See Chaplinsky v. New Hampshire, 315 US 568 (1942). There are lurking difficulties here with quiescent or nonviolent victims of fighting words, e.g., pacifists, or physically disabled people, or perhaps women.
29. Lehman v. Shaker Heights, 418 U.S. 298 (1974).
30. Greer v. Spock, 424 U.S. 828 (1976).
31. Id. at 2561 (Stevens, J., concurring in the judgment).
32. Id. at 2548.
33. Id. at 2546.
34. See Amar, supra note 18.
35. See Doe v. University of Michigan, 721 F. Supp. 852 (E.D. Mich. 1989); UWM Post, Inc. v. Bd. of Regents, 774 F. Supp. 1163 (E.D. Wis. 1991).
36. See Mary Becker, "Conservative Free Speech and the Uneasy Case for Judicial Review," U. Colo. L. Rev. (forthcoming 1993).
37. Bd. of Educ. v. Pico, 457 U.S. 853 (1982).
38. See Thomas Grey, "Civil Rights vs. Civil Liberties," in *Reassessing Civil Rights* (Ellen Paul, Fred Miller, and Jeffrey Paul eds., Cambridge, Mass., 1991).

Chapter 7: More Hard Cases: Pornography, Government Arts Funding, and Corporate Speech

1. Miller v. California, 413 U.S. 15, 24 (1973).
2. See, e.g., Ronald Dworkin, "Do We Have a Right to Pornography?" in *A Matter of Principle* 335–72 (Cambridge, Mass., 1985); Barry Lynn, "'Civil Rights' Ordinances and the

Attorney General's Commission," 21 Harv. C.R.-C.L. L. Rev. 27, 48–56 (1986).

3. See Catharine MacKinnon, *Feminism Unmodified* 146–62 (Cambridge, Mass., 1987).

4. See, e.g., Rae Langton,"Whose Right? Ronald Dworkin, Women, and Pornographers," 19 Phil. & Pub. Aff. 311, 335–36 (1990). MacKinnon's own position on this is complex. Subordination is her principal target, not simply violence; but I think that violence or coercion in some form underlies much of the argument and almost all of her examples. See MacKinnon, supra note 3.

5. See Robin West, "Women's Hedonic Lives: A Phenomenological Critique of Feminist Legal Theory," 3 Wis. Women's L. J. 81 (1987).

6. See the summary in US Department of Justice, Attorney General's Commission on Pornography, *Final Report* 888–89 (Washington, D.C., 1986).

7. The Court recognized this point in the context of child pornography in New York v. Ferber, 458 U.S. 747, 760 (1982).

8. See generally Edward Donnerstein et al., "The Question of Pornography on Sex Crimes," in *Handbook of Sexual Assault* (W. L. Marshall et al. eds., New York, 1990); S. Murrin and S. Laws, "The Influence of Pornography on Sex Crimes," in id. at 73; Edward Donnerstein, "Pornography: Its Effect on Violence against Women," in *Pornography and Sexual Aggression* 53–81 (Neil Malamuth et al. eds., Orlando, 1984); Attorney General's Commission on Pornography, *Final Report* (1987). On the problem of causation, see Frederick Schauer, "Causation Theory and the Causes of Sexual Violence," 1987 Am. Bar. Found. Res. J. 737.

9. For various reviews, see Richard A. Posner, *Sex and Reason* (Cambridge, Mass., 1992); Cass R. Sunstein, "Pornography and the First Amendment," 1986 Duke L. J. 536; Berl Kutchinsky, "The Politics of Pornography Research," 26 Law & Society Review 447 (1992); Steven Alan Childress, "Pornography, 'Serious Rape,' and Statistics: A Reply to Dr. Kutchinsky," 26 Law & Society Review 457 (1992); Steven Alan Childress, "Reel 'Rape Speech': Violent Pornography and the Politics of Harm," 25 Law & Society Review 177 (1991).

10. See Hendrick Hertzberg, "Big Boobs: Ed Meese and His

Pornography Commission," New Republic 21 (July 14, 1986).

11. See Ronald Dworkin, "Two Forms of Liberty" 100, 107–9, in *Isaiah Berlin: A Celebration* 100, 107–9 (Edna Ullmann-Margalit and Avishai Margalit eds., London, 1991).

12. See American Booksellers Assn v. Hudnut, 771 F.2d 323 (7th Cir. 1985), aff'd mem., 475 U.S. 1001 (1986).

13. See Joseph Raz, *The Morality of Freedom* (Oxford, 1986); Dworkin, *A Matter of Principle*, supra note 2.

14. We have seen that in *Rust v. Sullivan*, the Supreme Court upheld the so-called "abortion gag rule." The Court indeed seemed to suggest that government can establish a funding program limited to the government's preferred point of view. But we have also seen that *Rust* should not be taken to allow government to do whatever it wishes with funds devoted to speech-related activity. The *Rust* case involved a restriction on medical counseling that was ancillary to a restriction on certain services; it was not a simple case of viewpoint discrimination.

15. See, e.g., *Canons* (R. Von Hallberg ed., Chicago, 1986).

16. The word "understood" shows the problem: the approval of democracy is a form of viewpoint discrimination even if there is everything to be said on behalf of the viewpoint being approved.

17. This is not an undisputed proposition. See Mark Yudof, *When Governments Speak* (Berkeley, 1985).

18. 435 U.S. 765 (1978).

19. Austin v. Michigan Chamber of Commerce, 110 S.Ct. 1391 (1990).

Chapter 8: Deliberative Democracy

1. These points are treated in more detail in Cass R. Sunstein, *The Partial Constitution* (Cambridge, Mass., 1993).

2. Brutus, 2 *The Complete Antifederalist* 369 (H. Storing ed., Chicago, 1980).

3. The Federalist No. 81. Hamilton is speaking here in favor of a bicameral legislature, but the point captures much of federalist thought. See Samuel Beer, *To Make a Nation* (Cambridge, Mass., 1993).

4. 1 Annals of Cong. 733–45 (J. Gales ed., Washington, D.C., 1789) (emphasis added).

5. See, e.g., Norman Frohlich and Joseph Oppenheimer, *Choosing Justice* (1992); John Orbell, Alphons von de Kragt, and Robyn Dawes, "Explaining Discussion-Induced Cooperation," 54 J. Personality and Social Psychology 811 (1988).

6. I speak here and in subsequent paragraphs not about certainties or about laws, but about possibilities and mechanisms. We might think that deliberation will correct facts, and we can show how this can happen; but it would be wrong to say that deliberation in the real world always corrects facts. On some problems with deliberation, many of which are relevant to the discussion here, see Jon Elster, *Sour Grapes* 33–42 (Cambridge, 1983). On social science as a set of mechanisms rather than law-like generalizations, see Jon Elster, *Nuts and Bolts for the Social Sciences* (Cambridge, 1990). My discussion should be taken as a depiction of how a well-functioning system of free expression will work, not as a predictive claim about what invariably happens in our world.

7. Jon Elster, "Strategic Uses of Argument," in *Barriers to Conflict Resolution* (K. Arrow et al. eds., Stanford, forthcoming).

8. La Rochefoucauld, *Maxims* 65 (L. Tancock trans., New York, 1959) (1665).

9. See Robert Goodin, "Laundering Preferences," in *Foundations of Social Choice Theory* (Jon Elster and Aanund Hylland eds., Cambridge, 1986).

10. See the definition of a republic in The Federalist No. 46.

11. K. Arrow, *Social Choice and Individual Values* (2d ed., New Haven, 1963).

12. A helpful discussion in this regard, on "how common sense can be self-critical," appears in Elizabeth Anderson, *Value in Ethics and Economics* (Cambridge, Mass., 1993).

13. 3 Elliott, *The Debates in the Several State Conventions on the Adoption of the Federal Constitution* 536–37 (New York, 1888).

14. For helpful discussion, see Jon Elster, *The Cement of Society* (Cambridge, 1989).

15. I do not discuss here the complex issue of what sorts of arguments are admissible in the political realm. For relevant discussion, see John Rawls, *Political Liberalism* (Cambridge, Mass., 1993).

16. See, e.g., Jonathan Riley, *Liberal Utilitarianism* (Cambridge, 1988).

17. See, e.g., John Dewey, *Freedom and Culture* 108 (New York, 1989): "The assumption that desires are rigidly fixed is not one on its face consistent with the history of man's progress from savagery through barbarism to even the present defective state of civilization"; id. at 22: "A certain complex culture stimulates, promotes, and consolidates native tendencies so as to produce a certain pattern of desires and purposes"; "The idea of a natural individual in his isolation possessed of full-fledged wants, of energies to be expended according to his own volition, and of a ready-made faculty of foresight and calculation is as much a fiction in psychology as the doctrine of the individual in possession of antecedent political rights is one in politics," John Dewey, *The Public and Its Problems* 102 (Chicago, 1927). See also John Dewey, *The Quest for Certainty* 258–59 (New York, 1929), stating that his "objection is that the theory in question holds down value to objects antecedently enjoyed, apart from reference to the method by which they come into existence; it takes enjoyments which are causal because unregulated by intelligent operations to be values in and of themselves. The suggestion almost imperatively follows that escape from the defects of trancendental absolutism is not to be had by setting up as values enjoyments that happen anyhow, but in defining value by enjoyments which are the consequence of intelligent action. Without the intervention of thought, enjoyments are not values but problematic goods, becoming values when they re-issue in a changed form from intelligent behavior. The fundamental problem with the current empirical theory of values is that it merely formulates and justifies the socially prevailing habit of regarding enjoyments as they are actually experienced as values in and of themselves. It completely side-steps the question of regulation of these enjoyments. This issue involves nothing less than the problem of the directed reconstruction of economic, political and religious institutions."

18. See Amartya Sen, *Commodities and Capabilities* (North-Holland, 1985); Amartya Sen, *Inequality Reexamined* (Cambridge, Mass., 1992); Martha Nussbaum, "Aristotelian Social Democracy," in *Liberalism and the Good* (A. Bruce Douglas, Gerald Mara and Henry Richardson eds., New York, 1989).

19. See Samuel H. Beer, *To Make A Nation* (Cambridge, Mass., 1993); Stephen Holmes, *Passions and Constraint* (forthcoming 1994).

20. See id.; see also the first principle of justice in Rawls, supra note 15, involving political liberties; John Rawls, "Kantian Constructivism in Moral Theory," 77 J. Phil. 515 (1980).
21. See J. S. Mill, *On Liberty* (New York, 1926). Of course a fundamental commitment to political equality underlines the discussion of equal political liberties in Rawls, *Political Liberalism*, supra note 15, at 5–7.
22. I am generalizing from some complex ideas; there are many ambiguities in the liberal tradition, and there are important internal debates within the liberal tradition. Many of the points I am making appear in Mill, *On Liberty*, supra note 21; William James, *Pragmatism* (Cambridge, Mass., 1905); John Dewey, "Propositions, Warranted Assertability, and Truth," in *Dewey and His Critics* 265 (Sidney Morgenbesser ed., New York, 1977); John Rawls, "Kantian Constructivism in Moral Theory," 77 J. Phil. 515 (1980). See also Jürgen Habermas, *The Philosophical Discourse of Modernity* (Cambridge, Mass., 1987) on this general conception of truth. A perfectionist version of liberalism is powerfully defended in Joseph Raz, *The Morality of Freedom* (Oxford, 1986). A version of liberalism emphasizing democratic choice can be found in Elizabeth Anderson, *Value in Ethics and Economics* (Cambridge, Mass., 1993). A version of liberalism placing little premium on democratic deliberation is set out in Ronald Dworkin, "Liberalism," in *A Matter of Principle* (Cambridge, Mass., 1986). Rawls, *Political Liberalism*, supra note 15, defends a form of political rather than comprehensive liberalism. Rawls' discussion is highly compatible with what I have suggested here: see e.g., id. at 5–7 (defending political equality); id. at 324–31 (defending need to ensure "fair-value" of political liberties); id. at 363–65 (distinguishing political from nonpolitical speech).
23. Abrams v. U. S, 250 U.S. 616, 624. (Holmes, J., dissenting).
24. See *The Philosophy of John Dewey* 652 (J. McDermott ed., New York, 1981).
25. See Robert Entman, "Putting the First Amendment in its Place," University of Chicago Legal Forum (forthcoming 1993).

Index

285